BROKE AND PATRIOTIC

STUDIES IN SOCIAL INEQUALITY

This book series is devoted to examining poverty and inequality in its many forms, including the takeoff in economic inequality, increasing spatial segregation, and ongoing changes in gender, racial, and ethnic inequality.

Broke
and Patriotic

Why Poor Americans Love Their Country

FRANCESCO DUINA

STANFORD UNIVERSITY PRESS
STANFORD, CALIFORNIA

Stanford University Press
Stanford, California

Printed in the United States of America on acid-free, archival-quality paper

Library of Congress Cataloging-in-Publication Data

Names: Duina, Francesco G., 1969– author.
Title: Broke and patriotic : why poor Americans love their country / Francesco Duina.
Description: Stanford, California : Stanford University Press, 2017. | Series: Studies in social inequality | Includes bibliographical references and index. | Description based on print version record and CIP data provided by publisher; resource not viewed.
Identifiers: LCCN 2017005639 (print) | LCCN 2017012085 (ebook) | ISBN 9781503603943 | ISBN 9780804799690 (cloth : alk. paper)
Subjects: LCSH: Patriotism—United States. | Poor—United States—Attitudes.
Classification: LCC JK1759 (ebook) | LCC JK1759 .D77 2017 (print) | DDC 323.6/50869420973—dc23
LC record available at https://lccn.loc.gov/2017005639

To the women and men who opened their minds and hearts to me. I hope I have faithfully captured what you shared in this book.

Contents

Photograph section follows page 106

CHAPTER 1

A PEOPLE'S COUNTRY

Eddie,[1] a fifty-six-year-old African American, lives in Birmingham, Alabama. Once a spelling-bee champion in school and "smart kid" who used to draw and love music, he now aspires to work in food services but earns less than one thousand dollars a month working at informal and irregular jobs, taking life day by day, and hoping—as his grandparents taught him long ago to do—that "maybe tomorrow will be better." Though he served in the army for three years, he receives very few benefits from the government. He resides in the fifth most dangerous city in the United States, where the poverty rate is more than 30% and robberies, aggravated assaults, and arson attacks are commonplace.[2] He knows that incomes for the people in the middle and lower classes in the country have been stagnating and believes that "the top percentage seems to be making all the money." There are problems in the United States, for sure, and "no society is perfect . . . we have our dark shadows." Still, despite all the difficulties in his life, he is convinced about one thing: America "is an exceptional country." Indeed, as he puts it, America is "the last best hope for mankind on earth . . . the last best hope for countries on earth."

Eddie is like millions of Americans. Many are poor and face serious adversity, and much in their lives is a daily struggle. They have access to very limited social services and support—partly a reflection of the fact that the majority of their compatriots, including those with very little, believe in the fairness of existing class differences. The odds that their children will enjoy a better life in the future are low. They also work very long hours while the gap between themselves and the rest of society, already considerable, continues to widen. On these and other dimensions their situation is lacking in both absolute and relative terms: by many measures, America's poor are worse off than their counterparts in other advanced countries. To have no money in America is tough in itself, and tougher than being poor in most other rich societies.

And, like Eddie, these millions of impoverished Americans are highly patriotic. Given their predicaments, it could be reasonable to expect them to feel some dissatisfaction, if not resentment, toward their country. With the American Dream eluding them and little in their lives suggesting that things will improve, the American poor—understood in this book as those belonging to the most economically disadvantaged class in society—could understandably be critical of the society in which they live. In some respects, they certainly are. Many believe that, in a practical sense, a lot needs fixing—a sense of disgruntlement that the likes of Donald Trump and Bernie Sanders tapped into during their 2016 presidential campaigns.

But their fundamental belief in the country remains unshaken and, indeed, by any measure stunningly strong: 80%–90% of America's poor (and even more, depending on how exactly we define the "poor" and measure their "patriotism") hold the United States in high esteem. They are proud of their nation, believe in the greatness and superiority of the United States, and would rather be citizens of America than of any other country in the world. In fact, their patriotism—defined in this book as the opinion that their country is fundamentally better than other countries—is extraordinary. They are more patriotic than the poor in almost all other advanced countries in the world, even though the latter are in many ways better off than they are. In the United States their patriotism exceeds in many instances the patriotism of working-class, middle-class, and upper-class Americans. So, although America's least well-off have reasons *not* to love their country, they hold it dear to their hearts and in many ways idealize it.

The sentiment is widespread—cutting across race, gender, political, and religious lines. Patriotism is high among impoverished white, black, and other nonwhite Americans. It is high among poor men and women, liberals and conservatives, religious believers and nonbelievers. While there are certainly variations across regions of the country (in the Middle Atlantic region, for instance, it is less widespread), their patriotism is high in absolute terms in every region of the country. It is also a resilient sort of patriotism: among all classes in the United States, the patriotism of Americans living in poverty has been affected the least by the economic crisis of 2008–2009, and by some measures it has actually increased.

This book is about Americans like Eddie and their patriotic views. It is about impoverished Americans and their intense love of their country. Why are America's poor so patriotic? Specifically, what attributes do they ascribe to the United States? How do they think those attributes shape their lives? What are the limitations that they see in other countries that make the United States superior to those countries? And, crucially, how do these Americans reconcile—if they in fact do—their own difficult situation with their positive view of the country? This is a book about what sociologists would call the "narratives" of patriotism among the poor: the conceptual threads, images, stories, and visions that the economically worst-off Americans articulate about their country. It is about their stories and perspectives. It is an effort to investigate, hear, and understand firsthand the logic and reasoning of this particular segment of the American population—a segment that our wealthy and extremely powerful society seems to have forgotten in many ways or to have left behind with little consideration.

Why should we try to understand the patriotism of America's least well-off? Two reasons concern the country's social and political stability. First, the maintenance of the social order depends on widespread trust and positive feelings toward the public sphere.[3] The same can be said for the institutions and practices of successful democratic governance: they, too, require trust and the positive disposition of citizens.[4] High levels of patriotism certainly promote (and reflect) such trust and positive feelings. The patriotism of America's poor contributes to social cohesion and, thus, the peaceful and daily unfolding of life in society. Put in perhaps more dramatic terms, their patriotism may keep them content enough not to seek a major overhaul of society—with implications for the agendas of political parties, the direction of policies, and the continued availability of labor to provide basic services.[5] There are certainly concerns in the United States and elsewhere about widespread discontent among America's most economically challenged people and what this could mean for social stability: "Why aren't the poor storming the barricades?" recently asked the *Economist* when reflecting on inequality in America.[6] "Why don't the poor rise up?" wondered Thomas Edsall in his regular column in the *New York Times*.[7] And in the words of former US secretary of labor Robert Reich, "Our incomes are declining, the ranks of the poor are swelling, and almost all the new wealth goes to the wealthiest. So why aren't Americans rebelling against the system?"[8] The patriotism of the poor is likely part of the answer.

At the same time, rather than act as a force for stability, that same patriotism could be leveraged by populist movements looking to bring major changes to society. The recent rise of far-right parties in countries such as France, Austria, and Denmark offers one example of how that might happen. Their agendas, with "a focus on national identity," have included the rejection of international forums of cooperation, threats of protectionism, and xenophobic initiatives.[9] The patriotism of the poor need not necessarily be leveraged in this way, of course; yet the potential for populist appropriations of various kinds is always there. For many observers, the 2016 presidential elections in the United States featured precisely such rhetoric—in particular, Donald Trump's campaign and its calls to those who have been left behind for big changes in the name of "making America great again." This is the second reason why we would do well to understand the mind-sets of America's least-well-off citizens.

Geopolitical considerations should also encourage such an investigation. America's poor contribute greatly to its military, which is the most powerful the world has ever seen and constitutes a fundamental pillar of American society. As has been the case throughout the decades—consider that 80% of soldiers serving in Vietnam had a high school degree or less[10]—the majority of American military personnel these days come from the lower and middle economic classes, with only 13%, for instance, having some college education.[11] Much less than 10% have a college degree.[12] To be sure, in a controversial study in 2008 the Heritage Foundation reported that Americans from poorer neighborhoods (those with household income levels in the lower two quintiles) appeared to be underrepresented in the 2006 and 2007 recruiting years.[13] But many other analyses show otherwise: large numbers of recruits reportedly do come from poor neighborhoods (those with income levels in the second- and third-lowest deciles),[14] and the military has struggled to meet its target goal of recruits with high school diplomas, with just above 70% of recruits (rather than the desired 90%) in 2007, for instance, actually having those diplomas.[15] In addition, base pay for enlisted military members has for decades de facto relegated many military families to the ranks of the poor or near poor.[16] The military greatly depends, then, on Americans with limited means to fill its ranks. This need would not be met if America's worst-off citizens did not have at least some patriotic feelings toward their country. What is the nature of those feelings?

Relatedly, on the international stage, where American power remains unmatched, a sense of national identity, along with a sense of purpose and national unity, shapes how the United States acts in the world and is perceived by others. Surveys and research data alike consistently show over time that much of the world still admires the United States and the values—freedom, individual rights, the pursuit of personal happiness, optimism, equality, and opportunities for all—for which it stands.[17] Such international admiration of the United States is predicated, in part, on the perception that Americans stand united, strong, and committed to those ideals. The assumption is justified, since most Americans do appear to subscribe to those values, as recent research and polls by the Pew Research Center and the World Values Survey on optimism, the pursuit of happiness, and freedom show.[18] Americans of all stripes need to believe in America's ideals if the country is to project itself successfully onto the world as a shining city on a hill. Again, we should have a clear understanding of those beliefs.

Two more important reasons should compel us to better grasp the patriotism of America's least well-off. Being poor affects a large percentage of the American population. The US Census Bureau estimated in 2014 that around 15% of Americans (forty-seven million) live below the poverty line.[19] Many are children: UNICEF reported in 2012 that the United States has the second-highest rate of child poverty among the world's developed countries.[20] Their situation is at best stagnant and in fact probably worsening: household income for those in the bottom quintile of incomes, when adjusted for inflation, dropped by more than 15% from 2000 to 2014.[21] Indeed, inequality in America is among the highest in the world, is persistent, and has widened steadily over the decades.[22] A 2015 Pew Research Center Report showed that the middle class is shrinking.[23] Politicians, the mass media, academics, and many members of the public have accordingly called for a deeper understanding of the poor of America: the problems they face, the values they hold, their aspirations, and their preferences.[24] Understanding their patriotism seems an essential step in this regard.

Finally, we should recognize that the patriotism of the American poor contributes directly to the country's understanding of its essential qualities. Modern nation-states depend on shared understandings among citizens of "belonging" and of being part of "imagined" communities.[25] National identities, in other words, are not simply given but are instead socially constructed. With this in mind, sociologists have described American national identity as consisting, in part, of the celebration of individualism over the supremacy of the collective (as in communism) or over the imposition of preestablished notions of the good or righteous life (as in theocratic governments).[26] In the United States, people can do as they wish, provided that their actions do not infringe on the rights and well-being of others. This combination of beliefs is in turn matched by an unusual sense of exceptionalism, by a conviction that America's celebration of individual self-determination is unique and unprecedented in history, and that, as a result, America is the greatest nation on earth.[27] To work, such a vision of what it means to be American requires the participation of most members of society regardless of rank or place in the social system. It is, perhaps counterintuitively, a collective endeavor. The least well-off are therefore an indispensable part of America and its sense of self.

Much depends, then, on the patriotism of the American poor. Thus, it is rather surprising that few researchers have asked people who suffer from considerable financial hardships why they feel so positively about their country. There certainly is considerable research on American patriotism in general and on the patriotism of categories of people such as women, African Americans, or Native Americans. There is also some research on the principles of group cohesion and why disadvantaged members can at times feel very attached to a group. These works can offer us some potentially useful ideas about the patriotism of the American poor. Yet these remain only untested insights, since they do not focus on America's poor as a specific group worthy of study and investigation. We simply do not know much about the extent and logic of their belief in their country's greatness. Thus, this book tackles two questions: Why do America's poor think so highly of their country? How do they reconcile their economic difficulties with their appreciation of their country?

The best way to answer these two questions is to hear the voices and reflections of America's poor themselves. Eager to do so, I conducted in-depth, face-to-face interviews (each lasting between thirty and sixty minutes) during 2015 and 2016 with sixty-three low-income patriotic Americans in two areas of the United States that are arguably hotbeds of patriotism among the poor: Alabama and Montana. These interviews yielded nearly nine hundred pages of single-spaced transcribed conversation texts. I discuss in more detail in Chapter 3 the methodology I followed for selecting the sites (Birmingham and Vernon in Alabama, and Billings and Harlowton in Montana), identifying and selecting the interviewees, conducting the interviews, and analyzing the transcripts. I should nonetheless state here that the respondents included people living in cities and rural areas and were of different races, genders, political and religious orientations, and histories of military service. Importantly, my objective going into the interviews was not to generalize about any particular subgroup of America's poor: in-depth interviewing necessarily limits the sample size of respondents and therefore does not allow for that sort of analysis. Rather, the aim was to have exposure to as broad a number of perspectives as I could, explore those perspectives in great detail, and weave together the most comprehensive portrait possible of the patriotism of America's least-well-off citizens.

Why are poor Americans so patriotic? The interviews yielded three overarching narratives. First, the people I met shared a firm belief in their country's promise of *hope* for every one of its citizens and, indeed, every human being on earth. The American social contract offers to each person deliverance from the ills that have plagued humanity throughout history to this very day. There is something universal and even transcendental about the United States, even if its own history has had troubled moments, with race above all. America's spirit thus brims with generosity and a readiness to do the right thing in the world. It is an optimistic place, always oriented toward a better future. It is, not coincidentally, also God's country: from its inception, it has been thought to hold a special place in God's plans. One need only look at other countries to appreciate the greatness of the United States: most of the interviewees felt that even in the most advanced countries on earth ruthless and arbitrary punishment reigns, and backwardness and poverty deprive their citizens of the essentials for life. America, then, offers incredible hope and, with that, a sense of dignity that no other country can offer. To someone who struggles to end the day fed, clothed, and sheltered, this sense of hope has extraordinary importance.

The second narrative depicted America as *the land of milk and honey*. The interviewees saw in the United States great wealth, much of it accessible in the form of public goods and services. There are parks, public libraries with free Internet access, electricity, and potable water everywhere. America's roads, I was told, are paved in gold. The availability of government benefits and private charities helps a great deal. One does not starve in America unless one chooses to. Such abundance of riches makes suffering from very limited resources more bearable. Inequality is not a problem, for anyone can still make it in America: all one has to do is try. Someone is always ready to help, if one is determined to succeed.

Indeed, everyone from all over the world wishes to come to this wealthy and beautiful country. With these beliefs in mind, many of the interviewees expressed a sense of contentment. Again, as they told me countless times, all one has to do is look at the deprivations afflicting the poor in other countries. Opportunities are much more limited, people are barely surviving, and economies are depressed. America, then, is the place to be, especially if one has no money.

The third narrative was about *freedom*. Only in the United States can one truly determine one's physical and mental existence. This is the basis of the country—its origins and history. One may not have money, but in America one has freedom—and this is the most precious of things. The ability to own guns is central: Guns represent liberty, for the country began with a violent revolution against tyranny. Guns are needed for hunting, too, which is key for feeding oneself and one's family—something again of great importance if one lacks other resources. We should always remember that such liberty has come at great cost. Generations have served in the military, and this must be honored. In Alabama, the civil rights struggle was especially present in the interviewees' minds. No other country on earth, I was told, can boast such commitment to freedom. Deprived of much else, such freedom is of the utmost importance to America's poor. I encountered a fierce and almost instinctive attachment to it. This narrative took on Confederate flavors in Alabama and libertarian tones in Montana.

These were three grand narratives. In many conversations, after discussing these ideas, I pressed the interviewees to reflect on their own situation and life trajectories and asked them directly if they saw no tension between their steadfast belief in America and their own personal situations. Surely, America may be a great, unique country, but did this not contradict their own life experiences? How did they reconcile their love of country with their poverty—their struggles and difficulties?

I discovered that, in a sense, there is *no* contradiction or puzzle. The interviewees listed four separate reasons. First, everyone deserves what he or she gets: failure is one's fault, not society's. Why blame America for one's bad choices? Second, the future looks brighter already: better things are coming soon, and there is no reason to lose faith in the country. Third, America is founded on the principle that we are all worth the same. Money is only one, and not the most important, metric: in the most fundamental of ways, because of the American social contract, a homeless person is worth as much as the president. There is nothing, in fact, to reconcile. Finally, some of the interviewees recognized that they indeed lack accurate knowledge of other countries: America is all they know, and it is impossible to entertain alternative possibilities.

Upon reflection, after returning from my travels and spending time analyzing what I heard, it became clear to me that all these themes are tied together by one underlying idea: a belief that while one belongs to America, *America also belongs to each American*. The Americans I met saw themselves reflected in their country: their images, and those of their ancestors who built the country, are reflected in the Pledge of Allegiance, the Declaration of Independence, the Constitution, and the American flag. America is a country of, for, and by the people. Struggling and facing innumerable personal challenges do not diminish one's faith in the United States; in fact, in the case of the interviewees, they provide grounds for further strength and commitment to the country.

We delve deeply into these ideas in this book. We should start, however, by first considering the dire circumstances poor Americans face and, in turn, their very high levels of patriotism.

CHAPTER 2

BROKE AND PATRIOTIC

America may still be seen by many as the most dynamic, inspiring, and rich country in the world. Patriotism, of a populist sort, has deep historical roots in the country. But the most impoverished Americans get very little from their society, especially when compared to the poor in other advanced nations. There are good reasons for poor Americans to *not* love their country. They are instead deeply patriotic. We examine in this chapter both the plight of America's least well-off and their extraordinary patriotism.

Tough Times in America

Definitions of "poor" abound. Policy institutes, academic researchers, the government, and others often differ in their specific language. All agree, however, that the poor are those belonging to the most disadvantaged economic class. This is often defined as those found at the bottom 20% of income and wealth levels in American society, those who identify themselves as belonging to the lowest income brackets or class ranks, or those who are below the poverty threshold set by the US government for different household sizes.[1] These are all sound definitions that I use as I examine data on the poor and their patriotism.

In recent years, the plight of America's most economically challenged has attracted considerable attention in the mainstream media. Books like Sharon Hay's *Flat Broke with Children: Women in the Age of Welfare Reform* (2003), Jane Collins and Victoria Mayer's *Both Hands Tied: Welfare Reform and the Race to the Bottom in the Low-Wage Labor Market* (2010), and Kathryn Edin's *$2.00 a Day: Living on Almost*

Nothing in America (2015) have given us painfully detailed accounts of struggling adults, families, and children barely managing to survive. Stable and well-paying jobs are hard to come by; wages are depressed and hardly growing; benefits such as health-care coverage and retirement contributions are elusive; and money to support children and their educational growth is missing. Indeed, entire neighborhoods stand in disarray, with malfunctioning schools and public services and high crime rates. On their own, these accounts leave little doubt that the bottom tier of America's class structure is hurting and caught in a negative spiral.

The already troubling picture becomes even more dispiriting when we compare how America's poor fare relative to their counterparts in other advanced countries. Is it better to be poor in the United States or in places like Europe, Japan, or Australia? To start, consider social benefits. There is wide agreement among academics, policy makers, the media, and leading public figures that impoverished Americans are unquestionably worse off. A large amount of research has accordingly gone into explaining the uniqueness of the United States.[2] Comparative analyses consistently show, for instance, that Social Security benefits in the United States are much lower than those in continental Europe.[3] Unemployment benefits, health coverage, parental leaves and child-care support, housing support, public education funding, and retirement benefits—some of the most important programs that can alleviate poverty's damaging effects—are less generous in the United States than in most other advanced countries.[4] Indeed, data from the Organisation for Economic Co-operation and Development (OECD) itself (the world's club of rich countries) for the latest year available, 2014, show that public social spending (which is aimed at vulnerable segments of the population, such as low-income households, the unemployed, and those who are disabled) in the United States amounts to 19% of GDP, significantly lower than the total for the OECD and placing the country twenty-second out of twenty-eight of the most advanced economies in the world (Fig. 1).

Thus, research shows that Europeans pay, for instance, at most one-sixth the cost for child care as Americans do, while retirement benefits

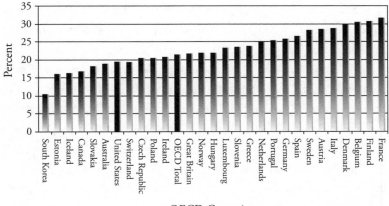

Figure 1. Public Social Spending as Percentage of GDP, 2014. Source: Based on data from OECD, https://data.oecd.org/socialexp/social-spending.htm.

in the United States are around 33%–40% of one's final salary—far below the OECD average of 57% and the European Union's average of 62%. Americans must also self-finance their old-age care by three times as much as their European counterparts.[5] Those who lose their jobs are often covered for longer periods of time, and with more money, in European countries than in the United States.[6] Americans with financial means can shoulder these burdens, but those with fewer economic resources cannot.

Comparative studies also show that, contrary to the myth of the United States as the land of opportunity, poor Americans have relatively low chances of intergenerational upward mobility. Indeed, by most measures, those chances are among the smallest in the advanced world;[7] the same applies to social mobility in general.[8] Broad OECD-wide evidence indicates that the children of the poor in the United States face bleaker prospects than the children of the poor in other OECD countries.[9] Studies show, for instance, that relative to other OECD countries the effects in the United States of parental socioeconomic status on the educational achievement of their children are very high.[10] In this vein, a study comparing Denmark, Finland, Norway, Sweden, the United

Kingdom, and the United States found that the sons of the poorest American fathers have a particularly high likelihood of remaining in the lowest earnings quintile.[11] In other studies, evidence indicated that the correlation between parental earnings and the later income of their children in the United States is high; the figures for other European countries (except the United Kingdom and perhaps Italy) and Canada are lower.[12] Thus, American children from below-average-earning families experience less mobility than most of their counterparts elsewhere.[13]

America's least well-off also face the difficulty of working exceedingly long hours in absolute terms.[14] For the period 2000–2013, Americans averaged the longest working hours among workers in OECD countries.[15] Specifically, data show that low-educated American men work longer hours than their counterparts in many continental European countries (especially Nordic countries—precisely where the poor enjoy some of the most generous benefits). The same applies to women (with the exception of women with low levels of education in southern European countries, who work longer hours).[16]

Even as they work long hours and therefore perhaps earn more than the poor elsewhere, those in the lower economic classes of the United States are worse off than their counterparts in many other advanced countries in yet another respect: They experience some of the largest income and wealth gaps relative to the richer members of their society. In 2011–2013, for example, among all OECD countries, only Turkey, Mexico, and Chile had higher levels of internal income inequality (i.e., larger Gini coefficients) than the United States.[17] To make matters worse, income inequality within the United States has widened since the 2007–2008 crisis;[18] the wages of poor Americans have not benefited from the recovery, while the income of rich Americans has increased. Indeed, income inequality in the country has been steadily on the increase since 1970.[19] Figure 2 shows the Gini coefficient for the United States relative to the OECD average for the years 2007 to 2014 (figures for 2015 or 2016 are not yet available). If perceptions of well-being are formed in part through comparison to others, the poor in America find themselves in a very unenviable position.

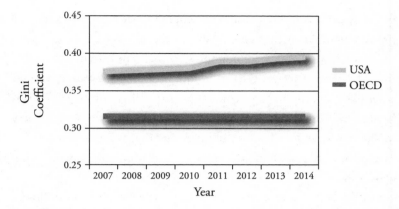

Figure 2. Gini Coefficients, United States and OECD Members, 2007–2014. Source: Computed from data available at http://www.oecd.org/social/income-distri-bution-database.htm. See OECD, 2015, 20, for the coefficient for the 2013 OECD average. The OECD average for 2014 was estimated from available data and existing projections. Note: The Gini coefficient is a measure of the income distribution in a country, where zero represents perfect equality (where everyone has the same income) and 1 perfect inequality (where one person has all the income and everyone else has none).

All this points to a rather disheartening situation. Those living in the poorest economic segments of America's population are facing dire circumstances in absolute and relative terms when compared to their counterparts in most other advanced nations on earth. The American Dream may be just that for the tens of millions of Americans who struggle every day to get by. It is not a picture that paints the United States in an especially positive light. But the very people who find themselves in this unfortunate position feel quite differently.

The Patriotism of the Impoverished

Given the unfavorable situation in which poor Americans find themselves, it would seem reasonable to expect them not to approve, or feel proud, of the society in which they live. This would be consistent with a strand of research suggesting that identification with one's nation is weaker among subordinate groups in society.[20] Even if their knowledge of the situations of disadvantaged people in other countries may be limited, poor Americans could still be expected to feel a high degree of dissatisfaction and therefore not view their country in a favorable light. In many respects, there is no question that they are critical of what is happening in their country and the direction in which it is headed. But in regard to their feelings toward America, as a country in the world and in history, it turns out that poor Americans are extraordinarily patriotic, and more so than the poor in many other countries.

Patriotism, of course, does not have a single meaning. According to some political theorists, it has to do with devotion and commitment to a large group of people who identify with a political entity.[21] If defined in terms of identification, patriotism could be said to be quite similar to the term "nationalism" as understood by many sociologists and political scientists. In this book, however, the term "patriotism" refers to something different: a sense of pride in one's country. It therefore means more than identification with the country: patriotism, as defined here, contains elements of approval, recognition of the goodness and possibly greatness of one's country, and beliefs in the superiority or higher standing of one's country relative to others. A nationalistic sentiment would then be one's identification with the American flag, while a patriotic sentiment could be the belief that the United States is the greatest country on earth.[22]

America's least well-off are unquestionably very patriotic. Consider Figure 3, data from the World Values Survey for the years 2005 and 2006—the most recent years for which data on national pride are available for several European countries. The figure reports data on pride in one's nation for the lowest income brackets (the bottom out of ten) in four major European countries, Canada, and the United States. Of the poorest Americans, 100% reported being either "very proud" or "quite proud" of their nationality. In none of the other countries did the poor exhibit such nationalistic pride, though certainly Canada came quite close.

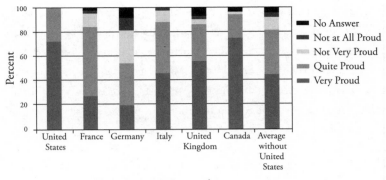

Figure 3. National Pride among the Poor (Lowest Income Group), 2005 and 2006. Selected samples: Canada 2005, France 2006, Germany 2006, Italy 2005, United Kingdom 2005, United States 2006. Source: Computed from data from the World Values Survey, Wave 5 (2005–2009). Question V209: "How proud are you of your nationality?"; and Question V253: "On this card is a scale of incomes on which 1 indicates the 'lowest income decile' and 10 the 'highest income decile' in your countries.'" We would like to know in what group your household is. Please, specify the appropriate number, counting all wages, salaries, pensions and other incomes that come in."

The same question was asked again in the 2010–2014 survey. The comparative picture remains the same between the United States and Germany (the only major European country polled). In Germany, only 37% of the poor (again, the lowest income group) reported feeling either "proud" or "very proud" of their nationality. In the case of the United States, the figure was 75%.[23] This survey includes Japan: there the figure was 65%—also lower than that in the United States. Of course, here it seems worthy to note in the case of Germany and Japan the findings could have been expected, given those country's efforts during the decades following World War II to promote a very cautious sense of national pride.

During the 2010–2014 survey, the same question on national pride was posed to respondents who identify themselves as "lower class" (the lowest possible class classification). In this case, European countries included Germany, the Netherlands, Poland, Slovenia, Spain, and Sweden; the survey also included Japan. The data hence offer us more comparative insights from additional advanced countries. The results confirm that patriotism among the American poor is high both in absolute terms and relative to that of other European countries and Japan. Specifically, we find the following:[24]

1. Across the polled European countries, on average 45% of lower-class respondents reported feeling "very proud" of their nationality.

2. Across the polled European countries, on average 74% of lower-class respondents reported feeling either "very proud" or "proud" of their nationality.

3. In Japan 24% of lower-class respondents reported feeling "very proud" of their nationality. Some 57% of lower-class respondents reported feeling either "very proud" or "proud" of their nationality.

4. In the United States, by contrast, 55% of lower-class respondents reported feeling "very proud" of their nationality, and 81% reported feeling either "very proud" or "proud."

If we expand the comparison to all OECD countries included in the survey (Australia, Chile, Germany, Japan, Mexico, the Netherlands, Poland, Slovenia, Spain, Sweden, and the United States), lower-class Americans again stand out for their patriotism, though less dramatically so when compared to only large Western European countries or Japan. Across the polled OECD countries (excluding the United States), an average of 50% (versus 55% in the United States) of lower-class respondents reported feeling "very proud" of their nationality. An average of 78% (versus 81% in the United States) of lower-class respondents reported feeling either "very proud" or "proud" of their nationality.

Despite the unfavorable circumstances that poor Americans face, and despite considerable data suggesting that the poor in other advanced countries seem better off on several counts, the American poor appear to think very highly of their country—and more so, the evidence suggests, than the poor elsewhere.

If we turn our attention to patriotism within the United States itself, we discover that there, too, poor Americans exhibit a remarkable appreciation for their country. We have seen that in the 2005–2009 World Values Survey a full 100% of lower-class respondents affirmed their pride in the United States: this, it turns out, was higher than the percentage in any other class in the United States—with upper-middle-class, lower-middle-class, and working-class Americans showing rates in the 90%–92% range (themselves very high) and the upper class with a 57% rate. The data for the years after the 2008–2009 financial crisis point to weakened patriotism rates in general for the US population (perhaps this might have translated simply into a return to pre–September 11, 2001, levels, as a June 2015 Gallup Poll on national pride indicates).[25] Consistent with this, data from the 2010–2014 World Values Survey show a drop for the lower class to 81%. That figure is still very high in absolute terms and remains higher than that for the upper class, though a bit lower relative to the other classes.

If we consider data from the General Social Survey (GSS)—one of the most authoritative surveys of attitudes and social trends in the United States (run by the National Opinion Research Center at the University of Chicago)—the patriotism of lower-class Americans stands out again in both absolute and relative terms to other classes. The GSS in 2014 presented respondents with the following statement: "I would rather be a citizen of America than of any other country in the world." The results are shown in Figure 4.

Of lower-class Americans, 93% indicated that they would rather be citizens of the United States than any other country in the world. This is a very high percentage and higher than those for the working, middle, and upper classes—which, at 85%, 87%, and 85%, respectively, are very high in their own right. In addition, 66% of lower-class Americans "strongly agree" with the statement, while Americans in the other classes seem somewhat less enthusiastic: middle-class Americans are second (63%), and working- and upper-class Americans a fairly distant third and fourth (58% and 41%, respectively).

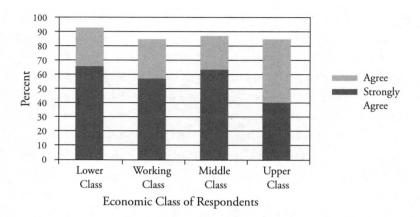

Figure 4. Class and Percentage of Respondents Agreeing in 2014 That They Would Rather Be Citizens of America Than Any Other Country in the World. Source: Computed from data from General Social Survey, 2014. Variables: Subjective Class Identification and Agree I Would Rather Be a Citizen of America.

Using these data, the positive views of the United States by the worst-off Americans actually *increased* after the 2008–2009 financial crisis. If we compare the results from 2014 to those available for the years before the 2008–2009 crisis (data are available for 1996, 2004, and 2014), we discover that the percentages of lower-class Americans either "agreeing" or "strongly agreeing" with the statement that they would rather be citizens of the United States than of any other country surged, while those of others decreased or increased by less. Lower-class Americans increased by 5 percentage points, while working-class and middle-class Americans decreased by 5 percentage points. Upper-class Americans did show an increase, but of only 2 percentage points (Fig. 5).

The GSS has approached Americans with a second statement that can be considered a proxy for a sense of patriotism: "America is a better country than most other countries." In this case, too, impoverished Americans come across as very favorably inclined toward their country. Combined data for the years 1996 and 2004 indicate that around 45% of those who identified as lower class (the lowest class category possible, indicating very limited economic means) "strongly agreed" that

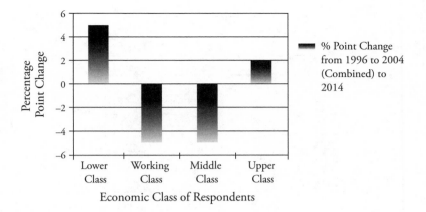

Figure 5. Percentage Point Change from 1996 to 2014 among Respondents Agreeing That They Would Rather Be Citizens of America Than Any Other Country in the World. Source: Computed from data from General Social Survey 1996, 2004, and 2014, Variables: Subjective Class Identification and Agree I Would Rather Be a Citizen of America.

America is a better country than most other countries, a higher figure than for working-class (39%), middle-class (40%), and upper-class (44%) Americans. Another 33% of lower-class Americans "agreed" with the idea—which means that 78% of lower-class Americans viewed their country as better than most other countries, with none saying that they "strongly disagreed"—a response true for only the lower class.[26]

GSS data from 2014—the post-crisis year when the question was asked again—provide additional evidence in the same direction. First, lower-class Americans continue to have the highest percentage of respondents "strongly agreeing" that America is better than most other countries (31%). Second, 77% of lower-class Americans either "strongly agree" or "agree" with the idea of America being a better country. This is a very high rate in absolute terms (just slightly lower than the 80% for the period 1996–2004) and also higher than rates for working-class (71%) or middle-class (74%) Americans. Only upper-class Americans beat the 77% approval rate (by half a percentage point) found among lower-class Americans (Fig. 6).

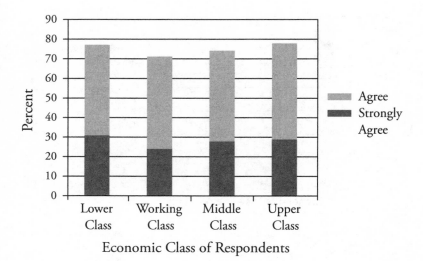

Figure 6. Class and Percentage of Respondents Agreeing in 2014 That America Is a Better Country Than Most Other Countries. Source: Computed from data from General Social Survey, 2014, Variables: Subjective Class Identification and Agree America Is a Better Country.

When we track changes over time, although every class shows a decrease after the 2008–2009 crisis in the percentages of those agreeing with the statement (strongly or not), lower-class Americans had the smallest decline of any group (3 percentage points), as shown in Figure 7. The biggest drop is observable with the middle class (15 percentage points). Again, we find that the patriotism of the economically worst-off in the country appears to be very resilient.

Overall it seems very clear that lower-class Americans continue to see their country as better than most other countries, do so at a very high rate, and have held on to that viewpoint throughout the worst economic crisis since the Great Depression.

Importantly, and not surprisingly given the high percentages of lower-class Americans holding on to such positive views of their country, poor Americans of all different categories—racial, gender, political, and so on—are very patriotic. The vast majority of lower-class blacks and whites, women and men, conservatives and liberals, young and old,

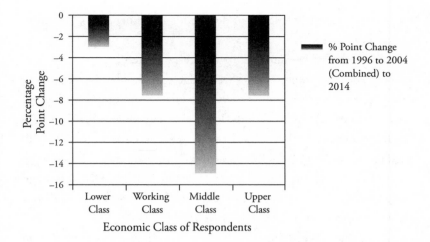

Figure 7. Percentage Point Change from 1996 to 2014 in Respondents Agreeing That America Is a Better Country Than Most Other Countries. Source: Computed from data from General Social Survey, 1996–2014. Variables: Subjective Class Identification and Agree America Is a Better Country.

and of other categories are patriotic. While some categories perhaps stand out for their especially high rates, the overall picture is one of pervasive patriotism. *Poor Americans of all stripes are very patriotic.*

Table 1 shows percentages of lower-class Americans agreeing that America is better than most other countries in the world across racial, gender, and age categories for the year 2014. It also shows those percentages for political affiliation and rural versus urban location for the years 1996, 2004, and 2014 (more years are considered in this case because the sample sizes were too small for 2014).

The data are clear: when we consider the combined figures of those who either "agree" or "strongly agree," the percentage of poor Americans thinking that their country is superior to other countries is very high and varies very little across any of the categories in question. The lowest figure is 74% (the young), and the highest is 85% (blacks). *All other categories fall within that range.* There is clearly widespread agreement across all categories of poor Americans in the superiority of their country. This means that no single category (being a Republican, for instance) is especially critical for determining whether a poor American is patriotic or not.

Importantly, the same can be said, even more decisively so, when we consider the statement of whether one would rather be a citizen of the United States than of any other country—the second measure of patriotism from the GSS. For the lower class as a whole more than 90% of respondents said they wished to be American citizens; for 2014, all age groups exceed 90%. The same applies to men and women, white and black Americans (with the latter reaching 100%), Democrats and Republicans, and rural and urban residents. In *all these categories, at least nine out of ten poor Americans are patriotic*.[27]

Note that it is certainly possible that very similar rates of patriotism across categories do not mean that people's patriotism, in substantive terms, in any one category is identical to the patriotism of people in the other categories. For instance, women's and men's, or Republicans' and Democrats', meanings may differ when they agree that America is "better" than most other countries. In addition, some minor differences across categories do exist. It is difficult to know what to make of those differences, but they may be indicative of something meaningful and are therefore worthy of note. A few data points stand out. Consider again the data in Table 1 on the belief that America is a better country than most others. The 85% figure for black Americans is very high indeed and contradicts research suggesting that black people are in general less patriotic.[28] Urban residents also stand out somewhat, as they are more likely to agree than rural ones. Gender and political affiliation appear not to matter. The same applies to age, except for young people, who stand out for being the least likely of all groups to be patriotic. This is actually consistent with the Pew Research Center 2011 data on patriotism showing that patriotism increases with age.

If we focus only on "strongly agreeing"—which can be considered a measure of the intensity of patriotism rather than overall likelihood of being patriotic—we note additional categories standing out somewhat. Middle-aged Americans are especially likely to "strongly agree" that America is a superior country. The same applies to Republicans (which is consistent with

	STRONGLY AGREE (%)	AGREE (%)	AGREE + STRONGLY AGREE (%)
White	32	46	78
Black	35	50	85
Other	42	33	75
Men	33	46	79
Women	34	45	79
Democrat	44	41	85
Republican	50	33	83
Independent	35	40	75
Rural	41	36	77
Urban	38	43	81
20–40 years old	18	56	74
41–60 years old	48	34	82
61–80 years old	32	50	82

Table 1. Categories of Lower-Class Americans Agreeing in 2014 That America Is a Better Country Than Most Other Countries. Source: Computed from data from General Social Survey, 2014; data for political affiliation and rural vs. urban are from 1996, 2004, and 2014 because the 2014 sample was too small. Variables: Subjective Class Identification, Race of Respondent, Political Party Affiliation, Gender of 1st Person, Expanded NORC Size Code (rural includes towns between 2,500 and 9,999 people, smaller areas, and open country; urban includes cities of 50,000–250,000 and greater than 250,000 people), Respondent's Religious Preference, Age of Respondent, and Agree America Is a Better Country.

recent Gallup data on the general American population and what percentage feel extremely proud to be American: 68% of Republicans, 53% of Independents, and 47% of Democrats polled).[29] We note in particular the high levels of other races (42%) "strongly agreeing" that America is a better place. "Other" likely includes Latinos and Asians above all. However, there are no real differences between men and women, black and white, and rural and urban respondents. On this last point, it seems important to note that rural respondents, though overall slightly less patriotic than urban ones, tend to "strongly agree" quite a bit more than to simply "agree" (41% versus 36%) in regard to recognizing America as a better place. Thus, there might be something important about the rural-versus-urban split as well: rural folks are, as a group, intensely patriotic.

These small but potentially meaningful differences in Table 1 can be summarized as follows:

1. Black Americans and older people appear to be more likely to either "agree" or "strongly agree" with the idea that America is a better country than most others.

2. Being Republican, elderly, or a rural resident all seem to increase one's chances of "strongly agreeing" with the idea that America is a better country. Being of a race other than white or black also seems to improve those chances.

To this, we can add data on an additional category of possible difference not covered in Table 1: religion. If we consider all responses from 1996 to 2014, 82% of Protestants and 81% of Catholics either "agreed" or "strongly agreed" with the idea of America being a better country. For those identifying their religion as "other," the figure was 83%.[30] The percentages are again very high and certainly similar across the various denominations. However, some difference can be seen when we turn to nonreligious respondents: the figure for them is 73%. This means that being religious seems to make a difference. Of those who "strongly agreed," only Protestants (46%) were significantly higher than Catholics (40%). The point seems fairly clear: being religious increases one's chances of being patriotic, especially so for Protestants.

These differences are minor and concern only one question related to patriotism, of course. Other proxies for patriotism may reveal similar or alternative differences. The differences nonetheless help us recognize something important: if we are interested in understanding the patriotism of America's poor, we would do well to keep in mind that poor Americans find themselves at the intersection of various societal categories with potentially different (and always pervasive) patriotic tendencies. Our analysis of patriotism should therefore without question take stock of the perspectives of all kinds of poor Americans and not limit itself to only one category.

The Greatest Patriots

The discussion so far points to one overarching conclusion: a very high percentage of poor Americans are patriotic. The rates are impressively high in absolute terms and in comparison to those of the poor in other advanced countries. They are also generally higher than those of wealthier, and themselves very patriotic, Americans. The high level of patriotism among the poor is prevalent in all the major demographic categories—women, men, black, white, conservative, liberal, rural, urban, and so on. We observe minor but potentially meaningful variations across some of those categories and recognize that categories that look quantitatively very similar may still differ, in substantive terms, in their patriotism.

Such high rates of patriotism across all different kinds of poor Americans are puzzling. It would be reasonable to expect them not to love, and in fact resent, their country. Instead, the evidence points exactly in the opposite direction. Two questions thus present themselves: Why do they think so highly of their country? More specifically, what are the different logics driving their appreciation of the United States? What are the building blocks of their patriotism? Second, how do America's poor reconcile—if they in fact do—their situation with their love of country?

We need insights into these questions. The patriotism of America's worst-off people matters to the country and the world. We ought to understand it. This book embarks on an unprecedented investigation into the beliefs and mind-sets of this important segment of American society.

CHAPTER 3

HEADING TO ALABAMA
AND MONTANA

How should we go about investigating the patriotic beliefs and mind-sets of America's most economically disadvantaged people? We would certainly do well to start by consulting any existing social scientific research that might give us some initial insights. Three strands in particular seem promising: a large body of work on patriotism in the United States and its evolution through time, an extensive scholarship on the patriotic sentiments of marginalized segments of the American population, and research on group cohesion theories and the unexpected attachment of disadvantaged members to their communities. None of these strands of research focuses on America's poor as such and cannot, therefore, provide us with a direct answer to our puzzle. Yet what they reveal may offer clues into the patriotism of America's most impoverished people. We should consider the key findings.

Ultimately, however, the most productive step we can take is to speak directly and at length with America's poor. We should ask them about their ideas, feelings, reasoning, and understanding of the country and the world. We should explore the associations and emotions that America invokes in their hearts and minds and what they find so special about their country. And we should also pose questions about their patriotism given their challenging circumstances. In brief, we should set out to conduct extensive, face-to-face interviews with patriotic poor Americans. The ideas we can gather from a review of existing research can help us plan for our interviews and formulate our questions. But the interviews should ultimately be wide ranging, to allow for all relevant perspectives to emerge. We want to hear the most patriotic of all Americans tell their stories as freely as possible. Throughout, the interview processes should be consistent with social scientific best practices: everything from the selection of interviewees to the capturing and analysis of the answers ought to be done in rigorous methodological fashion.

In this chapter I turn first to the existing research for initial insights and then spell out the methods I followed for the interview process. Readers interested in jumping directly to the core findings of the interviews can proceed to the next chapter.

Research on American Patriotism

We start by turning to the existing research on American patriotism and its evolution through time. A broad and general observation about the United States is that its citizens, as a whole, are intensely patriotic. Americans by and large believe in the greatness of the country, as comparative studies over the last few decades have consistently shown.[1] In fact, beliefs in the uniqueness and exceptional qualities of the country can be traced back to the founding of the country itself and its development over the centuries.[2] Today, the story of American greatness is learned in elementary school and is repeated again and again in public speeches, events, and media outlets. The abundance of American flags in public and private spaces, the reciting of the Pledge of Allegiance in many (even if perhaps no longer most) public schools, and the playing of the national anthem at almost all major sporting events help reinforce it. All sectors of society—including those at the bottom of the social hierarchy—are exposed to it. Indeed, as historian Peter Baldwin has argued, there has been a magnification of the country's uniqueness for all to hear and internalize.[3] There is almost a spiritual devotion to country. "Lacking a national religion," write sociologist John Hall and anthropologist Chuck Lindholm, two seasoned observers of the country, "America has made a religion of the nation."[4] Thus, as historian John Bodnar argues, American patriotism has taken "the discordant interests of diverse social groups and [has] united them into a 'unitary conceptual framework.'"[5] As a starting point, seen from this perspective, it is not too surprising that a strong sense of patriotism should be pervasive across all classes of American society.

But what exactly is the nature of that patriotism? What is its essence? Four elements stand out as especially important. Perhaps the most central has to do with what historian Woden Teachout calls the country's "humanitarian" dimension, which ultimately amounts to a special commitment to *individualism*. This dimension is "incontestably, inarguably American" and is best articulated in "the principles of the Declaration of Independence and the Bill of Rights." Americans love their country because it is committed to democracy "as a political and social system" and because it serves as the "source of civil liberties." Put somewhat differently, Americans love their country because it seeks to advance "the potential of each of its citizens," "individual equality," and "individual rights."[6] This was at the heart of Thomas Jefferson's words in the Declaration of Independence of 1776—that "all men are created equal . . . endowed by their Creator with inherent and inalienable rights . . . life, liberty, and the pursuit of happiness"—and has been systematically echoed throughout American history, not least, as Teachout points out, by Martin Luther King Jr. in his speech of March 1963 in Washington when he referred to the Declaration and the Constitution as "a promissory note to which every American was to fall heir . . . a promise that all men—yes, black men as well as white men—would be guaranteed the unalienable rights of life, liberty, and the pursuit of happiness."[7]

This means that, as Liah Greenfeld, one of the leading scholars of nationalism, argues, American patriotism celebrates a social contract and a sense of the nation that are based neither on ethnicity—as might be the case for Japan or, until very recently and perhaps even today, Germany—nor a sense of collective belonging but instead on a fierce commitment to individualism and the civic values it needs to thrive. This is a love, as she puts it, of "principled individualism," which was first invented in England starting in the 1500s and was exported, with great success and for its purest articulation, to North America.[8] Historian Hans Kohn used similar words when writing that "American national consciousness is based upon the conviction of being different from other nations—different in . . . realizing, as the first people, with the greatest possible approximation to perfection, the general trend of human development towards a better rational order, greater individual liberty, and basic equality."[9] It seems reasonable to expect this perspective to pervade all levels of American society, including its lowest economic ranks: after all, its call for equality and the recognition that each person matters are good news, in some ways at least, to those with the fewest resources. Everyone matters, and each person should be valued as much as anyone else.

There is a second, related, element to American patriotism: the *American Dream*—the belief, however realistic or not, in the possibilities of upward mobility in society's ranks. As two psychologists recently observed, "American culture is filled with anecdotes about the promise of equal opportunity and the pursuit of happiness. Beliefs in the American Dream permeate our parenting decisions, educational practices, and political agendas." In fact, Americans are prone to grossly overestimating the actual chances of "social class mobility in society."[10] Mobility was likely quite high for much of the history of the United States (compared to that of Europe) but has decreased in recent times. Regardless of actual trends, however, what matters is the widespread rejection of exclusive and closed societal ranks and with that a refusal to recognize anyone's "innate superiority" as legitimate, as Hall and Lindholm note, and instead the acceptance and even celebration of "achieved status" as a mark of distinction. This logic, Hall and Lindholm continue, has been in place since the early days of the nation: "American settler-farmers thus bore some resemblance to nomads in being able to get up and move, and were therefore resistant to control by any establishment. . . . For Americans, success existed both in fact and as aspiration."[11] Commitment to the American Dream remains widespread today: "The American Dream," observes sociologist Robert Hauhart, "is among the United States' most recognizable and revered symbols of our national heritage."[12] It stands to reason then that it should continue to inform the love that its poorest members feel toward their country.

To these two elements we can add a third, and very important, one:

deliberate self-determination as a distinguishing mark of human beings, and America as the first society explicitly designed to allow for such self-determination.[13] The commitment to individualism is in fact logically premised on the possibility of individual deliberation and choice: without the potential of human beings to reflect, exercise their reason, and chart for themselves their future, individualism would lose its significance and uses. The same can be said of the American Dream. There is, therefore, in the American case an element of willfulness and intentionality: the United States is a country born out of a plan, rather than historical or geographic circumstances, and one that gives every one of its citizens the opportunity to be truly human.[14]

Put in slightly different terms, Americans are patriotic because they see in their country an unshakable and singular commitment to the ability of all people to define for themselves their lives and future. Other countries in this regard cannot match America, for none was founded with this very idea in mind. Crucially, this also means a high degree of comfort with the notion that things are open-ended: there is no vision of a "good" or "end point" that every person should aim for, and the same applies to society as a whole. Each person can determine her or his end point. This makes America in a sense more about process than outcome, and the patriotism of its people one of deep appreciation of that process. So it is also about the belief that such a process ultimately unleashes fantastic creativity and leads to the most amazing accomplishments. Not coincidentally, therefore, a recent Pew Research Center report shows that Americans see freedom as the most important factor that explains the country's success.[15] It is easy to see how this third element should prove attractive to Americans of all classes, including those with the fewest economic resources: It amounts to a celebration of possibilities, openness, and hope that applies to all individuals regardless of their economic standing in society at any given point in time. It is also devoid of prescription or judgment because people can choose who they wish to be, and no one is a better human being because of differences in wealth or other outcomes.

Research on American patriotism points to a fourth element: a long-standing sense that America occupies a special place in God's mind and plans—that it is *God's country*. The notion of Manifest Destiny, for instance, included for some at least the precept that the nation's expansion would happen because of divine design. Indeed, the very founding of the country was seen by many as reflective of divine will or, at the very least, as a special historical occurrence meant to ensure the proper worshipping and serving of God on earth.[16] Over time, despite the desire by some to keep God and country separate, references to God found their way into America's mythology and sense of self. Phrases such as "One Nation under God" in the Pledge of Allegiance, and "In God We Trust" on coins since the 1860s and bills since the 1950s, have both reflected and contributed to the belief that the country holds a special connection to God.[17] Thus, according to a poll conducted by the Public Religion Research Institute in June 2015, 62% of Americans either completely or mostly agree with the notion that "God has granted America a special role in human history." In addition, 52% thought that "believing in God" and 33% felt that "being a Christian" were very important for "being truly American."[18]

In sum, existing research offers these four insights into why Americans, in general, love their country and think of it as exceptional:

1. The dignity and rights granted to each individual by America's founding documents
2. The American Dream and the possibility that anyone can succeed
3. The freedom of self-determination that America guarantees to each citizen
4. The bond between God and the United States

It seems reasonable to expect these insights to apply at least in part to the patriotic perspectives of poor Americans, though the details of how this might be the case are unclear.

Research on the Patriotism of Marginalized Groups

Research on patriotism in America among disadvantaged groups points to other potentially useful insights. The creation of the American nation has not been a smooth or uncontested matter.[19] At many critical junctures in the country's history—such as the Civil War or the Vietnam War—everything from the flag to the Constitution has been contested.[20] Most pertinent, scholars with critical viewpoints have stressed that the universal, democratic, and individualistic qualities of American identity applied first only to white men and that everything that today contributes to a seamless singular narrative of patriotism (the flag, the national anthem, the Constitution, etc.) was the object of division, exclusion, and struggles.[21] Here scholarship tells us that not everyone could, in the history of the country, easily participate in the patriotic narrative: African Americans, Native Americans, women, various categories of immigrants (Irish, Italian, etc.), certain religious groups, and other groups all had to fight, with varying degrees of success, at one point or another for their place in American society.[22] Exclusion and the struggle to be included, in other words, have long been part of the American story.

How might this matter for our understanding of America's poor and their love of country? These stories of exclusions and contested inclusion in the American social contract, even if not directly concerned with the poor, in their own right might reveal something about the poor and their patriotism. Perhaps the most important point is that many of America's underprivileged groups have fought for their proper place in the American project not by challenging its core tenets but by forcefully arguing, with irrefutable logic, that the essence of the country's founding documents guarantees their inclusion in American society. Women, black Americans, Native Americans, gays and lesbians, and even militias made up mostly of working-class citizens (such as, for instance, the Kentucky State Militia) have put forth their claims not by seeking to change the foundational social contract of the country but by arguing that that contract is correct and complete in the first instance and is simply being violated by existing arrangements (such as subsequent policies and laws and informal repressive and exclusionary practices).[23] The American social contract applies to them, too, in other words, and any thoughts or practices to the contrary must be reversed.

Examples of such assertions abound. Native Americans' protracted struggle is perhaps among the most recent to be recognized and documented. Historian Paul Rosier's book on the difficult path toward full integration serves as a good illustration. The fight, he writes, "for three generations of Native politicians, intellectuals, and activists" was not one of challenging American values or foundational texts but of insisting that "the United States recognize its obligations to and the value of its indigenous people": anything short of that would be contrary to the United States' view of itself as the promoter of "liberty" at home and abroad. Native Americans have accordingly asked, in line with the values of America, for recognition as equal citizens and for their continued ability to protect their cultural heritage. As Rosier puts it, "American Indians defended their right to be both American and Indian, representing that right as the promise of American life."[24]

The historical record is accordingly full of claims and statements by Native Americans asserting their de facto right of belonging to the American nation. Consider, in this respect, the words of George Heron, president of the Seneca Nation, when addressing the US Congress in 1960: "I am proud to be an American citizen and have four years in the United States Navy to prove it. I am just as proud to be a Seneca Indian. And I do not see any reason why I cannot be both."[25] Or consider the opening pages of journalist and author James Robbins's recent book on Native Americans and patriotism:

Are you a native American? I am. I was born here, raised here, and seldom go abroad. I am indigenous to the North American continent, as is my culture. So I have as much right to the title of American as anyone else of similar circumstances. . . . I have a right to live here, and the Native Americans have a right to live here, too. We have the same rights—no more, no less. . . . The U.S. government describes me as "white non-Hispanic," along with two-thirds of the population. It is a strange non-hyphenated identity, like non-dairy-creamer—we know that it isn't, but what exactly is it? But as an American I am free to reject my government classification. My Americanism needs no prefix or suffix.[26]

Indeed, he adds, "American nationalism is not based on race, or blood, or land. People become Americans by choice."[27] These are powerful words, most of which could have very easily been pronounced by representatives of the gay and lesbian, civil rights, or other similar movements.

These sorts of assertions about the inherent Americanness of every citizen of the country make the patriotism of the American poor, rather than surprising given their difficult predicaments, quite logical and even something to be expected. Their unfortunate economic conditions in no way should interfere with their inclusion in the American social contract—much like being a woman, a gay man, a Native American, or an African American. There is no tension or contradiction between their situation and their love of country. And to the extent that they do suffer from marginalization, the correct antidote is not a rejection of the promises of America but, instead, an insistence that those premises be honored and extended to them as well.

A second major lesson that emerges from the history of marginalized groups in American society and their struggles to belong concerns their contributions to the nation: they have done as much as anyone else to build the country. Research suggests that contributing to one's country promotes patriotism.[28] It follows that if marginalized groups feel as central to the national project as anyone else, they would also think that they deserve recognition as full members. Their patriotism should therefore neither be questioned nor surprise us: it is legitimate and, in fact, earned. The history of the women's movements offers many illustrative examples. Women have served their country with ardor—in the domestic sphere, traditionally, but also in areas like medicine, law, the sciences, and even the military—and should be accepted as full and very patriotic members of their country. This is what we learn, for example, from the work of historian Kimberly Jensen on the mobilization of women to serve in the military during World War I.[29] Women physicians pushed hard to join the army's Medical Reserve Corps by, among other things, sending a resolution on behalf of the Medical Women's National Association in November 1917 to President Woodrow Wilson underscoring their love of country, "undivided loyalty," and desire to contribute.[30] Such service, in turn, would further bolster their claims to full citizenship and belonging: they "sought service with the military as a way to claim more complete female citizenship and increased postwar equality."[31]

Other important examples come from immigrant communities, such as a recent study chronicling Croatian Americans' claims of belonging and patriotism in the late 1940s and 1950s. Historian Scott Duryea tells us that "Croats took pride in qualifying their work as contributions to the advancement of the nation. Croats' hard work in the mills and mines built machinery for the war and the domestic infrastructure. By their labour, these Croats could justify themselves as the builders of twentieth-century American civilization. . . . [They] also paid dividends during World War II [when] Croatian men joined the American armed forces and left their families behind . . . and popular gender roles shifted to accommodate women filling the work that absent husbands left." Hence, "all of us," declared Stephen Brkich in the Croatian Fraternal Union's (CFU) *Zajedničar* newspaper, "helped build the America we know today."[32] CFU's president Vjekoslav Mandich would echo the same sentiment, when at a public gathering of thousands of Croatian Americans in 1948 in Pittsburgh, Pennsylvania, he declared that "there are none among us today who will not depart from this park with a new pride for our ancestry and a deep sense of satisfaction over the contributions our fine sons and daughters are making to the American scene."[33] He then characteristically followed the claim with a powerful statement in *Zajedničar* about Croatian Americans "recogniz[ing] but one Flag and but one authority, and that is the Flag and the Constitution of the United States" and, with that, the publication of a Freedom Pledge that began with "I am an American: a free American" and ended with "This heritage of freedom I pledge to uphold for myself and all mankind."[34]

If these accounts of hard work and love of country are accurate, it seems reasonable to expect that similar dynamics apply to America's poor and their patriotic sentiments. Many among the least well-off in American society are military veterans (or come from families with a long history of service), work (or have worked) at tough jobs—in construction, transportation, manufacturing, and so on—and make everyday life possible in America as fast-food workers, fruit pickers, yard and landscape workers, taxi drivers, nannies, and cleaners. Though not necessarily a cohesive group with the potential for a compelling collective narrative (such as African Americans, for instance), they have given a lot to America and, therefore, might ground their ownership and love of country in their contributions.

The literature on marginalized people in America gives us, then, potentially useful ideas about why America's poor are so patriotic. They add to the list of four insights from the previous section:

5. The inherent inclusiveness of America's founding documents and social contract

6. Their own hard work and having contributed to the building of the nation

Of course, how exactly these ideas might apply to the poor remains unclear. There clearly is no research on the patriotism of America's least well-off that we can ultimately consult or, even more broadly, on the relationship between economic class and patriotism.

We should note here two partial, worthwhile exceptions. One is a study by sociologist Yoshito Ishio.[35] Based on 2004 American National Election Study (ANES) survey data, Ishio found a positive association across income levels: as income increases, so do patriotic sentiments. This challenges the data presented earlier in this book. However, the definition used for "patriotism" is more in line with "nationalism" as understood in this book (patriotism is measured by Ishio in terms of love of country, feeling good or not when seeing the flag, and the importance of being American), and the population in question is white Americans. It is also purely a quantitative analysis that does not probe deeper into respondents' logics and beliefs. Its relevance to our question is therefore limited. Ishio does, however, generate another data point of possible interest: controlling for other factors, patriotism decreases as levels of education increase. Perhaps education levels may explain something about the patriotism of poor Americans. A second relevant source is the popular book *Deer Hunting with Jesus: Dispatches from America's*

Class War. The author, Joe Bageant, observes that working-class, poor Americans are "patriotic to their own detriment."[36] This is in line with our observations and a useful reference point. However, Bageant offers limited insights into the logic of that patriotism, other than describing the poor as hopelessly ignorant, alienated, and ultimately gullible.

Research on Social Cohesion

Psychologists, sociologists, and other social scientists have developed several theories about group and social cohesion. A subset of these theories focuses on members who are in the lower ranks of the group hierarchy but exhibit an unexpected attachment to those groups. To be sure, plenty of research points exactly in the opposite direction. Scholars such as Jim Sidanius, Yesilernis Peña, and Felicia Pratto have argued that the most disadvantaged people in a community do not, in fact, feel a sense of belonging and ownership. Those feelings are more widespread among members of dominant groups. This reasoning is extended to "the nation and its symbols,"[37] so in the case of European and North American countries the expectation is that white citizens should feel "greater ownership of and attachment to the nation than members of subordinate ethnic groups."[38] Yet, parallel to those studies, a line of inquiry has emerged into why the least-well-off members of groups at times actually exhibit a remarkable commitment to their groups. This research has not specifically considered the poor of the United States and their patriotism, but its insights might nevertheless be relevant.

The most important work concerns "system justification theory."[39] Its proponents argue that it is usually the least well-off who, in counterintuitive fashion, believe strongly "that existing social arrangements are fair, legitimate, justifiable, and necessary." The reason is that those at the bottom of the social hierarchy "have the greatest psychological need to reduce ideological dissonance" and are, therefore, "most likely to support, defend, and justify existing social systems, authorities, and outcomes."[40] Put in simpler terms, those who find themselves in the worst positions have the most pressures to find legitimacy in the social order. The alternative—believing that the system is unjust, unfair, or even random—is in fact painful and generates more stress. Approving of the system therefore serves a "palliative function," even though in practice it discourages seeking beneficial changes that might concretely redress existing inequalities. In this spirit, researchers report that low-income respondents and African Americans in the United States are more likely to believe that economic inequality in the country is both "legitimate and necessary,"[41] while a number of studies show that social exclusion leads those who are left out to assume that people deserve the outcomes they receive and that the system is meritocratic.[42]

This research could easily extend to patriotism. America's worst-off might indeed have very strong incentives for believing in the greatness of their nation, the American Dream, and other core aspects of their country. Why? Because their own conditions become more tolerable when contextualized as outcomes that are bound to happen if one lives in the most open and dynamic system the world has ever seen—a system that allows people to succeed but also, by necessity and definition, fail. The system is fair—great, in fact—and those at the bottom have not managed to make it. This line of reasoning has an important logical extension: The responsibility for one's conditions (wealth or poverty, success or failure) does not lie with others, the government, or the system. Rather, each person is the master of her or his destiny. This too can help make the outcome more tolerable, since it removes from the equation any possibility of injustice or wrong. Poor Americans might be patriotic because this helps them rationalize and accept their position; it is an effective sort of self-help strategy.

An older intellectual tradition on social cohesion puts forth a less benevolent, and one could say condescending, possibility. Thinkers like Karl Marx, Herbert Marcuse, and Karl Mannheim have argued that misguided perceptions and "false consciousness" among the lower classes of capitalist nations help them feel good about themselves and reduce the likelihood of disgruntlement and revolt.[43] To achieve this, the poor must be convinced of the goodness of the system they live in. This is accomplished by concealing reality, creating blind spots, and distorting facts among the worst-off. The poor see inaccurately, think inaccurately, and embrace values that are ultimately against their own interests. Capitalist corporations, a corrupt media, a warped political system, and a biased education system have helped make that happen, as contemporary intellectuals such as Noam Chomsky argue.[44] Indeed, blinded, the poor often adopt the values of wealthier classes—in particular those of the bourgeoisie and, in the United States, to the puzzlement of many analysts, of the Republican Party and its more conservative ideology[45]—and thus feel fairly content about their country and ultimately their personal lot. Their patriotism could easily be explained in light of this sort of misinformed and inaccurate worldview: it signifies a naïve embracement of positive sentiments that manages to placate the lower classes and further advance and replicate a system that deprives them.

To these two bodies of work, we can add the more general theories of cohesion that are not specifically developed with marginalized groups as their core population. One strand of this research might be particularly promising. Drawing from rational choice theory, researchers have described the "instrumental attachment" that members of a group feel based on "subjective cost and benefit estimations of belonging to a nation" or, for that matter, any other type of group.[46] The idea is that citizens may feel more positively inclined toward their country if they sense that they can reach goals that would not be available as single individuals. This is potentially applicable to America's poor: it could very well be the case that their patriotism is driven in part by a sense of appreciation of the society they live in because of particular benefits they receive (access to good public resources like libraries and the Internet, or access to disability benefits, Medicaid, unemployment benefits, and so on) and because they feel supported by other Americans (via donations and volunteering services).

Research on group cohesion, then, suggests three additional and rather different factors that might explain the patriotism of America's least well-off:

7. A desire to rationalize one's unfortunate situation by celebrating American society

8. Ignorance and misconceptions about the true state of things
9. Rational calculation of the net benefits associated with being an American citizen

Again, these are only initial ideas and amount to untested possibilities. Only an in-depth and direct exploration of the mind-set of America's poor can reveal the logic behind their patriotism.

The Road to Alabama and Montana

Our discussion so far has yielded potentially useful insights into the patriotism of America's poor. But we still know very little about the nature of that patriotism. Our next step is to probe further into the minds of patriotic poor Americans: this can be done best with in-depth, semistructured interviews. To determine where to hold those interviews and how to select respondents, I followed the rules of social scientific research design and kept squarely in mind that poor Americans of many different and potentially consequential (for the sort of patriotism that is being embraced) backgrounds are highly patriotic.

The most appropriate approach in our case is to purposely seek out poor patriotic Americans as respondents and attempt to capture the full variety of patriotic views that might be out there among poor Americans. We want to speak to as wide an array of poor patriotic Americans as possible to hear all the key narratives. Our findings would be much less interesting if we heard from only a very specific subset of respondents and narratives. In the social sciences, this approach is known as "purposive maximum variation sampling."

Using GSS data, we can identify regions of the United States where patriotism among the poor (those who identify themselves as belonging to the lower class) seems especially widespread; this can help us select "hotbeds" of patriotism among the poor and thus increase the chances that we will speak with relevant and representative respondents. If we use the statement that "America is a better country than most other countries in the world" as a proxy for patriotism, cumulative data from 1966 to 2014 suggest that the hotbeds of patriotism among the poor are what the GSS classifies as the states in the Mountain (Arizona, Colorado, Idaho, Montana, Nevada, New Mexico, Utah, and Wyoming) and East South Central (Alabama, Kentucky, Mississippi, and Tennessee) regions. In the Mountain region, 85% of lower-class Americans "agree" or "strongly agree" with the idea that America is a better country than most other countries; the figure is 86% in the East South Central region. These are the highest percentages in the country (matched only in the West South Central region, with 86%; but there only 32% "strongly agree" with the idea, which means that more than 50% only "agree"; the other two regions have higher percentages of respondents strongly agreeing), as shown in Table 2.

Importantly, East South Central would stand out as well if we were to use the second proxy for patriotism from the GSS data set ("I would rather be a citizen of the United States than of any other country in the world"). The combined scores for those who "agree" or "strongly agree" is 100%: this is the highest of any region. The score for the Mountain region is 89%, which is overall in line with the average for all regions.[47]

Because we are interested in maximizing the breadth of patriotic narratives we will hear, we should start by selecting one state each from the East South Central and Mountain regions. Bearing in mind that each region is a hotbed of patriotism, we are especially interested in states that are otherwise very different in historical, political, and cultural backgrounds. I selected Alabama, which has a history of poorly funded public programs (education, unemployment, etc.), recently suffered from the Federal Emergency Management Agency's incompetence after Hurricane Katrina, and still has strong elements supporting its Confederate and secessionist past. The patriotic voices of the American poor in Alabama should be both revealing and fascinating. I then chose Montana because its northern location, independent and rugged spirit, and vast openness set it very much apart from Alabama. It seems reasonable to expect the narratives there to have a very different flavor from those in Alabama.

To identify the specific sites for the interviews, we should consider that important differences are likely to exist between urban and rural

GSS Region	Strongly Agree (%)	Agree (%)	Neither Agree nor Disagree (%)	Disagree (%)	Strongly Disagree (%)
New England	50	30	20	0	0
Middle Atlantic	31	34	17	7	10
East North Central	42	39	12	7	0
West North Central	43	33	19	5	0
South Atlantic	46	33	17	4	0
East South Central	53	33	7	7	0
West South Central	32	54	5	8	0
Mountain	45	40	5	10	0
Pacific	41	38	10	10	0

Table 2. Lower-Class Americans across Regions Agreeing That America Is a Better Country Than Most Other Countries. "Lower Class" is the lowest class identification available to respondents. Source: General Social Survey 1996, 2004, 2014. Variables: Subjective Class Identification, Agree America Is a Better Country, and Region of Interview.

settings. We saw from Table 1 that rural residents, when patriotic, are often intensely so. Research has also shown that unique strands of patriotism are found in rural America.[48] It seems appropriate to have interviews take place in both urban and rural settings. Using US Census data we can pick ZIP Code Tabulation Areas (ZCTAs) in Birmingham, Alabama, and Billings, Montana (both cities with populations greater than 100,000) with a high concentration of poor people: these will be ZCTAs with high percentages of families (for those cities) living on incomes of less than $25,000 per year.[49] This is very close to the $24,250 that the US government uses to determine whether a family of four lives below the poverty line.[50] Thus, we avoid ZCTAs where fewer poor people live, both because they would be harder to find and because we want to speak with poor Americans who by and large experience life in a poor setting, as most impoverished Americans do.

For Birmingham, I selected two ZCTAs: 35203 and 35234. The first is at the very center of the city where, per the US Census Bureau,[51] 44% of families earn less than $25,000 a year. The second is adjacent (to the north) to 35203 and has 47% of families living on less than $25,000 a year. I chose two ZCTAs for Birmingham because of the relatively high numbers of them in that city, their small size, and a desire to ensure that I would find sufficient numbers of venues to recruit respondents. Billings, however, has only a handful of ZCTAs. In this case, I selected its least well-off, which covers a significant portion of the city: 59101. There, nearly one out of five families lives on less than $25,000 a year.

We should select one ZCTA in rural settings (towns with population less than 10,000) in both Alabama and Montana where there are sizable concentrations of families living on $25,000 or less.[52] The rural ZCTAs chosen should be confined to those within two hundred miles of Birmingham and Billings, respectively, for purposes of limiting travel times and costs and those that have at least a town, to ensure that at least several interviews can be set up through some public facility (library, community center, etc.), and organizations (the town newspaper, for instance, or a local church). Given our interest in ensuring that we capture a variety of narratives, and because many scholars of patriotism in America emphasize the importance of race in shaping people's experiences of their love of country, we should disregard highly homogeneous ZCTAs in terms of race.

ZCTA 35592 meets these criteria in Alabama—and, within that, the town of Vernon, with a population of almost 2,000, and a total population for the ZCTA of around 4,700. Vernon is ninety-six miles almost directly west of Birmingham, very close to the border with Mississippi. The percentage of families living on less than $25,000 is around 28%. For Montana, it meant ZCTA 59036 and within that, the town of Harlowton, with around 1,000 residents. The broader ZCTA has

1,500 people. Here, around 19% of the families earn less than $25,000 a year. Maps 1, 2, and 3 show the interview sites.

How should we select respondents in these urban and rural settings? By analyzing GSS data, we have already determined that all categories of respondents have very high levels of patriotism. At the same time, we saw some differences in terms of overall propensity to be patriotic and intensity of patriotism and reasoned that similar numerical values do not necessarily mean that the substance of the patriotism is identical across categories. We also learned from the academic literature that different groups of Americans have had distinctive histories with patriotism and that they likely subscribe at least in part to distinctive patriotic narratives. It would be very useful, therefore, to ensure a diverse pool of interviewees. To be clear, the purpose of ensuring this sort of variation in the interviewee pool is not to generalize about those differences in background but to hear as wide a variety of perspectives as possible to best capture the sorts of patriotic narratives being articulated.

Thus, how many interviews are necessary for a study such as this? A general social scientific rule for in-depth interviews is that one should strive for "saturation" in the answers being collected: new respondents should be recruited until the interviewer hears the same ideas repeated over and over and conversations with additional respondents yield little that is new. In studies that rely on extensive interviews based on purposive sampling, this means that researchers typically conduct thirty to fifty interviews.[53] Given that we have two primary sites (Alabama and Montana) and that differences are likely to exist between those sites, we can consider sixty interviews as a good number (thirty or so in each state, with at least some in rural settings).

The recruitment of respondents went as follows. A few weeks before my arrival, I asked local schools, public libraries, community resource centers, senior centers, homeless shelters, coffee shops, community newspapers, and government offices to inform the public in those ZCTAs of the possibility, if they were below the official poverty line as set by the US government for 2015 ($11,770 income for a single person; $15,930 for a family of two; $20,090 for a family of three; and

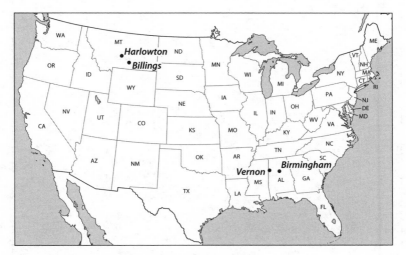

Map 1. Interview Sites in Alabama and Montana.

$24,250 for a family of four)[54] and felt themselves to be very patriotic, of participating in an extended interview (around thirty to forty-five minutes) for a small monetary compensation. Interested respondents were asked to contact me via e-mail or phone and provide me with some basic information (location, race, political orientation, income, age, gender, etc.). In line with the working definition of "poor" in this book, one individual who felt herself to be in the lower class of society and expressed interest in being interviewed was also considered (her income was just a little above the poverty line). Around 50% of the interviewees in Alabama were set up in this manner ahead of my visit there. However, no one contacted me ahead of time from Montana.

Once in Alabama and Montana, I also approached individuals in various public places (Laundromats, fast-food restaurants, bus stations, used-clothing stores, homeless shelters, sidewalks, senior citizen centers, and other such sites) with expected high numbers of low-income people. In some cases, I began by asking immediately if they were patriotic and loved their country. In other cases, I initiated conversations about unrelated topics (the weather, for instance), made some general comments about the country, and then eventually inquired about their

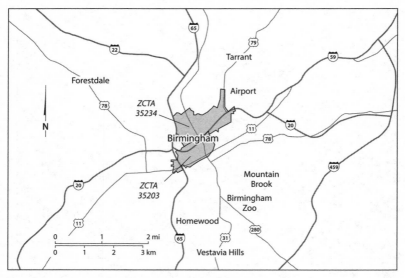

Map 2. Birmingham (AL) Interview Sites' ZCTAs.

levels of patriotism. In those cases where individuals emphatically stated that they were patriotic, I asked whether they would be willing to be formally interviewed, provided that they were low income (something that I verified later in the interview as well). If they answered positively, I would find a quiet space, provide them with the relevant information and consent forms, and proceed with the interview and the recording. Importantly, this on-site recruitment allowed me to ensure the right demographic mix of respondents: as I proceeded, I was able to select respondents to keep my sample as diverse as possible.

For Birmingham specifically, I conducted most of my interviews in November 2015 at three sites: the Birmingham Greyhound Bus Station, First Light Women's Shelter, and the central branch of the Birmingham Public Library. In Vernon, I conducted the interviews during the same month at the town library, a local barbecue restaurant, and a used-clothing store. I arrived in Billings, Montana, in April 2016. The majority of my interviews were conducted at two Laundromats; others took place in the Billings Public Library, in the front yard of a dry house for recovering alcoholics, and the Jefferson Lines Bus Station. In Harlowton, the interviews took place at the town library, the Harlowton

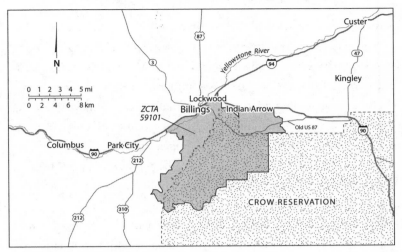

Map 3. Billings (MT) Interview Site's ZCTA.

Senior Citizen Center, and a small real estate office. I unexpectedly also interviewed a couple in a very small town on the way back to Billings, after driving by a house and stopping to admire the American flag flying in the front yard.

The Appendix offers details about the interview process, questionnaire, and coding methodology for the transcribed interviews and lists the interviewees and their basic demographic profiles. The reader will likely find it useful to refer to the Appendix when needing a reminder of who any given interviewee might be. Overall, of the total sixty-three interviewees, thirty-six identified as white, four as white and another race or ethnicity (Hispanic or Native American), seventeen as black, two as Hispanic, one as Asian, and three as Native American. There was a balanced mix of conservatives, liberals, and politically inactive or independents; married and singles; and young (below forty), middle-aged (forty to fifty-nine), and older respondents (sixty and older). Many, but not all, of the respondents described themselves as religious. The gender balance was close to 50% male and 50% female. Some twelve respondents had served in the military, with several more coming from families with members who had served. Most of the interviewees either had no permanent job or worked at part-time and often informal jobs. Approximately 15% of the interviews took place in rural settings.

Two interviewees in Alabama and one in Montana were not patriotic: I included these because I was interested in capturing at least a glimpse of what alternative narratives might exist. Their views, along with the reservations that some of the other sixty interviewees had about America, are captured briefly in the Appendix. A handful of respondents had incomes somewhat above the official poverty line but felt that they were either poor or living on a very limited income. I noted this and included them in the pool.

The interview itself was semistructured, with an initial section of questions designed to capture basic background information about respondents (age, race, occupation, political orientation, etc.) and screen the respondents for their levels of patriotism (using primarily the GSS questions on whether a person would rather be a citizen of the United States than of any other country, and whether the United States is better than most other countries on earth) and income levels. The core sections of the interview then delved deeply into the nature of their patriotism—the values associated with America, the relative standing of America in the world, the merits and limitations of other countries, and so on—and how respondents reconciled (if in fact they did) the potential contradictions between their love of country and the challenges facing them, inequality in America, and other potentially contradictory facts. Several of the questions took into consideration the potentially useful insights from the existing research discussed earlier. I asked, for instance, whether the United States shared a special relationship with God. But most questions ultimately gave the respondents as much freedom as possible to elaborate on their perspectives and sentiments.

For example, one question asked whether we should teach our children to be patriotic. If the respondents answered yes, a combination of related questions followed: Why is it important? What sorts of things should we teach our children about America? Why does the interviewee care so much about this? Do those things set America apart from other countries? Questions like these served as open-ended prompts for interviewees to articulate their patriotic views. Another question asked whether the United States should do more to help its low-income and disadvantaged people. Additional questions on inequality, hard work, rights and privileges, America as the land of opportunity, and immigrants and racial groups often followed. These sorts of questions offered much latitude for broad and far-ranging discussions.

Taken together, the questions offered numerous valuable opportunities to explore the respondents' love of the United States, their relationship to the country as it might have evolved over time, and their understanding of the core characteristics of the country. Importantly, as stated from the outset, my primary objective was to gain insights into the thoughts and beliefs of the interviewees. As a result, each of the following three chapters is organized around one of three major patriotic narratives I encountered and, within those, more specific themes and threads. I sought to give voice to the interviewees: the chapters are rich with quotes and, hopefully, devoid of critical assertions or speculative interpretations.

The sixty-three interviews were recorded, transcribed (894 single-spaced pages), coded, and examined for themes and overall narratives following the most recent methodological guidelines for such an analysis.[55] The Appendix specifies in more detail how this was done. The following pages include extensive quotations. For those, minimal editorial changes were made to minimize interjections that were irrelevant to the intended meanings.

CHAPTER 4

THE LAST HOPE

For me to give up hope on the country in which I live in is almost to give up hope for self. So I gotta keep the light burning for me and for my country or I'm gonna be in the dark.

Shirley, Birmingham, Alabama

Many of the people I met had no stable jobs, and a good number did not have permanent housing. Often, they recounted that at some point in their lives things went terribly wrong—with substance addiction, for instance, or an abusive partner or parent—and ever since they had found themselves unable to hold on to a steady job or provide properly for themselves and their children. Some were convicted felons, just released from prison and looking to make a fresh start with a few dollars in their pockets. To be sure, a good number did work, received government benefits (often for disability), or enjoyed some kind of retirement benefits. But even in these cases their income was so limited that they often found it impossible to make ends meet. As Michelle, a middle-aged black woman in Birmingham told me, a relatively senior job as manager at a McDonald's restaurant means a paycheck of only eight hundred to nine hundred dollars a month, while working in construction in Billings translates, at least for Kevin, a young white man, into ten thousand dollars a year. Even without children or other dependents, these are inadequate amounts for a decent living.

These Americans struggle. But in their minds and hearts there is little doubt that their country is exceptional. They feel that there is something transcendental about America. It has a special place in the history of the world. They view the United States, despite its shortcomings, as still the shining city on a hill: a place designed and intended to represent deliverance from the ills that have plagued humanity throughout history to this very day. America, in a word, represents hope, both for humanity and for each individual person in the country, including, crucially, themselves.

This belief in the exceptionality of the United States became all the more stark when the interviewees spoke of other countries. Pictures of oppressive and destitute places were frequently evoked. While other countries deprive their citizens of all kinds of basic necessities, America—with its principles and immense practical generosity—offers reprieve and the possibility of a better future. For someone struggling every day to make ends meet, such promises are particularly valuable. The idea of exceptionality was further reinforced by a belief that, while God is kind and loves everyone equally, he holds America in a special place in its heart: America is God's country. And with this there was also an almost tragic sense, described by several, that one *has* to believe in America: when all else seems to be a struggle, faith in country, and in America in particular, is a must.

Elements of this narrative resonated with the first, fourth, and the eighth insights we considered in the previous chapter as potentially useful for understanding the patriotism of America's poor: America's founding documents offer individuals unprecedented dignity and rights, God is closely connected to the country and its people, and considerable ignorance and misconceptions about other countries make it easier to think of America as superior. But some of the other ideas, such as the almost existential need to believe in the country, proved much more unexpected. Let us begin listening, then, to the words and thoughts of the sixty-three interviewees.

For All of Humanity

Ray is a black army veteran in his mid-fifties, looking forward to the start of a new job selling gardening tools, after a long stretch of unemployment and homelessness. He spent three years in Germany as a soldier and was able to travel across Europe. He was one of many to put forth a picture of the United States as a reference point for humanity at large—as a country whose greatness is of benefit to people everywhere. When I asked him for the first three words that come to mind when imagining the American flag, he said he thought of "pride, duty, and honor. That's what I see. You know, I'm proud to be an American, and it's an honor to be American." "Why," I probed, "is it an honor to be American?" Ray answered that "we lead by example in every form or fashion, whether it be financial, education, military of course, as a whole. You know, some guys in other countries, they have an edge on us in certain things, but on the overall . . . we're ahead . . . we lead." The United States, in other words, sets the standard and serves as the *example* for others. While sometimes other countries outperform the United States, in "the major areas, the more important areas," the United States is ahead.

I encountered repeatedly this idea of the United States as a leading and inspiring country. Jill, a white conservative married mother in her forties who works in a very modest real estate office in Harlowton and who has suffered from extended spells of poverty, likened the role of the United States to that of a parent:

Well, yeah, I think there were a lot of times historically when the US has stood out, especially if there was a time of political upheaval. . . . And they're looking for us to kinda . . . hello, we need your help, you know, or if there's some financial problem and they're wanting more money or just things that . . . community-wise across the world that, when people start to look to the US to be a trendsetter or if something happens, if there's an incident in the world, and they, and they . . . look to the US to see how we're gonna respond. That says something about, about who . . . what kind of influence we have and who we are. It's kinda like if I liken it to my family. If something happens who's the first . . . my children always look to the parents and go, how is this . . . is this a good thing or a bad thing, how are we supposed to respond to this? . . . [This] presents a bit of authority, and I feel like in a lot of ways the United States operates in that way, and other countries do look to us. What's our response gonna be?

When questioned whether America's responses have invariably been good for the world, her reply was somewhat balanced at first but eventually became more assertive:

I think we've done good, yeah. We've done some bad too, but I mean everybody has. We're . . . we're . . . we are not a perfect people, and so every human being has an issue, so I bring my imperfections here, I bring my imperfections to my church, I bring my imperfections to my family. . . . When I was like . . . I've been on a school board previously, so I brought my imperfections to that board and made it imperfect. It kinda just, you know, just . . . you know what I'm saying. . . . You know, . . . I'm very proud of the United States, but in the same respect, I'm not ever, I'm not ever gonna apologize for being American. I will not do that.

It was, however, Eddie, a struggling, somewhat liberal, black man in his late fifties originally from New York City and now in Birmingham, who spent the most effort discussing what could be called the transcendental qualities of the United States. A self-described avid reader who has struggled with addictions and other personal problems, he thought of the United States as a unique experiment in the history of humanity:

First of all I think America is the last best hope of man on earth. That's why it's a man-run country. We try to uphold the principles of liberty and freedom to the best of our ability, and many countries even today do not have the rights and freedoms, and it was bought dearly, in this country . . . my people and patriots of this country who believed in the principles of America. . . . Well, of course, we know that the human race isn't perfect, but I think the ideals that the forefathers had envisioned were to liberate and raise man to its highest level that it can achieve and not keep our, to keep us in bestiality basically.

The exceptionality of America, for Eddie, lies in its explicit intention to free each person's spirit from external oppression or, simply, primitive types of existences. Hence, in a dictatorship, human fulfillment is "not impossible, but it's unlikely because its [fulfillment] starts with the human spirit. . . . I think, in a free society man is able to achieve much more than he might think possible." And America has excelled at this:

Look at the achievements America has . . . I need to rephrase that. Look at the achievements that the people of America have built upon during its existence. I would say probably half of the population of the world, if they could, would attend American universities and schools. . . . There's high achievement and art, literature, science, and me even as an African American, unfortunately Africa has a lot . . . has a ways to go, but because of places like America, African Americans have been able to achieve a lot more educationally and economically than most other people who came to those countries the way we did in chains and shackles and managed to work our way out of these situations. And part of the key to that has been education. To free a person's mind is to free, is to free them from a chain and to become the best they can be, and we fall in that category also as African Americans 'cause it, principles and . . . these principles and liberty and freedom are not restricted to the white man. I believe all of us have that ability in us if given the opportunity. It's an exceptional country because nobody does what we do. There's no country as diverse as America. . . . Nobody does what we do.

The promise of the United States, then, extends to all human beings: "There's a place for everyone in society, and I think that we try to live up to those principles for the most part." This, Eddie continued, is unlike other countries, especially those with religions that are in need of "reformation." "America," therefore, "is the last best hope of countries on earth." Along with Canada and perhaps some other European countries, the United States recognizes

the human capacity to improve itself, and, and, and they try to allow the human spirit to flourish. Whereas in these second and third world countries, that's not the case. But you can't . . . you also notice that once some of these countries get a sense of their self-worth and what they can achieve and what they would like to become in their life and what they choose to become, once these countries get an inkling and a sense and a taste of freedom and opportunity, none of them want to go back, I would say for the most part unless the government crushes the, tries to crush the human spirit. And I mean human spirit; I'm not talking about American . . . the human spirit.

What the United States has done is to respond to the call of the human spirit: therein lie its universal qualities and, therefore, its appeal. Many of the interviewees subscribed to this point of view. For Phil, for instance, a former government cartographic technician in Billings who had to retire early because of an accident and is living on no income, the United States "has influenced a lot of countries in, in that their ability to create their own constitutions that tried to improve upon the Constitution that we had"—countries that he would one day like to visit, "but I don't have a means of, of doing that."

The idea that the United States stands for something bigger than itself became an early theme with many of the interviewees. It took on more specific qualities when the interviewees shared with me their views of the country's actions and stance in the world. What does the United States stand for on the world stage? What does it offer the world? Two things in particular stood out: generosity and answering the call to do the right thing.

Generosity

America has a magnanimous spirit. Its promise extends beyond its borders and reaches out to every human being on earth. America is for many the promised land and has an outsized heart, and this is a source of immense pride. As Anne, an elderly white woman who retired as director of a senior citizen center in Harlowton put it, the American flag "has earned the right to fly, and I don't think it should ever be burned, because we are a nation that helps others, have always been. . . . Oh yes, yeah. I think we've always been." Ray expressed a very similar sentiment in Birmingham: "I mean, we, we care . . . the heart is in the right place, we caring, we, we generous, . . . We're very generous and, we don't mind helping people, you know?"

Several interviewees encouraged me to think about America's generosity. Shirley, a forty-six-year-old unemployed black woman with plans to become a chef, pointed to the loftier achievements of the country and the readiness of Americans to share them with others. Americans of all ethnicities and backgrounds have planted "the seed of ambition, love, pride, bravery, strength." And America has selflessly spread the fruits of all that throughout the world: "Here we have all come to a point where we have gifted the world from America . . . technology, science, music, arts, theater . . . just the cooperative engagement in . . . reaching out to others. Some things that we knew were developed here in this country, we could have kept it to ourselves, but we didn't. We shared it."

America's "sharing" and "gifting" spirit has extended to the basic necessities of life. America gives "aid, foods, shelters to other countries," as Angie, a young white mother from Alabama on her way to Colorado, said. We "send food to other countries," said Hubert, a self-described borderline schizophrenic in Birmingham, who marched with Martin Luther King in the 1960s and witnessed firsthand the turmoil of the civil rights movement. It was the same sentiment expressed by Oscar, a fifty-six-year-old Hispanic concrete finisher in Billings, who said that the United States is a force for good in the world because "we give a lot of good . . . aid out, you know what I'm saying? . . . Billions and billions of dollars." For many of the interviewees, like Gabby, a twenty-seven-year-old unemployed white woman waiting for a bus in Birmingham, America's contributions boil down to one word: "protection."

The comparison with other countries was sometimes implicit and other times explicit, even if done on rather shaky grounds—something that we see again at various points in this book. Denzel, a black man who works seasonally by helping put up tents at events, for instance, told me that

the United States does a lot of things that are good for Ethiopian kids, Ethiopians . . . look at what, look at the UNICEF program. What other country is trying to help Ethiopians? The kids? You don't see commercials on TV where Germany is trying to help Ethiopians; you don't see China on TV where they're trying to help Ethiopians; you don't see that. So that's the good of coming out of America, trying to help neighboring countries. I don't say neighboring countries right next door, but neighboring countries trying to do the right thing.

Jeff, a white/Native American truck driver waiting for a bus in Billings, while talking about God's plans for the United States, felt that "he gives us the freedom and power to help other people, you know. I mean, look, look, look what we do in Africa . . . and what does Africa do for us? But it's not, it's not that way . . . it's not a give and take . . . it's a give and help." The direction seemed one way to many: The United States gives more than it receives. But, as Jeff suggested, this might have something to do with God. He was not alone in thinking so. As Sidney—a young, white woman who began doing drugs at the age of nine and recently spent three years in federal prison in Arizona for drug distribution—explained,

I believe that God wants us to help the less fortunate, and that's all over the world. He wants us to go out into the other countries and help those, those people. . . . Yeah, of course, he does. He wants us to take our wealth, to take what we've got here and go to share it with those that are less fortunate. And to just always [mumbles] love and what's fair. I don't know what's fair . . . treating people kindly, treating people how you want to be treated and loved and respected and honored . . . integrity, you know, what's right, do what's right.

And thus it makes sense that both the public and private sectors participate in this. "Why do you think . . . we are trillions of dollars in debt?" Jeff asked me. "Do you think we should be less generous?" I asked. "No, no. As long as they don't start raising taxes." To my suggestion that the money could "go to something else," Jeff noted without hesitation that "a lot, a lot of that stuff is done by charitable stuff, you know, like doctors going over and, you know, killing viruses and stuff that are infecting people over there . . . HIV and all of that stuff and whatever. . . . I think that's, that's what the United States is all about, helping. Giving a hand out. Not a push down."

Generosity means as well a remarkable "openness" to letting others come into the country and do well for themselves. America is a better country than most " 'cause we bless others," reasoned Kysha, an aspiring homeless black woman artist at a woman's shelter in Birmingham: "We let people come over and get rich, and we're the land of the free." For some of the interviewees, such as Lanai, a young Asian woman who has served in the US military, this sort of openness holds deep personal meaning. In a Laundromat in Billings, she described America as being "my savior . . . because of what my people went through; it's the Americans that helped us, my people get here to the US. . . . We came here during the Vietnam War [from Laos and Thailand]."

This openness has an almost romantic quality. As I listened, the image of the Statue of Liberty kept coming up. Darrius and Janice made an old, beaten-up Saab their home. He was in his forties, and Janice was in her early twenties, recently served in the army, and was pregnant. Both smoked throughout the interview, even if they complained of not having enough money to pay rent of three hundred to four hundred dollars per month for an apartment. Though fairly cynical and worried about the direction of the country, they consistently found themselves recognizing their love of the United States and the ideals on which it was founded. As Janice put it,

A lot of the times yes, you know, we offer refuge to those who can't necessarily get it elsewhere, even, I mean, obviously not to the Syrian refugees now . . . but we've always kinda been that country that, that had the open arms that said come here, we have everything you need: we have the freedom, we have the jobs, and we have the opportunity for you to make money.

To this, Darrius interjected that "there's an old saying like 'give me your huddled masses . . .' something like that." "And then," Janice continued, "I kinda still believe that we're like that, and a lot of people don't, but I still see us as that country that welcomes people with open arms."

Answering the Call to Do the Right Thing

I encountered a widespread sense that America is moved by an almost moral imperative to do for other countries what they wish to, but cannot, do for themselves—even if this can sometimes come at a great cost for the United States. Put differently, without the United States, chaos and disaster would ensue. This, too, was an important source of pride. "We're trying to keep the peace," stated Sam, a sixty-year-old black man in a bus station in Birmingham. He continued, "Trying to keep the peace 'cause some people can't even keep the peace in their own country, they need help. They don't have the resources . . . because, you know, the United States is a good place to live. You know, like I said, land of opportunities. So you teach them other ways," though, he quickly added, "and then gonna get killed anyway." There is a need for the United States to act. As Cole, a white ex-felon originally from Texas, told me on a street in Billings, in front of the dry house where he was spending time to stay sober and rebuild his life,

Yes . . . I think sometimes we put our nose in other people's business. . . . However, I think other countries look to us as the world's protector, the world's policeman because, you know, everybody's like, look how rich the United States is and, you know, then . . . with, with Iraq and Afghanistan and I mean, I feel like Saddam needed to be taken out of power; Gaddafi needed to be taken out of power; Osama Bin Laden, I think, he needed to be killed.

All this had to be done, and only the United States could do the job, even if the cost was high, as Cole added, "Do I think we should be twenty trillion in debt? No."

This is similar to what Chad, twenty-six years old, now a farm inspector after years of active duty in Iraq, thought the United States does in other countries: "Defending the freedom . . . not only defending the freedom but defending the other people's freedoms. It's . . . over there, it's, it's a lot different. They even . . . decapitate . . . they decapitate people just for speaking out; I mean, unlike here where you can say what you want, over there, no, you couldn't say what you wanted. They were the head of the household, women were below a house cat . . . right, and it was just horrible." Americans came to the rescue of defenseless people.

The image of the United States as a savior, protecting locals in faraway places from wrong, was evoked by several Vietnam veterans. "What do you think you were fighting for when you were in Vietnam?" I asked Jeff in Billings. The exchange that followed was educational: "Fighting for people that couldn't stand up for themselves. . . . You know, while I was over there, you know, I seen a lot of stuff that wasn't right, but for the most part I just felt that we needed to be over there." I wanted to hear more: "You felt that way?" He replied with conviction: "Yeah, because those people couldn't defend themselves. . . . It's like when we fought in Korea, you know." This made me wonder what he would say about America's defeat in Vietnam, so I interjected, "Korea, well Korea we, in the end, we cut in half, but the Vietnam War, the communists, didn't they in the end run over the whole country?" Jeff's reply surprised me and was emblematic of many of the conversations I had, which were for the most part quite coherent but occasionally veered into significant confusion or factual inaccuracies: "Yeah, they tried to. But they didn't. There's still a separation."

The moral imperative to intervene was made stronger by the simple fact that other countries ask the United States to intervene: other countries actively turn to us with hope. As Chad put it,

I think it's, it is kinda a little bit of arrogance that some . . . we do hop into some other countries' business, but then again sometimes those countries do ask Americans for help. . . . Just because it doesn't go in the media, like, you know, the president of Iraq came over and said, hey, we need help with dealing with ISIS or something . . . or back then it was Al-Qaeda.

His thinking was echoed by his partner, Lanai: "Yeah, like, I don't know 'cause I'm not . . . I don't know much about history, but, but the way I see it . . . I haven't seen the US go in now and attacking people or start a war. We usually just stay until you ask for help, you know?"

It follows that America, as Shirley told me, acts with the right intentions, even if the outcomes are at times far from perfect. It is as if, blessed with material richness and abundance, America also has a noble heart:

When, when things are done from the proper intent, which is normally the heart, the blessing of, the gifting of, I want to see you drink water like I drink water. Look how special that is now; we'll share a glass of water together. Look what I can . . . look what I've given you and what you've given me back. You know when things are done from the right motive and intent, then it blossoms and it blooms across nations, and mountains, and rivers, and countries. Now when America acts from that point of love and empathy, then that I love . . . that brings about a greater appreciation.

At the same time, to be sure, America's intentions can be misunderstood, and this, I heard frequently, means that other countries do not like us. But this does not mean that America's heart is in the wrong place. As Fiona, a white mother of a foster child, who had just lost her job in Harlowton, told me, "We used to be one of the world leaders. . . . We're now looked on as a, as a bad guy by a lot of people . . . the other countries. And . . . I don't know, I can't explain how that happened for sure, but I know that the heart of America is not like that."

In any case, there is clearly a sense that the world still greatly admires the United States. Will, a former marine now landscaping in Birmingham, told me, "Well, actually the people over there in other countries make you feel . . ." He could not quite find the words to complete his thought, so I suggested "make you feel proud?" "Yeah, yeah," Will continued. I then asked, "What do you think they admire you for?" The answer was revealing: "You know, being American." I followed by asking what he thought this meant to them. He answered, "I think it's . . . you know, that's kinda hard because I really really don't exactly know, but I know they mostly wanted to be American, they wanted to know other stuff about America, they wanted to know what's going on in this state; I guess they wanted to come here, and they couldn't." I decided to probe further: "What do you think the US represents to them?" "I think freedom," Will replied. "I think it's that and freedom and wealth. . . . Yeah, I mean, they can't get out of poverty so . . .'cause what I'm thinking about is the Philippines and the low income, the low area poverty in the Philippines . . . grass huts, mud huts, and stuff like that. Yeah, I've seen that; I sure have."

I would hear this line of logic multiple times. Reflecting on his time in Germany in the service, Ray recalled that "I got a lot of respect, and the Europeans, the majority of them, they respected Americans, and, you know, we have a reputation of being the world police. . . . Actually . . . pretty much everybody over the world thinks you run into some conflicts or issues, they tend to look at, to look at the US." To this, Ray added his perception that Europeans view America as the best country on earth because, while policing the world, "the democratic way of the United States and the laws and the government overall . . . I think we top the world." When pressed to specify how the United States "tops" the world, Ray replied, "Once again, like I said, opportunities number one, you know, and of course our military, we got the best military; I don't have to . . . I don't have to explain that, right [laughs]?"

Perhaps not surprisingly, some, still very patriotic, interviewees questioned whether America "teaching" others or exporting its ideas of freedom was problematic. It was something I heard especially in Montana. My conversation in Billings with Daniel, a fifty-something, colorful, burly, bearded white man in denim overalls who worked as a floor installer, captured well this line of thinking. "I would change," he said, "the views that we're the police force of the world. I'd bring our troops home and do like it was before Roosevelt. Before WWII. You know, we take care of our own. I ain't saying be isolationist country, but I'm saying it's none of our affair. That's the reason they can come and terrorize our country, because our people scatter all over the damn world." I asked him to elaborate:

I'd take them home and tell them, "Y'all handle it; it's y'all's problem." We got more food than any other country on the planet, we're feeding half the others, and when they get their belly full, then they wanna start shit with us, you know. I just . . . starve, I don't care. Or behave your damn self, and I'll give you some! You don't got to send troops over there, stop sending groceries.

Given his earlier admission to being a Christian, I suggested that "that's not very religious of you to say; it's not very Christian is it?" "It's very Christian," he retorted,

'cause the Lord said that you will go into the house, and if you ask peace to be upon a man and if they say no, then they don't want you there, then you turn, kick your dust off your shoes, and walk away. You don't go back, they don't wanna hear what you gotta say, they don't wanna be a part of it, they don't wanna try to get along, then you don't have to force . . . that's their right, you know?

This was a line of reasoning that others in Montana, such as Anne at the Harlowton Senior Citizen Center, shared: "We're not minding our own business, we're sticking our noses in where they never belonged, and they still don't. And the fact of it is they're not really doing any good. . . . You can't, you can't make countries change 'cause you think what you want is the best way. We had our start as America. They each got theirs, and there will always be third world countries. There will always be the poor with us." Her feelings were echoed by another elderly white woman living in the countryside in Alabama. The owner of a very modest barbecue place next to her home, Charlotte, a rather direct person, simply stated that American soldiers in the Middle East are "trying to civilize people that's never been civilized and that ain't gonna work, and a lot of American soldiers are getting killed because of it. Now that's the way I see it. I may be wrong, I may be way out there in left field, but that's the way I see it."

Perhaps in some cases America risks too much for too little gain when looking to save the world from evil. There were certainly skeptical interviewees who felt that way in both Alabama and Montana. But the predominant theme was positive for many of the interviewees. The majority shared the viewpoint of Erica, a white fifty-seven-year-old woman in a homeless shelter in Billings, now unemployed but formerly a caregiver. "Americans," she told me, "are much more optimistic than Europeans; they're much more positive than them. There is a sort of hopefulness, yeah." America remains the shining city on a hill founded on the noblest of principles and is ultimately always ready to offer hope to the world.

In Germany, They Cut Your Tongue Off

Heading to Alabama and Montana, I hoped to hear people tell me something about other countries. How does America stand out? Why would they rather be citizens of the United States than of any other country in the world? The interviewees painted disturbing pictures of other countries as often places of brutality and destitution, and of America as a place of reprieve and safety. Inaccuracies and inconsistencies abounded. Their statements can be organized around three key themes: ruthless and arbitrary punishment, backwardness and poverty, and basic rights.

Ruthless and Arbitrary Punishment

Other countries are ruthless and arbitrary, rather than fair and balanced, in their administration of punishment. Sitting on a bench in Billings, I asked Oscar why he would not contemplate being a citizen of any other country. The conversation we had is worth recounting in some detail. "Because," he replied, "other countries they cut people's heads off, they do morbid things to people, which is not right. Yeah, we got crime in the United States, yeah we do, but we don't do public hangings, we don't do beheadings, you know . . . start people on fire . . . we don't stone people to death, so, yeah, I'm very proud to be from the United States." I asked Oscar why the United States does things differently. As he explained,

I think it comes from . . . I don't know if it's more, not socialized or more grown from the world, but . . . we have, I've seen, I've seen videos on the phone where people take people out and they stone them to death. . . . That is, that is . . . totally morbid, you know. I've seen them take them out and hang them, you know; I've seen take them out and burn them. . . . On, on the Internet and stuff. It's like . . . this is not what the United States is. The United States is . . . you go to the court, you're seen in front of the judge, you got a lawyer, and you get tried and sentenced. And then . . . you get whatever your sentence is; you get sentenced. . . . It's a very fair process, I think. . . . It's, it's, it's very respectful. It is, I would say. Instead of having somebody drag you out of jail and stone you to death. It's very respectful, yeah.

Aware of the proximity of Billings to Canada, I asked Oscar whether he thought Canadians also did not follow due process. He responded by pointing out something quite central to his thought process (and representative of what I would hear from many others): other advanced countries do not matter much ("Well, I've got friends that live in Canada, and they don't think too much of it," Gil, in a very small town between Billings and Harlowton, told me). "I, I don't," Oscar said; "you see in America, you don't hear very much about the Canadian laws or the Canadian people or what they . . . how they . . . their justice system. In America you don't . . . in the United States you don't hear very much about that. But like in . . . Libya, Africa, you hear Iraq . . . they're very savage people. . . . You know, they're very savage people."

I pressed Oscar a bit more on Canada: "What if I said move to, move to Canada. You would rather be dead than live in Canada?" He seemed to have a positive opinion of Canada at first but then quickly changed direction:

I, I've never been to Canada. I don't know. . . . I wish, I wish America would have, like, more of their values like, like their medical value here in Canada. You get sick, you go to the hospital, no medical bills or nothing. It's all taken care of. I wish it was like that here. I, I think Canada's like, more like a dictatorship you know. . . . You do you this, you do that. . . . And not be like America, like, hey, this is how it is, this is how I'm living, and this, you know, you know.

Canada, then, appears to be more top down and authoritarian than the United States: perhaps it lacks freedom, after all. But then again, Oscar, like many of the interviewees in Montana, also told me that he would not hesitate to punish severely those who breach the American social contract. Indeed, despite his condemnation of savagery and violence in other countries, he seemed to have very little tolerance for criminals:

I mean . . . capital murder . . . I believe, like my dad believed, my grandpa believed, just eye for an eye, you kill somebody, you deserve the same. . . . That's the way it is. You know, I mean . . . I can see . . . I was turning the corner and accidentally run you over; . . . oh . . . that's different, but if I go out and shoot you or shoot your family or shoot you . . . bring back public hangings . . . uh-huh. Drag the motherfuckers out in the middle of the street, in the square, and hang them. Now the rest of you people . . . what's gonna happen to you if you start raping and killing people? . . . "This is what's gonna happen to you." Poof, hang 'em.

I could not help asking Oscar about due process. "That's, that's due process," he explained:

If you are convicted of it, I mean just don't go, just grab somebody out and just . . . accused of it, but if you get . . . prosecuted and found guilty, take you out in the square and hang your ass in front of everybody, and everybody is gonna know, damn, I shouldn't be killing nobody, because that's what they're gonna do to me. . . . Ain't nobody gonna get raped no more. I've seen videos on the, on YouTube, of the people take people out and they stone them to death. . . . That is a horrible way to die.

If Oscar seemed at this point to contradict himself about the savagery of other countries relative to what he would like to see in America, many others—especially in Birmingham—expressed unequivocally their fear of what happens in other countries, particularly around crime and the ability of felons to recover and have a second chance at life. "Well . . . some, some countries have, you know . . . prisons and prisons," stated Sam in Alabama. "You know, like, you'll go to prison in other countries; you don't have the opportunities in prison to bring yourself back. Don't have the programs in their prisons like we do. You can get your GED and go to college; you got to have a lot of programs in a lot of prisons, but other countries don't have that. They don't care. They want me to do your task, you know. That's it. They beat you till you do your task." And such considerations apply to both the poorest and more authoritative countries in the world. As Denzel reflected,

'Cause I know if I get in trouble in America, they'll slap me on the hand and put me in jail. If I get in trouble in Germany or Russia or somewhere, I don't know what they might do . . . cut my hand off, cut my tongue out, I don't know . . . depending on what kind of trouble it is . . . because look at Mexico, if you go over there and sell drugs in Mexico, what do they do? . . . You come over here and sell drugs you might go to ten to fifteen years, but Mexico you might be there thirty to forty years. It's not the land of the free. What do you learn in thirty to forty years that you can't learn in ten to fifteen years?

Indeed, as Angie at the bus station in Birmingham put it, "I heard that when you steal, you get your hand chopped off in some countries, stuff like that."

In contrast, thankfully, the American justice system respects life and the individual. The words of Doug, a black veteran who works temporarily for the Veterans Administration (VA) in Birmingham, captured this sentiment well:

Our justice system is more lenient compared to some other countries' justice systems. Just like if you go to somewhere like Japan or a Muslim country, you get, you get caught with drugs, you can get the death penalty. I mean over here, you know . . . I mean it's, it's probably one of the, one of the best legal systems in the world. I mean there's no legal system and no society that is perfect, one hundred percent, but I think that the Founding Fathers tried to put together a good . . . good system for us to go by. And I admire them for that.

In fact, as Antonio, an unemployed black man in his fifties in Birmingham, reflected, "I think that our laws are a lot less laws than a lot of other countries, 'cause I know some countries we'd probably be dead with some of the mistakes that we may have made."

Backwardness and Poverty

Many of the interviewees spoke of other countries as backward and destitute. I met Jeannie at a secondhand clothing store in Vernon. White, Democrat, and in her late thirties, she expressed resolute love for the United States. As occurred with most of the interviewees, the conversation turned almost immediately to freedom. As also occurred with almost all interviewees, I asked Jeannie whether other countries lacked freedom. "I think they do," she said, and then she quickly added that those countries suffer from another very serious problem: "But you know, it's just like the Amish country, that's what I'm trying to think of . . . and you know, people you know they don't have electricity, they don't have . . ."

This image of nearly primitive conditions afflicting countries all over the world would be evoked many times in my travels. Katie, a former prostitute and drug addict in Birmingham looking to get disability support from the government, recalled her visit to Mexico, just over the border. "Did you like it?" I asked. "No I didn't." "Why did you not like it?" "Because it's the worst, it's nasty, and they don't have like fresh bottled water, and it's like the people bike and the women out there flaunt themselves, and, like, they sell their bodies and stuff for like five dollars, you know, and it's just not a place to be." For Kevin in Billings the logic was that "I [would] rather not die of dysentery or diseases . . . which is fairly common" in developing countries.

Jeff's reflections at the bus station in Montana offered another telling example:

But there's some countries then . . . you gotta from the time that you're born, basically, until the time that you're out on your own, whatever . . . you know, you're trying to help your family eat . . . so you're not paying rent, 'cause you're not living in a, an apartment building, you know . . . and then . . . when I was over in Vietnam, I mean . . . those people were just happy to have a rice field, you know. And some, some oxen and some goats . . . and they're happy with that. But that was . . . that's pretty poverty . . . people living in shacks.

What about the fact that many of the interviewees themselves had very limited financial means? There is, in fact, little comparison, as Will in Birmingham explained to me:

Well, this is our way of living; I guess you become immune and used to it . . . but other people in other countries are a lot worse even though we think we're bad, but you look at other people in other countries . . . and you feel glad that you're here because they, they have, you know, in the Philippines, I think, I think it used to be twelve dollars a month, not quite sure, so that's not money. You know, you got me taking your money . . . twelve dollars is your money income . . . c'mon . . . now compared to what, you know what, like back then maybe five hundred dollars a month or twelve hundred dollars a month now . . . which I'm sure is not that over there, so why wouldn't you be patriotic to your country? You know, and you're free to do what you want to do, go where you want. . . . You're not being dictated, you know, curfew . . . you can say what you want; you can make fun of the president.

Being poor in America, then, beats being poor anywhere else in the world.

Basic Rights

There was a general consensus that most countries in the world lack even the most basic rights. Though broad and often inaccurate, the statements were quite consistent. The words of Logan, a forty-one-year-old white man recently laid off from his job in industrial air-conditioning installment in Birmingham, were fairly typical: In "most other countries . . . democracy doesn't exist. . . . In another country they're like . . . we just do what we're told . . . what happens is what happens, you know . . . At least over here you, in my mind, you seem to have a bigger voice to voice your agreement or disagreement. You can vote or not vote, you can be political, be not political, and you don't . . . you don't have that stigma a lot of other countries have with not having that opportunity." When I asked for more concrete examples, Logan continued:

Meaning you can, you can choose to go to church or not go to church. You don't have to . . . forced into one religion, you know, or forced to agree with something that you don't want to. In other words you . . . here you have so many choices . . . in a lot of countries you don't have any choice at all; either you go along with things, or you don't. I would say . . . I would say like China, I mean you . . . you pretty much do what you're told. Over here, yeah, there is limits, but in a place like China or Russia or, you know, big countries like that, you . . . you're not given a choice. You, you, you go along with what's going on, or you're part of the problem. . . . It's just that at least here you have a choice, you have a voice, and you can exercise both of them if you want to, and if you don't want to, you don't have to. . . . If you don't have somebody standing over your shoulder telling you, well, you need to do this, you need to do that, or . . . you know, it's . . . that's the big difference for me.

Along this vein, Angie in Birmingham told me that America stands out " 'cause like I said, we are free. They, other countries are not. . . . I don't want to be a communist; that's the last thing I want to be."

Many felt that in other countries one is unable to do some of the simplest things in life. When I asked Chad, in Billings, what differenti-ates America from other countries, he answered that "you can say what you want, you know, you can, you can tell people how you feel about something, and you won't be, you know . . . get your head cut off or your hand chopped off. Even . . . we have somewhat equal rights, you know, I mean not everyone gets paid the same, not treated the same, but not everywhere does that." Freedom of speech and of opinion is crucial, as is the ability to go through one's day as one wishes. The fol-lowing reflections, put forth by Dennis, a retired cast-iron-pipe worker in Birmingham, captured both this very basic sense of freedom and the broad brush used to paint other countries. What makes America stand out? "Well, basically just, I'd say land . . . land of the freedom, but I don't know how much they have of that in other countries. . . . You know what I mean, being curfews and stuff like that . . . they have. They tell you what time you have to go to bed; they . . . go in for the night and stuff like that. I heard of that on TV where countries did that."

There are both physical and mental sides to the oppression found in other countries. Antonio in Birmingham had this to say about Africa and the Middle East:

It's good to be able to use your own mind to think, make your own decisions without being forced to do something, you know. I think that gives us that right to have our own way of thinking that's, you know, not being in prison to me. In other countries I feel like they're in prison. . . . Yeah, the mind in prison. Well, yeah, and be in control basically because to me if you can't do something because you decide to do it, you make this choice . . . you're being forced to do something when you go, to me, go to prison; they tell you when to be, they tell you when to get up . . . basically the same thing to me as for you and I here. . . . You don't have to be in prison to be in prison to me, you know?

If other countries have curfews and order people when to go to bed, Americans enjoy considerably more latitude. If in "some countries kids have been taken away from their parents," as Lynn—an elderly white retired female farmer visiting the Billings Public Library—told me, "we got to raise them; we got to end up with a good family." America's freedom, Ray explained to me as he reflected on his time in the service, extends even to the military, where once again Americans seem to respond above all to a higher sense of morality and individual choice rather than top-down authority. Ray made noteworthy observations about flexibility as it applies especially to the military. He began with a general observation:

Because we, for me Americans, Americans have a little more flexibility, you know? Versus a lot of other countries, I mean, a lot of the countries they don't . . . question things . . . you know, they tell a guy to do this by the T, the letter, that guy go normally straight and do that . . . but in America, in our case, we can pick one word out of a sentence and change one word . . . one word can change a whole sentence . . . and we question that, you know, versus other countries, they're like okay it's written down here . . . and we do that.

He then proceeded to make the following, rather powerful, observation:

And, like especially in the military, if a high-ranking individual in America, if a high-ranking individual give you an order, for instance, and their order don't look right or don't sound right, you have authority to question that . . . regardless what rank they have or they have whatever. . . . You know, as an American you have the right to question that versus some countries, the generals or whatever, the captain, you don't have the, either they don't have the right or they just don't do it, you know, but . . . if it's a lawful order and their order is, is nothing that's . . . you know that's gonna be, is gonna be detrimental to a group of people or a situation, you have the right to say, hey, man, we're not gonna do that.

The older interviewees especially felt that the governments and norms of other countries—including advanced and liberal democracies— intrude too much into people's lives. Will's reflections on Japan are instructive in this regard: "Well, a lot of other countries dictate the way you live and your money, income. . . . They don't do that here; this government doesn't do that here. They give you the freedom, the freedom of speech, the freedom of right. So that's one reason because in other countries they just don't have that, and a lot of them don't like the Western ways. You have communism like in some parts of

Japan; when I lived in Japan, you had people that just didn't like the American way."

The mischaracterization of parts of Japan as communist caught my attention. I asked Will to say a little more about Japan. He continued, "I haven't been . . . it's been about twenty to thirty years, so it's kinda hard to describe that because I can't quite remember . . . in Japan how certain ways you had to do things, some things you can't do there you can do here . . . freedom of speech; you cannot speak against other presidents over there without being beheaded."

Similar observations were made about Europe and Canada. When talking to Hubert and his girlfriend, Katie, in reply to my suggestion that in European countries and Canada the poor get more benefits from the government and they are, therefore, able to do more, Katie flatly rejected the ideas by saying, "No, I don't believe it, I don't believe it!" "You don't believe it?" I replied. "No," exclaimed Hubert, and then added that there "they worship the president and all that. Here you have the freedom of speech." I could have pushed back a bit more but decided instead to switch angles: "Yeah, yeah, okay. But if they give you more benefits, I mean . . ." Katie stood her ground: "I don't believe it," while Hubert interjected, "Probably not. America is number one. Everybody wanna come here."

In some instances, of course, comparisons to other countries seemed more informed. I spent a very pleasant hour speaking on a warm sunny day with Roger, a retired white/Native American, and Linda, a white woman in her fifties who owns a small Laundromat in one of the roughest areas of Billings. I approached them as they were sitting at a table in a courtyard behind the facility, chatting and passing time. Linda emphasized the repressive policies of China and North Korea. Concerning North Korea, "I mean they go to, you know . . . they do something slightly wrong, they're being forced into these work camps and . . . everything." In regard to China, she pointed to the reproductive policies in that country: "In China, you know . . . yeah, there's a lot of people there, but they all tell you, you can only have one child . . . where if you wanna have a dozen kids, that should be your choice." Roger nodded all along and remarked that, compared to North Korea, in the United States "we have less killings. . . . There's no wars going on in the United States." His source was television: "I've never been to, but I've seen on TV and all that."

Basic rights were often closely associated with safety. For Javier, a Hispanic roofer in his twenties who immigrated to the United States as a very young child from Mexico, the problem with other countries is that "it feels like right here I'm more free. If I go somewhere else, I just feel like people just watching me, or I don't know." "So," I asked, "what do you do with that freedom? You just live your life?" "Yeah, you do the things you do, you go to places . . . and just be happy, no worries about people coming to your door and telling you to get out of there or just people breaking your window and checking in on your house." Is that, I wondered, what other countries were like? "I don't know," Javier answered; "it's just 'cause I hear others . . . other countries with bunch of drama and wars, and it just feels like the United States is the safest place even though we still have war, but there's no military guys going in house to house just like . . . calm, you're free, you live your own life." It was a feeling that Fast Eagle, a Native American in Billings, shared: "I watch the news, yeah, I watch the world news, yeah, I watch a lot of the news, so . . . some of the things that I see that goes on in different countries just is not something . . . I'm very thankful for not having to go through that."

And safety and freedom were, of course, linked by many to the ability to own guns. "Well," noted Daniel when asked why he would not want to live in Canada, "for one thing in Canada, . . . I don't believe there is no firearms allowed at all is it? . . . As far as I'm concerned, for what I want out of life, you know, this [the United States] is the best one for me." What the interviewees thought about freedom and guns is discussed in greater detail later.

God's Country

The idea that God and the United States enjoy a special relationship was something I would hear often in Alabama and Montana. The relationship appears to have two important components. First, God has "blessed" the United States. To be sure, God loves all people the same. At the same time, many interviewees felt that God has selected America for something different and extra. I asked them why they thought so and what manifestations such blessing takes.

Sitting in her small real estate office in Harlowton, Jill took some time to explain. She noted God's infallibility, the fact that plans made in accordance with God's wishes never fail, and pointed to the very rapid industrialization in the United States as a feat that could not have happened without God's blessing:

Why do I think it's blessed by God? . . . Oh, well, I think it's blessed by God because whenever I believe the word of God, I believe it's infallible, I believe what he says is true, and when you found certain . . . when you, when you . . . when you create anything . . . a country, a family, a business . . . on, on some of those basic framework elements, I've never seen it fail. Now I'm not talking radical, I'm not talking wigged out, I'm not talking, you know, . . . being misconstrued to what I want it to be. I'm just talking basic framework, basic principles. I've, I've never seen those things fail . . . and so when I look at the basic framework of what the United States was founded on, it . . . it has prospered, it has endured, like I was saying earlier, it's gone very, very fast. To me that reflects blessing of God. If it was still struggling, if there was . . . if there was . . . you know, if we hadn't made any advancements on the level that we have made over the last few hundred years . . . I really wouldn't call that blessed.

This explanation, with its focus on America's rapid progress over a few hundred years, prompted me to ask about other countries. "Do you think there are countries that, that aren't as blessed?" Jill said, "I think there's countries that are in spiritual turmoil." I countered by asking whether she thought "that they're not as blessed by God. Do you think," I said, "that God holds them in less favor?" As many others, Jill first reasoned that God loves everyone the same but then proceeded to differentiate other countries from the United States:

Less esteemed? No, I don't think God holds them in less esteem, but I think that there's some elements, like we were talking about, that framework, if you're not operating within that framework, then you know there's certain spiritual laws that are in play that we can't change. . . . And I think, but I think that God loves all countries the same; it's just we have operated in a framework that has caused richness. It's kinda like farming; if you farm well, you harvest well. It doesn't mean that God loves you more than he does the farmer next door; it's just that faith and wisdom go hand in hand . . . and I feel like God's kinda poured out a revelation knowledge over the United States. Maybe not in the century that we know it, but I know previously.

I wanted to know more about the idea of "revelation." "What do you mean by that?" I asked. She elaborated:

Well, like the Industrial Revolution, I mean, there was a time when this country was making advances in things so fast, medicine and . . . and, you know, in . . . steel and in production and in travel, whatever. We were just advancing at a rate that was just unheard of before, and I really feel that is divine revelation that God allows us to have. Did it stay that pace? No it really didn't.

The attribution of America's success to divine blessing—and Americans making the right moral choices—clearly laid at the heart of Jill's thinking. She was not the only to think so. Jeff, in Billings, for instance, pointed to the abundance of "beautiful things" in America as proof of a close relationship with God. "In God, in God we trust. . . . It says it right there on the dollar bill," he noted. I acknowledged it and then asked: "Well that's us holding God dear, but do you think God holds the United States . . ." He quickly answered, "Yeah I do. Because, look at all the beautiful things he gives us, you know, and it's because of the, the . . . the honesty that comes from people, you know, and the beliefs." Americans are a truthful and righteous people.

Revelation and America's faith in God were also central to Antonio's thinking in Birmingham. "Yeah, I am a God man," he said, "and, and our country speaks to God and in God we trust . . . in God we trust it in the dollar we trust. . . . We keep God in the top of our prayers, and that makes me proud of our country because I love God and I know God would help us and in the situation that we in we allow him to." I was eager to hear more: "So you think God looks over the United States?" The answer was a familiar one, wavering between stating that God loves everyone and following up with something special about the United States: "Sure, I think he looks over everybody, the whole world." "You think so?" I asked. "Especially the United States," he added, "because I believe that, if you put God first, then he's always going to be there." He then continued: "This is to me just things that happen when you put him first, you know. I don't see those signs in some of those other countries."

Above all, then, many of the interviewees appreciated Americans' willingness to put God first. Fast Eagle praised in this regard the country's founding principles. "Do you think that the United States holds a special place in God's mind?" I asker her. "On the principles that the country was founded on I would say yes." I wanted to hear more: "Tell me, tell me . . . what kind of principles? What do you mean by that?" She continued:

Well just like our . . . the honor and the money that we have, the "In God we trust," which means we put God, we acknowledge him, and we put our trust in him, so that says a lot for somebody. . . . I mean, we trust him with our livelihood, our lives, this whole country. . . . It's, it's a lot . . . [and] I think he looks favorably upon those that acknowledge him.

So, Americans somehow acknowledge God more than people in other countries do. This is precisely what Todd, a young white banquet server in Billings, thought as well. As we talked about the desirability of reciting the Pledge of Allegiance in public schools, he reasoned that it is "a source of knowledge that you can give your kid so they could go to school, read the pledge, and know that their land is something that was given to them by God, and they should love it as much as they can because, you know . . ." I interjected to clarify the divine attribution: "By God, you think?" "Yeah, by God," he confirmed. "How do you know that?" I continued. "Do you think other people's countries were given to them by God? In the same way the United States was given to us by God?" His answer was revealing:

I mean a lot of other countries, I believe, they don't believe in the same God or believe in a higher power or different power of God . . . but as a United States, as a kid . . . I think an everyday pledge thing is gonna make you a greater person and respect, you know. I'm living here, and this is who I am, you know. . . . I just feel like God created the people and . . . maybe not the land itself, but he has a plan for everybody, so yeah.

It was with this sort of spirit that a good number of interviewees, such as Katie and Paula, a fifty-three-year-old white woman in Birmingham on disability with a history of drug abuse, answered when asked about the first three words that come to mind when picturing the American flag. The phrases "God bless America" and "One Nation under God" were often mentioned. This, interestingly, was also done at times with words of caution—with warnings that in the recent past the country has moved away from God. As Lynn in Billings put it, "I think we have more and more taken God out of the equation the farther along we've gone . . . and when you do that, I think you lose that; you lose that love thing that I was talking about." Or, in the words of Alicia, a thirty-year-old black woman in a homeless shelter in Birmingham working on her GED, this "whole nation should get back to the Bible and do what God tells us to do."

Freedom was the second component of America's special relationship with God that I would hear a lot about. Many interviewees readily told me that, by divine design, the very founding of America was a deliberate effort to allow for freedom of religion. America allows everyone to worship his or her God, and this, for many, is a clear badge of honor and distinction for the nation. I was reminded of the country's origins on multiple occasions, as during my conversation with Charlotte:

I'm a Christian, and . . .'cause of that I believe that it was ordained by God that people who are seeking religious freedom would be able to come and set up their own country and be able to worship him in the way that they want. And we've gotten away from that, but that, that's what I like about this country, is, is basically about freedom, and even if you don't agree with that, you know you're welcome to your own ideas. . . . That was in God's plan, that America be set up so that people could worship him unoppressed. To get away from the, you know, England and the oppression of the church there.

Anne, another elderly white woman in Harlowton, subscribed to a very similar point of view:

When, when we got our start, when America started, that was one of the reasons they left England and Holland and that was for so they could worship God the way they wanted to. Not some state like Church of England and, . . . that's the way we started out, and that's . . . I still think there's that element present in this country. I know there is. And I wanna see that grow. God knows how I feel; I talk to him often, daily. . . . We, he made us, and he made this world; there's no, in my thinking and in my heart, I don't think there's any other way to really go and accomplish anything. One with God's a majority. You know . . . and I know Mr. Obama doesn't; I've heard him say that we're not a Christian nation. Well, I got news for him; the world don't spin on his axis, and thank God it don't.

Thus, one can worship freely in America. On the details of exactly how this is the case, differences emerged. For some respondents like Charlotte, and clearly Anne, the God in question is "a Christian God." For this reason, while practicing other faiths, such as Buddhism or Hinduism, is acceptable in America, the president of the country must be Christian. Could Charlotte imagine, I asked, a Muslim president? "No," she firmly said. What if the person was "totally committed to American values" but just happens to read the Quran instead of the Bible? That would not be possible: "I don't think they can be committed to American values because . . . America was based on the Bible, not the Quran. Founding Fathers believed in the Bible." She further clarified: "Not if they're a Muslim who agrees with the Quran and it says the great Satan must die. . . . I do not want a president who wants to kill me." It was perhaps with this logic in mind that Grace, a white retired cotton packer in Vernon who was upset by the removal of the Ten Commandments from public sites and the end of prayer time in schools, and Jeannie in Vernon lamented the fact, as they saw it, that President Obama is a Muslim.

But for many America's unique protection of religious freedom does extend to all kinds of faiths. This is precisely what makes it so distinctive. As Timmy, a second person I met in front of a dry house in Billings who was on probation and trying to put his life back together and reopen his construction company, articulated quite clearly during our conversation: "It doesn't matter which God you believe in, you know; everybody's got the right to practice their own, and America has found a way to make that coincide with each other." In this way, Timmy noted,

"America allows God to work; it allows that freedom of religion where other countries don't, so, so . . . everybody can be molded by God . . . because America started to get that freedom from religion, freedom from the English church, you know, church running the country, and, and that was the foundation of the country."

Others would recognize that they believe in Christianity, but that this does not mean that other people should not be free to worship their own God. Antonio, for instance, reasoned that "I'm a Christian God. . . . I don't get into religion; I'm not . . . I'm a Christian God, and I believe in our Lord Jesus Christ. I won't mock nobody else, what they believe in 'cause I think, I believe that's what works for them. . . . If it works, you gotta go with it, and that's one the things I like about America, the freedom, the freedom of religion." And Sidney, a deeply religious young woman, attributed her appreciation of the United States as a country that is better than most because

we can still serve God. . . . We can still serve God without getting killed. I heard in other countries you can't really serve God. . . . You can't really worship and praise him in certain parts of the world without getting killed or without getting thrown in prison, and here we can worship him without getting killed or thrown in prison, without anything happening to us. That's the main reason I'm happy to be a citizen of the United States, because I can worship God, Jesus Christ, without going to jail and getting killed.

So what did she think about others worshipping someone other than Christ, say, Muhammad? Her reply affirmed clearly the idea of religious freedom in its broadest sense: "Yes, it's okay with me as long as I can worship who I choose to worship, you know. I can't be stereotyping over nobody else's religion because I get, you believe what you believe, but I'm happy that I'm able to worship who I want to worship as well."

It follows that many of the respondents believed that the president of the United States can be of any religion, including Islam. As Tom in Vernon, a retired black man who worked for many years as a truck driver and suffered from racial discrimination throughout his career, said, he actually "would welcome it" (a Muslim president). As he said this, Kayla—a black woman who worked as a bus driver and was now raising money for college for local kids—who was also in the room and participated in the interview, nodded approvingly.

Nothing Left to Lose

Some of the most intense and emotional moments in my conversations came when the interviewees recalled their lives as children, growing up in what seemed to many to be easier and better times for themselves and, in some cases, the country. Several recounted periods with more resources, such as a job, a house, or a car, and happy times with a spouse or partner. Because of one thing or another—such as bad choices, an illness, destructive relationships, or getting fired from work—many lost much or all they had. But all professed their love of country. What would happen, I generally asked them late in the interview, if someone were to deprive them of their American citizenship? How would they feel if they could no longer call themselves American and had instead been given, say, Mexican or Japanese citizenship? For many, this would prove intolerable because their national identity and pride was the one thing that they could still hang on to—something that they could still believe and hope in and that gave them a sense of direction.

Darrius was among the more cynical and educated persons I met in my travels. But as he spoke, I sensed that he had not given up on America yet. In fact, he still believed in it, and quite deeply so. I asked him why. His reply stayed with me for a long time:

You have to have some shred of dignity. Even the bottom-of-the-barrel person has to have some shred of dignity. That's just a human condition. We all want to have some sort of self-respected dignity about ourselves. And so when we're struggling and we're super poor and broke and going through all these things, you almost have to believe in something better or higher. That's why poor people are super religious. And that's why a lot of rich people aren't. Is because they have to have something in order to, like, hold on to that's, that's good and that's true. And the Americans' ideals kinda ring on that level because they're a lot different than maybe other countries' because the American ideals are supposed to embody those things that are, are like good for humanity, you know . . . and it's true. That's why Americans . . . that's why poor Americans are so patriotic. They have to.

Retaining a "shred of dignity" and the necessity to believe in the American ideals, because these are universally good for humanity and must be supported, no matter or in fact *because* of how destitute one is: these were incisive words. "They have to?" I asked. "They almost have to. 'Cause I mean . . . why be here? Why do the things we're doing? Why believe in that? If you take it away . . . it takes a lot out of a human soul, spirit. . . . I can go on and on and on."

Four months earlier, in a homeless shelter in Birmingham, Erica told me something similar. Here, however, necessity was blended with an awareness of the oneness of the people and the country. Could she give up her pride in the United States?

We can't give up. We can't give up. . . . If you give up, you're going to, your self-pride goes away. Your self-pride, self-worth goes away, you know. . . . You're going to start, you know, blaming other people. If you don't have yourself, you're not going to be able to make it in this world. . . . To me I think that that's, you know, your building block of who you are, and if we put all that together, then that's probably what we're feeling in that. . . . Does that make sense? . . . But what I have is I have hope, I have faith; I have faith, and I love my children and my family . . . and I love my country. We're all one.

Erica spoke of the deep connection between self, family, and country and of the need to have faith in all of them or otherwise succumb to the circumstances. It was the same oneness that Shirley described to me, almost poetically, in the Birmingham library:

Yeah, yeah. I just . . . for me to give up hope on the country in which I live in is almost to give up hope for self. So I gotta keep the light burning for me and for my country, or I'm gonna be in the dark. . . . Light go out in the country, then the country dark. Light go out in me, then my heart's dark. So one reflects, I think . . . is capable of illuminating the other.

Herein, I thought, lies one of the most important explanations for the patriotism of America's impoverished people.

CHAPTER 5

THE LAND OF MILK AND HONEY

*[The] luxury that we have. We do pretty well in this country . . . like
I'm not doing too bad and I live outside!*

Marshall, Billings, Montana

An abundance of riches that allows everyone to survive, a feeling that
one is being taken care of, and the conviction that anything is possible in
America: despite their own lives' often difficult trajectories, many of the
people I met took pride in America's great wealth and what, they felt, it
means for the country's poor. Twice in Alabama I heard, from Denzel
and Doug, that America is the "land of milk and honey." Voiced by
two homeless black veterans in the South who have struggled to make
ends meet for years, the statement seemed especially significant. Many
of the interviewees reminded me of the limitations of other countries:
run-down, unable to provide for their people, and oppressive. Everyone
still wants to come to the United States, they said. The country's natural
beauty may play a role, too. Many expressed contentment with their lot.

We have heard about the country's principled qualities and now
hear about its impressive material resources. There were differences between respondents in Alabama and Montana. In Birmingham, gratitude
to the government and private organizations was especially common.
In Montana, the ethos of self-reliance was more pronounced; this also
meant that there, in the eyes of some, being homeless or without a job
was a choice, not a matter of fate. In both states, many interviewees felt
strongly that anyone who is willing to work hard can achieve anything,

despite difficulties they face. And overall, women were more likely than men to appreciate the country's natural beauty and express contentment with their lives.

To some extent, these themes were consistent with the second and ninth insights derived from the literature discussed earlier, though the specific meanings they took on reflected the dire economic and personal challenges experienced by the interviewees: America's poor do seem to believe in the American Dream, and they actively recognize the net benefits of living in America. But there was also much that could not have been predicted on the basis of existing research. This included the extent to which the interviewees expressed an appreciation for the country's ability to take care of its own and their general contentment with life.

Overflowing Abundance

America is wealthy. "We need to respect what we have," Lynn, the elderly farmer visiting the Billings Public Library, asserted, "and we have a lot. I mean we have problems, but we have a lot. . . . We have a lot to be thankful for." How, exactly, did wealth play a role in the interviewees' love of country?

First, many noted with pride that America's wealth reaches its most vulnerable citizens. In Alabama, several expressed great appreciation for the fact that no one is left behind. Hubert's statements in the Birmingham Public Library captured this feeling well:

America is paved in gold [laugh]. . . . You know, they help people with food stamps. . . . That's why overseas they say this is . . . our streets . . . our streets are paved in gold [laughs]. I love America; I been here all my life. I ain't know nobody want to go anywhere else. No other country. No way.

I asked him to elaborate on the availability of food stamps. He continued:

We ain't gonna let anybody go hungry. We gonna help each other. That's what I like. We help each other. We all work as a team. The armed forces is to let you know that we have somebody back us up. Anything come here try to destroy us all, that's when our armed forces come in to protect us.

Hubert described a feeling of unmatched togetherness and mutual help.

Alex, in Birmingham's bus station on his way to Colorado, articulated something similar. How is the United States different from other countries? "We got a lot more . . . we got a lot more to give, like we got all these homeless shelters for homeless people; they got these Salvation Armies; they got all these bus stops and stuff like that." There is an abundance of wealth in the United States, and it reaches its poorest members. Jeff, in Montana, added to Alex's thoughts: "Because, you know, here in America you can go to the food banks; they got lots of them . . . Catholic churches, charities, you can go to Goodwill, get clothes if you need them, and here, you know, whatever . . . and you can't do that in a lot of places. You know, they don't have that many resources." The result is that, in the words of Eddie, "I'd say the poorest, the poor people here are probably, are probably well-off poor people. . . . I think the quality of life and living in this country is higher than most places in the world, even for the poor."

In other countries, those with limited means face a much harder time. It is as if they are outcasts and not allowed to belong or to be a part of the system. In the United States, however, initiatives are in place to help the needy. In America people care, and the government has extensive programs for those who need help. In Antonio's words, "We have a better place to me that has taken care of people, disabled or something like that . . . that's not able to do for themselves. . . . There are some programs that America offers that I haven't heard about in other countries to help the homeless." These are points of distinction and pride, as Fast Eagle, the Native American who as a single mom worked at a hotel clerk in Billings and supported four children, thought:

And I think . . . I go to work and I get taxes taken out of my check just like the next person, but they're making it for when you need it. . . . I mean, people who have disability, you know, that's the thing about our country, you know, there's people who . . . that's how we take care of the next person; we get it. . . . You get in other countries where they do not have the health care or the means or the money to take care of different things, you know. We have housing, we have food stamps, we have medical care that's all taken care of 'cause somebody . . . doctors have to get paid some way. And . . . our taxes help take care of the next person, you know . . . that's what we do.

Comparisons to specific countries or regions of the world were sometimes made. As Harley, a sixty-year-old black male on food stamps in
Birmingham put it, in "a lot of other places you can't live broke and survive. Some parts of Africa, you know. I would think the United States
is better than a lot of places." Roger, the elder white/Native American
sitting with Linda in the courtyard of her very modest Laundromat in
Billings, reasoned that he could not stand contemplating the possibility of being a citizen of any other country. Mexico was mentioned. "I'll
always be an American. No matter what, what they say," he told me.
I asked him why. "I'd start thinking, boy, all of a sudden I'm not an
American citizen. . . . I'd be deprived of a lot of things. . . . I wouldn't
be able to get Medicare, Medicaid . . . Social Security . . . you know.
I'd be pissed off." As I was about to suggest that perhaps those things
might in fact be available in Mexico or other countries, Linda offered a
preemptive rebuttal: "Yeah, 'cause down in Mexico they don't get any of
that stuff. 'Cause a girl I used to work with, she has her citizenship now,
but her mother lived down there, and she had to always depend on her
family for stuff."

Along these lines, Emily, a seventy-two-year-old black woman who
once worked in Alabama for a printing company and was now living at
a homeless shelter, offered details from a tour of North Africa and Europe she had the opportunity to participate in years ago. What she saw
there made her very glad to come back to the United States:

I still would rather be a citizen in the United States 'cause other countries they
have poverty there; they don't have system where they can take care of people,
people who are homeless, people who're old senior citizens; they don't have
programs like that for people in those countries. Most of those people when
I, when I toured through those countries, they have like flea markets on every
little spot where somebody selling something, and that's how they make their
living, because they don't have welfare; they don't have money to take care of
senior citizens or poor people.

America gives a great deal to its most vulnerable people, and this is a
significant mark of distinction.

America's wealth is a source of pride in a second way: The country has an extensive and easily accessible infrastructure. Potable water, electricity, free Internet access in public libraries, and other amenities are within reach of just about everyone. Many interviewees were acutely aware of this. Marshall—a white young man in Billings who describes his homelessness as a freely chosen "sabbatical" from the everyday constraints of life—spoke, for instance, about electricity: "Well," he noted, "at least seventy, eighty, ninety percent of the populated areas of the country have running water, electricity. . . . We have prosperity!" The same cannot be said of other places. In the same vein, Doug recalled talking to a friend in the Philippines: "You can't even go to . . . if you go to a library you got to . . . I couldn't believe it. I mean, when I told her we got free Wi-Fi at the library, it blew her mind!" Sidney in Billings echoed this line of thinking when speaking about Africa and its buildings:

I just hear about places that are . . . there's war, they're run-down, they're dirty, they're not put together nicely, run by the government. I don't know . . . I don't know much about the government or anything like that, but I just know that Africa and all those other places are poor. They're poor; they don't have buildings all over the place; they don't have, you know, what we have, and I've always known . . . I don't know, I guess . . . that we are a richer place.

Sidney was admittedly not knowledgeable of other places. She was certainly not the only one. Grace, a white woman in Vernon, stated, "Well, I think we have more, more here than other countries. Like I said, in a lot of countries these people are starving to death." When I pointed out that the same could be said of Europe or Canada, her response was, "Well, that's what you say, but I've never been over there." Several others, however, did draw from personal experiences. Emily's observations from her visits to Egypt, Croatia, and Greece were a good example:

I got the opportunity to go. And I was very happy to be back in the United States. . . . Well, I mean the condition, the conditions of people; there is a lot of poverty there, people . . . some . . . of course they have that here, you know; they live on the street, some live in buildings that don't have anything but just a shell, and, it's like, I don't think . . . for it's taxes, they don't pay taxes or anything; they don't do, like help, I guess, sanitary conditions. . . . They don't have like people that clean the streets, garbage collectors and all of those things; I mean, some of those things we take for granted in the United States. But when you go to other countries and you see how they live, I mean it makes you really appreciate America.

Indeed, the abundance of food in America was also often mentioned as something real and at times taken for granted. Ray, a black man in Alabama, reflected on this very fact in the much broader context of African Americans' struggle for equality in the country:

Black people . . . we think about the Hebrew slaves, so . . . this, this one guy, this one white guy I was just making, I was just talking, I said, "Man, they working me like a Hebrew slave." . . . He say . . . "But you guys were slaves." I said, "You don't know about the Hebrew slaves; they had it worse than us." They really did, so . . . you know, it's . . . it's the way it is, the mentality, the way of thinking. Regardless of how bad, how worse it is, somebody had it worse. I mean . . . we throw away more food in our garbage; I mean, look at those starving kids over in those countries and everything, I mean . . . the stuff we got in our dumpsters, man, they would think that's a feast over there! . . . So I, I like that . . . all the other stuff . . . you know, I work for a company, Salvation Army, worked for, for about a year and all the clothes that we didn't put on the shelf, you know, we, we would put them together and ship them to other countries overseas, and so, . . . and it's just too many people that got less than we got, and some Americans take it for granted. We take one bit of a hot dog . . . ah, it don't taste good, throw it away, but it's, it's a lot of people have it worse, not only the African Americans; of course, I know we not the, we're a long way from where we would like to be, but we making progress, individual progress . . . and, and that's why we keep going and don't look back. Yeah.

African Americans, too, have benefited from America's prosperity. And that prosperity is all the more impressive considering the very short span of time it took the country to develop from an unsettled and primitive place. "We created something from nothing in such a short span of time," Jill in Harlowton noted as part of her broader assessment of God's kindness to America. Some other countries might be developed, too, but in their case their economic and other systems were "created over hundreds and hundreds of thousands of years. Ours was only a few hundred years. That's what I think is incredible about it. . . . It went from being nothing, you know, there was no formation of a country at all; it was bare lands all the way across from one coast to the other, and to, to bring it up to a level of production . . . from 1640 all the way up to today . . . that's a very rapid growth."

America's wealth is impressive in a third way. The country has a good and functioning economy with jobs that pay decent and livable wages. There are choices, and those who wish to work will find good employment. Those who wish to improve their skills can take advantage of government loans and programs. The same cannot be said of a lot of other countries, where a very limited or dysfunctional economic system, often coupled with corrupt political systems, prevents people from earning a living.

We have "big cities, good jobs . . . [a] good economy and stuff like that," Alex told me. Wages are better than elsewhere. As Denzel put it, America "is better than anywhere else that I know of because at least I can go make seven dollars an hour here. . . . In Russia and Germany I might not make four and a half to five dollars an hour on their jobs. . . . Which one is greater? Seven dollars or five dollars? I take seven dollars and run with it." When I asked Denzel what he would say if I showed him data that the chances of making it in Germany were in fact higher than in the United States, he showed little doubt: "I wouldn't believe it." "You wouldn't believe it?" I asked. "I'm not in Germany. I'm in America," he replied. "I know American soil; I know what I can do here, but I don't know what I can go do there. That makes me lean a little bit more toward America . . . than it does anywhere else." On this matter, too, Emily found interesting points of comparison with Europe and North Africa:

Everybody that's out there, they all trying to sell something, and that's their livelihood. I mean, you can go down when they carry you through these little towns on the bus, or you get out and walk through the town; everybody got . . . selling something. And that's how, and then they live off of the tourist, 'cause if the tourists don't come to those countries, they, they don't have money 'cause they live off of the tourists. When the tourists come, they have all everything; they make things, they have all kinds of fruits and vegetables and some of everything you can name, they have bread and all kinds of meats; I mean they be selling it. That's their income. But here in the United States, people can get jobs. . . . Some people are not able to work. So I mean, to me, the people that can work and able to work, they could, they could find them a job.

When I mentioned to Emily that it might actually be difficult for some people to find a job in the United States and that some interviewees had said as much to me, her response was stern and direct:

Well, I would just think they're not appreciative because I would say if they went to some countries where they don't have any laws, they don't have no kind of feel of homeless and shelter the homeless, if they go to some of those countries where those folk live on the street and they set up their little booth trying to sell their little goods, they'll be glad to come back to the United States.

America, then, with its advanced economy and stable legal system, offers valuable opportunities, and, as Sam in Birmingham reasoned, "Some countries don't have that. Some countries don't have that, you know? . . . It's important to me." Why, I wondered, do other countries lack those opportunities? "They're more depressing, and the job opportunities they don't have. You know, they don't have it; they just don't have it. Some countries are real poor; they don't have it. . . . Yeah, yeah, they need more opportunity, programs, benefits. They don't have, have the benefits that the United States have. Opportunities. A lot of poor countries don't have that." Choices and opportunities, then, make America stand out, and this was so even for people like Fiona, in Harlowton, who had just lost her job but not her faith in the country's economic system:

You have a choice of what you want your life to be like, in my opinion. Like I said . . . it's a little more difficult anymore to get a degree because college is becoming so expensive; that is the one thing, but . . . you have the ability to make the choice whether or not you want to go to school, whether or not you want that occupation or . . . you're not . . . I know that there are some countries that what you're born into is what you're handed in life basically. You can make whatever you want of your life here by your own choices.

With all this, competent government that supports (rather than gets in the way of) the economy and offers citizens valuable resources for improvement is key. There were certainly complaints about the intrusiveness of the American government, some of which are captured in the

Appendix. But there was also significant appreciation for the opportunities in the country, especially in comparison to other countries. When I asked Charlotte, in her barbecue place, if she thought the United States is a better country than most, her reply was immediate: "Of course they [the United States] are!" she affirmed. Did she really feel that strongly? "Yes, very strongly . . . because we have everything here. Everybody has a chance to better themselves, and everybody is held back in other countries 'cause they're only allowed to go so far and that's it." I followed up by asking, "How are they held back?" "Well," she said, "they're held back by the government. They're only allowed to do so much and that's it. Rest of the money is going to the government and not your pocket." "Oh, in taxes?" I wondered. "That's right!" she stated, though interestingly then added, with a dose of libertarian thinking, that "our taxes here are pretty steep too. If people had to sit down and write a check every month for what they pay in taxes, they'd be in uprisings!"

For others, like Jeff in Montana, good governance means useful public programs. "You know," he stated, "another thing I like about this country is the government loans to go to school . . . you know, and you gotta pay them back of course after you're working . . . after you're out of school, but that's how most people go to college."

They Give Me Everything

In Alabama I repeatedly heard people express gratitude to the government and country for the help they receive. These were men, women, black, and white; some were young, and others were older. They included conservatives and liberals. Very few thought that the government could do more for them, and almost none thought it *should* do more. While they believed that certain segments of the population (veterans most frequently) do deserve more support, they seldom stated that this applies directly to them. They spoke highly of the country and of private charities and did not seem to know that perhaps in other countries they would have the chance to receive more benefits from the government and other sources.

Katie and Hubert, one of a few interracial couples I met in my travels, offered an example. Considerably older, Hubert took Katie under his protection as she recovered from selling her body on the streets and from drug addiction. They both emphatically expressed their love of country. "What did they appreciate about the United States?" I asked them. As did the majority of people, freedom of speech was the first thing Katie said. But in the same sentence Katie spoke of her own experience: "How they help with the food stamps. They help with a lot of stuff in America, in the United States." Hubert then added, "Churches come and feed us and stuff . . . like they help the homeless. It's thanks to this town feeding me and stuff like that. I never would make it. . . . And love every minute of it [laughs]!" As Katie reached for her glasses and was perhaps poised to say something, Hubert added, "Free glasses. . . . She got 'em for free." "From whom?" I inquired. "The government," replied Katie. "The government," continued Hubert. "They pay for people with old age . . . so to get glasses and stuff. I paid fifty cents for my glasses!" "So you're grateful for that? You recognize that?" I asked. Hubert's reply gave me reason to pause: "Yes. I'm schizophrenic, suicidal. . . . Without that medicine I would probably kill if you were not dead. They give it to me, you know. . . . I paid fifty cent 'cause I got a government card showing the United States got me covered. So I'm straight. I love that."

Free access to medication, in this case marijuana, to treat the pain from poorly healed broken bones and many hours of daily work in construction, was what fueled Alex's appreciation of government programs—in this instance those of Colorado, where he moved precisely in search of this benefit:

We get to get marijuana legally, that's why, how everybody looks at it in Colorado, and I mean . . . look . . . look at Colorado, they're a, they're a multimillionaire state right now because they legalized it. They, they get free food . . . they give food away up there, man. You go up there, you get . . . it's so easy to be homeless up there it's fun. You live like a king up there homeless. Just 'cause marijuana is legal, and, and it . . . people's rich off of it, you know. Everybody's rich off of it, and it's steadily growing.

When I interviewed his partner, Angie, a little earlier in the day, I encountered a similar sense of gratefulness and even cheerfulness—despite the fact, as I learned toward the end of the conversation, that she was recently diagnosed with a brain tumor and, together with Alex and their children, was living on very little income:

That's another thing that's good about Alabama and America; there are things for people that don't have access to stuff. Like me, I'm on a check, don't make a lot of money; they help me pay my rent; they help me pay for food. . . . But, I mean, I went through school with programs; they paid me to go to college. . . . I don't believe you can get that in every country.

Somehow, then, even in the most difficult of situations, several of the people I met spoke about the benefits that living in America affords them. Kysha, the aspiring artist in a homeless shelter in Birmingham, even referred to her temporary home as "phenomenal" and of America as a place where one can always get out of poverty: "Lot of people real poor. . . . We poor here, we know. But to me, there's no reason to be real poor in America; we got too many . . . like this place here. We got too many phenomenal places to help you. So sleeping on the streets and all that . . . there's no reason for that. I, I just don't see it." I wanted to hear more and asked, "You don't see it?" She returned to a familiar theme: "You know we got running water; you know we can bathe; we can eat."

What about the veterans? I wondered. While many nonveterans thought that the government and country could do more for the veterans, the veterans themselves surprised me with rather positive rhetoric. My exchange with Harley was especially instructive and quite representative. "My love for the United States is deep. . . . It's deep," he exclaimed. "I won't live nowhere else, no other places except the United States. . . . Absolutely, right now I'd go fight, go fight for it. Suit up right now." His words of devotion to country followed a detailed description of the benefits he receives from the government and the VA:

Well, they give you, they give you food stamps, housing. . . . They help you with housing; you know what I'm saying? Like housing right now, 'cause I live in a home. . . . I'm homeless right now, and I stay at a place called [name]. You know, and through the military program, VA program, I'm waiting on new housing, waiting on an apartment right now through the VA housing program. . . . I just talked to my counselor this morning; she said it be sometime in January. . . . That's one thing about the United States and being a, you know being a GI or something, veteran. . . . You get a lot of help now. Oh yeah, a lot . . . that's another good thing about the United States. I don't know about other countries join Social Security or anything like that, but I know the United States do it. . . . Don't have to worry 'bout nothing else. Worry 'bout nothing else, you know, for the rest of your life. Getting a check coming in, your bill paid.

"What about health care?" I inquired. "Do you have access to that?" "Yeah, I, well, mine is free through the VA . . . yeah, free through the VA . . . oh yeah, yeah, it's good. I don't have to pay for it. That's another good thing."

Harley, one could be tempted to think, might have been an exception. But I ran into the same feelings with other veterans in Alabama. Douglas had similar words of gratitude and appreciation for the country:

Well, [I am] doing pretty good. I mean, they got programs, they got government, they got housing programs, they got Section 8, they give you food stamps, they . . . I don't have no complaint. I mean, I'm not saying that they can do more than what they already doing now. They doing, they doing enough. . . . I can't say what they can do more. They got the programs to find you shelter and clothing, and you can get your checks and pay your rent and all that kind. . . . What else? I mean . . . yeah, they doing, they do . . . yes, I'm taking advantage myself. Especially the food. . . . We have plenty of food; [that is] why . . . why, we don't worry about each other.

Overall, there was a widespread sentiment that, in Sam's words, "well you got, you got a lot of free stuff . . . free . . . free programs you can get into to make a living." It was a heartfelt sentiment—and one that, as we will soon see, some people in Montana felt uncomfortable with, as they articulated their own reasons for loving the United States.

Forget Inequality: Anyone Can Make It

Inequality in the United States has widened in the last few decades. It is also the highest among the rich nations of the world. What do America's least well-off make of such a trend? In particular, in light especially of their own predicaments, does the gap between rich and poor dampen their enthusiasm for the United States? I posed this question to every interviewee. Inequality, several people told me, is not symptomatic of any systemic barriers to success and is instead the inevitable result of a free society. Besides, inequality is everywhere, not just in America. Their answers quickly morphed into positive affirmations of what America has to offer: The United States remains the land of opportunity, and anyone who is willing to work hard and take advantage of what is out there will succeed. America is a great country where anyone can make it.

These were not original points, to be sure, but not ones that would necessarily be expected from those with the least financial security in the country. Yet I heard them very frequently in both Alabama and Montana and from people of very different backgrounds, even though at different moments in the interviews many recognized that too many people suffer from poverty in the country.

The interviewees often began by dismissing inequality as a concerning issue. When I asked Marshall, for instance, about inequality in this country, "Is there too much inequality?" His response was, "Well, there's always inequality. Show me a country that's equality in the world." I noted that, yes, it is everywhere, "but there's a lot, there's a lot in the United States, you know that right? . . . A big gap between the rich and the poor." He agreed and actually observed that "it's getting bigger." "Does that bother you?" I asked. It seemed of some concern to him, but he then stressed that "the very machinery that's doing it also provides us with a lot of . . . just our general well . . . luxury that we have. We do pretty well in this country; like I'm not doing too bad and I live outside [laughs]!" This line of thinking was nearly identical to Eddie's, who told me that he

ain't gonna search for no perfect society; they don't exist in no country. But when you live in a country like America, where you at least have freedom of opportunity and expression or religion, you know your chances are better than, you know, you may have a pretty decent life. Not everybody can be billionaires and millionaires; but you can be reasonably happy; that's what I think.

Inequality likely exists everywhere, then, and perhaps more so when you have a society that offers the opportunities that America does. In fact, inequality is probably inevitable, as Emma, a forty-nine-year-old, conservative, white woman who worked part-time writing for the local newspaper in Vernon, argued. When I asked her whether there is "too much inequality" in the United States, she replied, "I think it's about right because all throughout history, since the beginning of time, it's been that way. You cannot make everybody equal because they're just not made equal. They're equally loved, you know, equally deserving, I guess . . . but it, that's just how it is. You can't, cannot make everybody equal." When I probed a little further, she said that she would, in fact, prefer a smaller gap but added, "At the same time I do realize there's always going to be one. It may not have to be as wide as it is, but, ... but I can't ever see there not being a gap."

What most interviewees quickly turned to as they answered my questions was instead the idea that anyone can make it in America: this is a great trait, one that distinguishes the country from the rest of the world. As Sam, with in mind his Haitian father coming to America for a better world, put it, America is great

'cause you can be what you wanna be in America. You can be what you wanna be, you know. The life . . . the life . . . the best opportunities, yeah. Great opportunities. . . . You can be like a movie star; you can be . . . have your own business. America is be what you wanna be. You know, they got opportunities to be that. To be what you wanna be. . . . As long as you follow the rules and regulations. . . . Now, everybody have a chance in the United States. Everybody has a chance. People are coming from other countries have chances, we have chances, the people that live here has chances; everybody has chances in the United States. It's a good country.

Sometimes the statements were a bit shorter and to the point. Javier, the young Hispanic roofer in Billings, told me, "Yeah . . . you just think about what you want in life, and you just go for it, and there's nobody that can stop you but yourself, you know." Timmy, the young ex-felon and recovering addict in Billings, in a brief comparison of the United States to other countries, claimed that unlike other countries, where "one religion is killing another religion," in the United States, "over here we can all do our own thing, live our own . . . achieve our own dreams, and still . . . I mean, you can achieve anything you want in this country if you're willing to work for it and not have the fear of being . . . have your head chopped off for it or whatever. You know, like you do in other countries." And Ray, when explaining why he so enthusiastically wants to be in America and nowhere else, said that it is "simply because it's, of course, it's the land of the free, home of the brave, and there's numerous opportunities. I mean if a, if a person is willing, I think, such as I, as far as opportunities in America, that they're unlimited." For proof, he urged me to think about his children and their education: "I mean, my son he got a, an associate's degree in electronics, and my daughter, she has a PhD, yeah, at an early age."

Others elaborated more on the nature of these opportunities and the importance of being willing to work hard to improve one's lot. Choice and personal effort were often evoked. My conversation with Denzel offers an example: "This is the land of milk and honey. You know what I'm saying? I can come here, with nothing, and achieve something. Whereas I can go someplace else with nothing and not achieve anything. . . . That's what makes me more patriotic about America than anywhere else." "And how does one achieve something?" I wondered. Denzel elaborated:

Because here's the thing, like we just talked about, it's not what you do; it's how you do it. If I want to get to a level and stay at that level, I got to work at it. If I don't work at it, I can't achieve what I need to achieve. So I could be a multimillionaire if I choose to; I just haven't come up with a game plan to put it on paper . . . and done what needs to be done. How do you think multimillionaires did it? They started from the bottom and worked their way to the top. You gonna, you ask any multimillionaire how he made it, he gonna tell you about a lot of hard work . . . so if he worked hard, what makes you think I can't work hard to get the same thing he got? Easy.

These were powerful words, revealing a determined belief in oneself and the absence of obstacles, other than one's self, to success. "Easy," Denzel said. What made me think that he could not work hard and become rich? The only obstacle was coming up with a game plan, something he had not (yet) managed to do. Surely, I suggested, one could grow up in the wrong environment and not have those options: "But some people," I suggested, "may be born in the wrong family or the wrong situation." Denzel disagreed:

That has nothing to do with it. You still have all the options just like every-body else. I can drop out of school at the age of fourteen or fifteen; at the age of sixteen I can drop out of school and still get a GD and go to college, if I choose to. If I don't utilize that, whose fault is that? That's my fault. I can excel at my education as far as I want to, or I can not excel as far as I want to. So to me . . . I've had good jobs, I've had bad jobs, but I've had other kids. . . . I got a sixteen-, seventeen-year-old now telling me how do I go get a good job: apply yourself, go to school, go get all the education you can get; it's free . . . go get all the education. If you don't want to go learn anything, I can't help you.

Indeed, anyone in America can become anything he or she wants to, even president, "if you keep at it," as Roger in Montana said:

You know, they say that if you have a dream that you want to be president, if you keep at it, your dream will come true. And right now people can . . . it seems like people can run for offices, you know, if that's what they wanna do, they do it. In other countries it seems like they put a stop to it. Like you wanna run for president, say, in Russia, and you're, you're a nobody . . .'cause there's people in the United States that have been nobody and become millionaires or become mayors or you know.

Key, then, is the utilization of opportunities. And these, again, are given to everyone. On this point, I was struck by Fast Eagle's thinking, given the historical, and for many the current, plight afflicting Native Ameri-can people in Montana and places like it. "I've been given every oppor-tunity," she said,

to be able to go to college, work, single parent, married, having kids, you know it. . . . I've had to apply for food stamps before; I've had to. I mean, I've worked full-time jobs; I've gotten taxes back and being able to take a taxi and stuff like that. You know, so there are breaks and something to . . . but if you're willing to work, I don't see there's really any reason. I mean . . . you're able to go to college and learn skills, you know, and pay that back. I mean, some things may not be as . . . I mean, I'm not educated in every aspect or everything, and I don't know everything, but I've been given opportunities, and I don't see why the next person wouldn't be able to have as long as they do them, and I mean work . . . everything takes work. You've got to be willing to work and do whatever you want to get what you want.

Indeed, if anything, the system—the country, the government, and society in general—helps you take advantage of America's opportunities. This, too, is part of the attractiveness of the country. I asked Sam if he felt that the country did enough for him. He replied:

The country does enough. . . . They feed you, they give you free housing, they give you food stamps . . . the country does a lot for their people. The United States do a lot for their people. If you can't make it here, you can't make it nowhere. . . . If you can't make it here, you . . . you . . . there's something wrong with you . . . there's something terribly wrong with you. . . . Yeah, he [my father] taught me that. It's the land of opportunity to be what you wanna be. I helped you so far, and you have to help yourself.

I paused to think about the words "there's something terribly wrong with you" if you don't make it in America. It was as if America really gives people everything they need to succeed. Angie, in the same bus station in Birmingham, stated something nearly identical: "If you check into anything like college, you want a good job . . . there's the government, there's funds, there's programs, there's no obstacles if you know how to go get what you want, what you need. There's something always out there to help you." What is necessary on the individual's part is the will to progress. "If you, if you work for it," she added, "you can have what you want here. You go to school and do what you want. Before I had a wreck and broke my back and wound up on disability . . . I was a real estate agent making close to one hundred thousand dollars a year." The help extends even to criminals. In Sam's words, "Even in the prison they, they got programs in the prison. Trying to reprogram them, you know."

Everyone Wants to Come Here

I traveled to Alabama and Montana in the midst of the 2015–2016 presidential primaries and the Syrian crisis. The timing made immigration a very popular and hotly debated issue in the media. Perhaps because of this, immigration came to mind quickly when discussing America's greatness. As Doug put it, "You got a lot of people that want to come to this country . . . why? Why is that? Why we got that flood from Mexico to come over here? It's the land of milk and honey. . . . I mean, you got opportunities here. I mean, a lot, a lot of them come over here and get together and they make it."

The typical sequence of thought was that, when explaining why America is great, immigration serves as *proof* of the riches and opportunities that the country offers. My exchange with Kysha, in Birmingham, offered a good example. I asked her why she loved the United States and thought it was great. "We just shine," she replied. "You shine? What does it mean to shine?" She continued: "Everything we do, we do great. . . . We, we shine. They say the stars shine on Alabama, and they do! We have some brilliant people. . . . No, it's just, it's just something about the United States that's spectacular." "Spectacular?" I repeated inquisitively. "How so?" "We show a lot of love," Kysha replied. "To whom?" I asked. "Anybody that come from overseas or . . . they know about our greatness. They know about how we [interruption in the room], they, they, they know about our greatness; they know we give opportunity in acting, singing, sports, cooking. They just know." Chad, in Billings, the young white soldier recently back from years in Iraq, put it in fairly similar language, partly in reply to whether other countries, in Europe, for instance, offer similar things as the United States does. A "lot of people still come here. I mean, why . . . if, if the United States wasn't such a great country, then why do people still come here?" Sure, he admitted, a few other countries do offer quite a lot, but there are usually downsides. Eventually, people leave those countries:

I'm not for sure Sweden or one of those . . . one of the, one of the countries over there, but they do give out free health care and free education and free college or something like that, but the people . . . the guys . . . the people as soon as they get that, you know, the free health care, the free or the free education they get their college degree, they go somewhere else. . . . Is what I'm thinking of, is what I read or . . .'cause they don't wanna . . . they . . . yeah, the taxes are too high.

Alternative destination countries were often dismissed. What America offers is exceptional, and this explains the draw it has for so many people, especially, as the interviewees in Alabama told me, those from

Mexico. Erica reflected on this point while thinking back to her earlier, and financially more comfortable, life with her ex-husband:

And I think that that's the opportunity, it's the land of opportunity, and I think that that's probably one of the greatest things. What, and living in the United States we have so many people that want to come to the United States. . . . In California, my husband, my ex-husband, was in the construction field; eighty-five percent of his laborers were from Mexico, and they would have . . . live in an apartment, like eight of them, and they also had homes in Mexico, and what they would do is, you know, give the funds to their homes, to their families in Mexico. So you can see that in itself that they're another country coming to the United States because of financial jobs in that field, you know. It might not be, the housing is very bad right now in California, but I think it is the opportunity and the job market.

The son of Mexican immigrants himself, Javier in Montana confirmed such thinking. His parents, he said, "they're from Mexico, and they just came here to have a better life for us. . . . I think the United States is probably one of the richest countries out there, and that's why everybody wants to come here, for the money."

Mexicans, of course, were only one of many people being attracted to the United States. People from other parts of the developing world, such as Africa, also come to the United States because of its greatness. Alicia, the young black woman in her thirties in a homeless shelter in Birmingham looking to complete her high school education, reflected on an African pastor she knew:

He's African, and some of the advantages we have here in the United States is shelter, food stamps, that we don't really cherish, they don't have it in Africa; they don't have shelters; they don't have food stamps. . . . You know, those people have to come over here to get the resources that they need. I don't wanna be in a place like, now I'm homeless; if I was in Africa, I'd probably be just on the street. I'm thankful for some of the resources that we do have that other countries do not have.

In weaving together America's greatness and immigration, it is worth noting that some of the interviewees expressed doubts or outright negative sentiments toward those who come. Antonio, for instance, reasoned, "I think a lot of countries would think we're a better country; I mean, to me

I think it's like everybody is trying to come to America. I kinda have my little doubts about having all of them because I think America needs to do more for American people." Katie, whose ex-husband was Mexican, also expressed "doubts": "Me, immigration . . . now my husband, yes, was Mexican, but he was legal. . . . But I also feel that they're coming and doing stuff to us. Taking our jobs . . . taking our jobs and stuff like that. Yes, you know my kids are Mexican American, so I do have thoughts about the immigration." The same questions about people coming over the borders (i.e., Mexico) came from Emma, also in Alabama:

Yeah, some is okay, but what they're doing now, they're overflooding the borders, and they come in and get all this free help when the people that live here can't even get it. If they needed it, they couldn't get it because supposedly they broke . . . but they're helping everybody that comes across the borders.

But, interestingly, such doubts were sometimes quickly used to talk about patriotism and love of country again. Anne, in rural Montana, for instance, called on her fellow Americans to garner strength and deal with the influx of people:

Way back when people come to this country to accept life in America . . . where they had it a better chance to make a go of it, you know. Nowadays we got bad elements coming in by the hordes, and it's gonna take a lot of people that are patriotic and love this country that stand together and make it work. We don't, I don't want that other stuff. . . . You know, I'm, I'm sure I'm almost in a minority group anymore, but that don't lessen how I feel about my country.

But not everyone felt this way, of course. Jeannie, the middle-aged white woman in a used-clothing store in Vernon, took on a softer tone: "You know, the people that's wanting to come over here to America, I think they should; I don't think they should be denied. The reason why is because they're human beings and they've got every right, I think, in this world to go where they want to go to go live. . . . I mean, it's just like Americans; we go where we want to go and live."

Beauty and Contentment

Several of the women I spoke with explained their love of country by pointing to its extraordinary beauty. Their images and language added to the picture of the United States as the land of milk and honey. When, for instance, I asked Jeannie in Vernon what words came to mind when thinking of the American flag, she immediately replied, "beautiful, loved, and free!" I wanted to probe further and asked, "When you say you love America, why do you love America? What do you love about it?" She answered, "Well, the scenery. . . . [We have] got beautiful scenery." As did many other interviewees, she noted that she had not traveled outside the country, but the natural beauty of the country was central to her understanding of America. Kayla, also in Vernon, associated the American flag "with patriotism. I think about America the beautiful." I asked her "in what way is it beautiful?" She replied, "To me it's beautiful, I mean, you know, I've been, like I said, to California; it's beautiful, Arizona's beautiful, Carolinas is beautiful. I've been to all those states, and it, it makes you feel like you want to come. They welcome you sometimes." There was a warmth and softness to her description. Her words resonated very well with what Autumn, a young white woman who worked as a banquet server in Billings, said to explain why she loved the United States:

I like the land, I like the, the sights, I like Mount Rushmore, I like the waterfalls, I like the sky, I like the mountains. . . . If I think about moving to anywhere else, it just wouldn't be the same. . . . It's my home. Nothing ever . . . hits the heart like your home.

Indeed, for Valerie, a white veteran from the navy who had lived in various parts of the country, part of the reason people call the United States God's country is that it, and with it Montana, "is a beautiful country." Why, in turn, did Fiona love the United States? "I guess because I was born American, raised American . . . it's pretty much all I know, and I think America actually has a lot to offer people still no matter what other people might think. And it's a beautiful country. We've got some wide-open spaces that are just awesome."

Men were less likely to mention the country's physical aspects, but three did. Two appreciated its size and openness. Ray contrasted it to Europe, which, "land-wise it's too small—that's a personal thing—it's too small. I can visit the whole country, Europe, in less than six months.

Okay, versus the United States it would take me maybe a year or so just to visit every state in whatever, in the United States." Chad, in Montana, talked about the ability to leave cities behind and be in the open country: "Big sky, yeah, I love being able to go out in the country whenever and not having to drive twenty miles to go out in the country. I love being close, this close to nature. I mean, yeah, I live in the city, but I can live in a small town." And, humorously, Marshall spoke more about the varieties of climates one can find. What would he think if I took his American citizenship away? His reply was that "the first thing I can think of is the choice of climate control; there's a lot of places that you can live in this country; you can go wherever you want."

A second sentiment complemented the appreciation of the country's physical beauty: a feeling of contentment with one's situation. Though with clearly very limited financial resources at their disposal, several interviewees—mostly women, again—asserted that in fact they lacked little. Sometimes the logic was comparative: people in other countries have it worse. Fast Eagle, grateful to be working as a hotel receptionist and able to feed her children, said, for instance, "I watch the news a lot, and the opportunities that I've had and just where I'm at now, a lot of people don't have that. So I suppose I could be doing worse, maybe doing better, depends on the choices that I make, but I'm safe and I'm happy." Emily, comparing the plight of the poor in other countries to her own situation, told me,

[I am] very thankful for what I have because some of those people don't have anything. They live on the street; they live in abandoned buildings that don't have any windows, no doors, they just a shell. And I mean that's, that's real poverty; I mean, we have it here in the United States, but at least they have programs where you can work, where you can get, if you disabled, you can get some kind of income.

Poverty in America, then, is less severe than elsewhere. Interestingly, the comparison on one occasion extended to the past, when things were even harder. Recalling her childhood, Grace, the retired cotton picker from Vernon, felt that "we have more now than I did then 'cause when we was growing up, we was bad poor. And lived in houses where you could see chickens through the cracks. I don't have that problem today."

But there also was a fairly widespread sense that having very limited economic resources need not mean that one feels "poor" or is "lacking" something fundamental in life. Anne recalled growing up in a farming family in rural Montana. The fact is, she said, "when I was a kid, we were poor, but we didn't even know it. You know, we . . . we . . . my father was a farmer, and we always grew our own big garden, and we didn't even think about such a thing." Perhaps they were self-sufficient, or perhaps people today are too focused on feeling deprived: "Today, there's too many people that consider . . . they think about things that aren't productive. . . . There's nothing wrong with being poor, you know; you can still do the best you can do every day." Besides, she added in a rather revealing thought, "I wouldn't know what to do with a lot of money anyway. You know . . . I, I'm sure I could find places for it where it would help, but I don't think you should give people anything and everything they want all the time."

Anne would have to think about how to use any extra money. She was not the only one to express a feeling of sufficiency. Rainbow, a Native American in Billings who in her early forties was unemployed with four children, told me, "I'm fine; I'm happy where I'm at. . . . I'm fine where I'm at." Kysha, in the homeless shelter in Alabama, outright affirmed, "I'm not poor; I think I'm rich!" She premised that with the idea that according to the Bible the "poor is gonna be with you always" and went on to recall a "white doctor" who "gave all his millions and went and lived with the poor, but the poor just gonna be here." The logic, it seemed, was one of inevitability and therefore acceptance: the poor will always be around, and being poor need not mean that people should think of themselves as actually deprived.

Thus, a number of the interviewees were aware that others in American society have more—or that they themselves could have more—but expressed satisfaction with their own situations. "Yes," Katie said, "there's people that has better lives and stuff, but, I know that that, yeah, peoples do have better . . . you know, I'm happy where I'm at."

I asked her to elaborate. "I said, I said there's a lot of people that does different things, but I'm happy . . . that has more stuff, but I'm happy where I'm at." Antonio, also in Birmingham, similarly stated,

I can't have everything, you know, and actually at the age I'm at now, I'm not looking for everything; I'm not looking for things. . . . I just want to be comfortable with life. So I ain't stressed out like my wife would be; that's why I'm not . . . and I ain't no rich guy at all. I struggle to get to the end of the day, but I don't see the point of being frustrated for real because it's not gonna help nothing. It hasn't helped me in the past.

As it turns out, his wife, Paula, told me in a separate interview that, despite Antonio being unemployed and her receiving $530 a month for disability, "Well, I have it good. I'm, I'm, well, I'm married. We have a good life."

Difficult financial situations often coupled with dire personal situations did not translate into overall antagonistic feelings toward life or the country. Perhaps it was Angie's positivity that made the strongest impression on me. A recent diagnosis of a brain tumor, constant pain, and very little income to support her two children did not make her bitter. "I love my country," she told me with a smile. "I'm happy here." I asked about her tumor: "Yeah," she said, "they diagnosed me three months ago . . . so, like I said, though the government has helped smooth everything you need here, so why would I want to go anywhere else?"

Katie and Hubert (Birmingham, AL): Remembering marching with Martin Luther King, Hubert expressed a deep appreciation for America's freedom and the hope it gives to its people, while Katie, whom he helped stop working the streets, explained her patriotism in light of the sacrifice of many family members who served in the military and fought for the country.

Alex (Birmingham, AL): Alex shared his deep appreciation for the ability to go hunting in America, one's rights to be and do whatever one chooses, and government programs that help the poor. He owns a T-shirt showing both the Confederate and American flags.

The interviewees are listed, by their pseudonyms, in the Appendix along with some basic demographic information. These photos of some of the interviewees were obtained with their permission.

Doug (Birmingham, AL): Doug spoke at length about the Revolutionary War, the sacrifices made by so many to build a free nation, the role of America to rid the world of tyranny, and personal control over one's life.

Charlotte (Vernon, AL): A staunch conservative, Charlotte believed that God has special plans for the United States. She also felt that America is the freest country on earth, with a limited government that has, unfortunately, recently become more intrusive.

Kayla (Vernon, AL): Kayla was one of several people who talked about America as especially beautiful.

Roger (Billings, MT): Roger emphasized the fundamental equality of opportunity and worth among American citizens and the safety the country provides from violence and terror.

Linda (Billings, MT): Countries like China, North Korea, and Mexico, for Linda, limit people's beliefs and personal choices. America offers the most freedom.

Tanya (Billings, MT): Recently a victim of an assault, Tanya expressed great appreciation for gun ownership and the freedoms that only America offers.

CHAPTER 6

FREEDOM

I want to be who I am. I don't want somebody to tell me who to be. . . . I'm an individual, I'm unique, I'm not some robot, and I don't want to be a robot.

Angie, Birmingham, Alabama

"Freedom" was the word that nearly all interviewees mentioned when explaining their love of the United States. It was the term that most often came to mind when thinking of the American flag, the military, or what makes America unique in the world. It was uttered with reverence and conviction—like something sacred and dear that one has learned to respect and appreciate since childhood. "My freedom," Doug told me in Birmingham, that "freedom is the most important thing, just about as precious as eyesight." Questions of income, social status, or other metrics of personal success were secondary and often irrelevant. America is the country of freedom, and freedom is the most important thing anyone can have.

Freedom exists in other countries, too, of course. But there is an important difference, I was reminded, between the United States and all those other countries: Freedom is at the heart of the American social contract. America was born out of a yearning for freedom; it came into being because of freedom. The same cannot be said of countries in Europe, Japan, or any other place where today we find freedom: none can trace their origins to freedom as explicitly as the United States can. At turbulent times in their histories, some of those countries even turned their backs to freedom altogether, and they found freedom again because of American intervention. There is a purity of intent that is unique to the United States, even if admittedly at certain points in its history mistakes were made. Perhaps because of its origins, there is also "more" freedom in the United States than elsewhere: one can do things there that are not allowed in other countries.

These were broad and wide-sweeping ideas. They were deeply felt, despite, or perhaps *because* of, the more immediate and practical concerns most of the interviewees faced in their daily lives. They took more specific form as the interviewees elaborated on their appreciation of America's freedom. First, they valued enormously the possibility of individual self-determination, both in physical and mental terms. Those in Montana infused this narrative with considerable libertarian themes; black interviewees in Alabama tended instead to point to progress in racial relations. Second, women and men alike affirmed with fervor the importance of gun ownership for freedom: only America guarantees the right to bear arms. This is more than a matter of self-protection and rebellion against tyranny: one can hunt, and feed one's family, with guns. Third, many stressed that America's freedom was fought for, at great cost, by generations of Americans, including those currently in the military: it is both a duty and honor to cherish it and America for it. To these we should add more localized patriotic narratives: a Confederate view of freedom and heritage in Alabama, and an antigovernment version in Montana.

Some of these themes were consistent with three of the insights present in the existing research discussed previously. The interviewees put a premium on the dignity and rights granted to each individual by the country's founding documents (insight 1) and on freedom of self-determination (insight 3). They also talked at length about the inherent inclusiveness of America's founding documents and social contract (insight 5). Yet the specific articulation and threads those themes took on, as well as the intensity and devotion to freedom that the interviewees felt, could not have been captured by those insights. There was much more that only in-depth and in-person conversations could reveal.

Self-Determination and Open Skies

To determine one's existence: this, in a nutshell, was the primary reason given for one's love of America. America uniquely recognizes the importance, and moral necessity, of this prerogative. Most of the people I met had a fierce, nearly instinctive attachment to the idea. "We are all each different flowers," Shirley told me in one of the earliest interviews I conducted in Birmingham; "we all each look different, think different; we're all different for a reason." Alex put it in blunter tones:

A casket is only room for one person, you know . . . and that's why I want to live my life, how I live it regardless of what the government says or the president says or that dude over there says. . . . I don't care. That's me; I'm gonna live my life how I want it, not . . . I'm not gonna have nobody running it.

Individual lives must be expressed, or, at the very least, the conditions for expressing them must be assured. And this is precisely what America guarantees, as Alex reasoned:

'Cause it's more freedom, more free than, and I think, I mean, you got more rights here like all our, I don't know how to explain that . . . like you, your right, you got more rights and more freedom than you would anywhere else . . . like freedom to, like freedom of speech and everything. All the, like all the amendments and all that. We got all that freedom.

Many others echoed Alex's words. Linda, in Montana, when asked to contemplate living in Mexico instead of the United States, stated, "I would be fighting tooth and nail to stay here 'cause we have a lot more choices than they do down there." But it was perhaps Darrius who was able to articulate the connection between freedom and his patriotism most clearly:

The thing that attracts me about this country is the, the ideals that it was supposed to be founded on. . . . I love the fact that, well . . . that . . . how can I put this . . . I love, I love how Americans try to aspire to live by our Constitution and the American ideals and principles even though we've failed that a lot of times. Still, it's there, and still a lot of Americans like us believe in it, like wholeheartedly . . . like one hundred percent. Like, I mean, with the Bill of Rights and everything else, the Declaration of Independence, if you actually read those documents, you know, they're beautiful, and they're, they're written by very intelligent people, and, and, the principles in those things, they're timeless. They're . . . that all men are created equal . . . life, liberty, and the pursuit of happiness. I mean . . . those are things that everyone can relate to, everyone tries to do across the world. America actually tries to embody that, and growing up here and being educated here, they try to push that down your throat a lot, but there is a glimmer of truth in all that, and that's what I love about it. . . . It's that fact and how that differentiates America from a lot of other countries. We still have that sort of history.

The Declaration of Independence and the Bill of Rights: these "beautiful" documents embody "timeless" principles that, Darrius noted, reach back to "the American Revolution and how people here tried to revolt against monarch . . . monarchy." Many others, such as Angie in Birmingham, agreed with this sentiment, albeit with simpler language and sometimes by pointing to the absence of repressive laws: "I don't wanna be told what I can and can't do." America in this respect is superior: "I mean, we got laws to an extent, right; you see what I'm saying, but they're not as strong as some other countries' can be."

What, then, did self-determination actually mean to the interviewees? In what ways did they feel free to determine their own existence? Two primary narratives emerged: physical and mental self-determination.

Physical Freedom

Montana in winter is not a warm place. From December to March, temperatures can easily plummet far below freezing. Snow is abundant, and spring comes late. Yet Marshall prefers a homeless life there, describing it as a choice, an expression of a sort of freedom that only America offers: the freedom to be, physically, wherever one wishes. This is how Marshall put it, in reply to my asking why he loves the United States, with his companion, Marion, a mentally unstable Native American/Irish thirty-eight-year-old woman on Social Security, next to him, nodding in approving fashion along the way:

Well . . . it's, it's a very free country. I mean, I'm actually, I live on the streets, I'm kinda choosing to do that . . . sabbatical. Nobody bothers me for it; I'm not bothering anybody. I got my own little nook. . . . There are other places in the world where I'd be forced into some place to shelter up or you know herded off or . . . jailed.

"You can't live like that," interjected Marion, in reference to life in those "other places." Marshall continued, "Yeah, there's places [where] injustice like that happens every day." The idea of being forced into a shelter as an injustice intrigued me. I asked Marshall to elaborate:

There's, there's . . . you can still go and be, you know . . . left alone in this country. Freedom still exists in it. And I mean real freedom where you can be who you want to be without anybody messing with you. I would kinda like to go back to Alaska because we still got a frontier out there.

"Real" freedom for Marshall meant essentially physical isolation—the ability to be out of anyone's reach. He proceeded to tell me that the American government still "supports the cause of freedom, which is the core . . . it's what we founded the country on. . . . We wanted to be free of oppression . . . misrepresentation, basically downright exploitation . . . so the less, the less structure you have, the less opportunity there is for that to happen." Indeed, in a libertarian turn, he reasoned that the government's job should really be limited to administering justice and "maintain[ing] structure and order, keep[ing] things in operation—that's essentially its core role."

I asked Marshall how he made it through winter. He replied, "two sleeping bags. One's rating minus ten and the other one I don't know the rating on it, but it's decently heavy. Extra padding," he said smilingly. Did he ever want to go to the shelters? "No, they lock the doors, and I believe in my freedom!" He smiled again with a twinkle in his eye. Is this something he would continue doing? Would he make a different choice one day? He reiterated his ability to choose, informed me that he is working on a mobile game for smart phones and that he needs time to do so and that no one is bothering him: "Yeah, I've done it before, and I'll do it again. Like I said, I'm working on mobile games, so the best way, the best way to be able to focus on that is just become a starving artist. Nobody seems to mind too much."

I ran into this steadfast view with others, that physical freedom is a fundamental aspect of life in America. It was often described in terms of movement—above all, the ability to "come and go." What did Valerie in Harlowton appreciate the most about America? "All the freedoms, being able to come and go, speak our mind when we want to." When I asked Charlotte in Vernon why she was flying an American flag in front of her house, her reply was, "'Cause like I said before, we love this country." "What makes you love it?" I inquired. The answer began, "Well, you have the freedom to go anywhere you want to, do whatever you want to, to a certain degree; you have the freedoms." The language was nearly identical to that of Tanya, Daniel's wife, in Billings. "Considering how we're living, living to all the other countries, I'd say we have it pretty damn good." "Why is that?" I asked. "What does that mean to you?" "Well," she went on, "we can always come and do basically as we please." This was also very similar to what Kysha, homeless and living on less than one thousand dollars a month, shared when explaining that America is the best "'cause you can be free. I can go to New York; I can go to California . . . I can fly here; I can fly there. You know it just . . . yeah, eat the good of the land . . . it's just awesome."

As to why this ability to come and go was so important, some, like Valerie, could not provide me with much of an answer: "You know, I never really thought about it. It, it just is." But others did. For Charlotte it meant that no one was watching over her—not unlike the sentiment expressed by Marshall when describing the feeling he enjoyed being homeless. "Yeah," Charlotte said, "going where you wanna go, go and come as you please; you don't have somebody watching you all the time." Back in Montana, Oscar, a Hispanic, expressed a similar concept about some "other"—a Fidel Castro, for instance—constraining him:

What free means to me? . . . I have, I have no dictator telling me I can do this, I can do that, I can't do this, I can't do that. Free means I take my granddaughter to the park, I take my granddaughter to the store, I take my granddaughter, I take my sons . . . we go to a baseball game, and I haven't somebody dictating us like Fidel Castro or like saying, hey, this is what you gotta do, this is how you live, this is what you do, this is . . . no . . . nuh-huh. I, myself, I rather be dead than to live like that.

For some, then, there was almost an existential meaning to this ability to move around and do the things one wants to do. Shirley elaborated on this point when describing what freedom meant to her:

Simple things like getting up, going to the store, choosing the type of food that you would like to eat that day or put in your household to eat. . . . the ability to walk about freely, to go places and experience different things . . . concerts, theaters, movies . . . zoos . . . science museums and concerts. . . . I mean, it just depends on what interests you. . . . Art, literature, there's just so much that you can channel into, for let's say just for your own hobbies and leisure or your own talents and gifts.

Being able to move freely, it seemed, is part of self-expression and the utilization of talents and gifts. The logic echoed what Janice stated in Billings. Homeless and living out of a car, she told me, "I love it here; I love the diversity; and . . . I just love it here. I love that, you know, you can go to a restaurant and eat Italian food; or you can go to a restaurant and eat Chinese food; or . . . where in a lot of countries you don't really see that." Movement means the fulfillment of one's inclinations and interests. "A lot of countries" do not allow that, because they "stick to their own things."

Indeed, America itself did not use to allow such ease of movement for its black citizens. Today, however, those restrictions have lifted, at least in official terms, and several of the African American interviewees in Alabama made a point of saying so. Emily, for instance, who at seventy-two recalled well growing up in a segregated South, drew the following comparison:

If you did, it was like, you know, sometime you would get beaten and just, a whole bunch of things that happen to you if you went into other areas. . . . Your parents told you, teachers told you that you couldn't go to certain places; you couldn't do certain things. I mean, it was segregation; they had separated even water fountains.

The present is considerably better, though certainly far from perfect:

But now things are a whole lot better; I mean, it's not where it really should be, but it's better. I mean, you can go to whatever school you want to go to; you can go to whatever college you want to go to; you can be, you can apply for whatever job that you qualify for; you can go simply as riding the bus; you can sit anywhere you want to on the bus, on the train, on the plane; you can go to whatever store to shop that you want to go, restaurants, church. So of course it's still segregation, but it's not like it was. . . . Yes, it's a whole lot different now. I mean, even imagine back a long time ago, you couldn't even come to the library and sit down and read a book, or, well, of course, they didn't have computers and all that then, going online, they didn't have all that back a long time ago, but . . . I guess you, you, I mean this was off limits to the black people.

Denzel offered similar reflections:

That's what changed. The black race and the white race now we can coexist with each other now, whereas in the past we couldn't coexist with each other. It was either you did this and we did this, or we didn't do it at all. Now it's, we can do it together. We can go eat at the same restaurant, we can use the same bathrooms, we can drink out of the same water fountains . . . and things like that. It's not this is y'all restaurant, this is our restaurant, you can't come in our restaurant, we won't go in your restaurant . . . no, we go in any restaurant we want.

Of course, Denzel stressed, the continued existence of racism today "makes me angry; it makes me, it infuriates me because of the struggle that we've all been through in the past and is still trying to go on sometimes today." But, he added in pointed fashion, "America is the land of the free, and if I intend to be free, I need to act like I'm free." With this spirit in mind, I heard the expression "color-blind" often in Birmingham, as from Doug, who reiterated themes that had become familiar to me by then:

That was in the past, and I'm color-blind too; it don't faze me. It really don't. I mean . . . we all got to live here together, and there was a time, I mean, that was some dark history of, of our past, and that's the way it should be . . . in the past. As you know, Birmingham was one of the most segregated cities in the United States, and it was not too long ago I couldn't be sitting up here with you; I couldn't even go, I couldn't even go over there to sit at all or anything. And now we got our own black city hall, council members, and so we got progress; we need to put that crap behind us. We got to live us here together.

Kysha, speaking to me in a homeless shelter in Birmingham, expressed a similar sentiment: "Well, I've never had any problems being black. I know our ancestors . . . but I don't have anything to do with what happened back before I was born. But I just always been just free . . . able to do what I want." Michelle repeated nearly the same idea when saying that "I haven't seen any [racism]. . . . I seen it on TV, but I have never seen it in person."

Three times these discussions on freedom and race in Alabama eventually touched on sex and marriage (and extended sometimes to homosexuality as well). Denzel, for instance, said,

That's what keeps us together because I can go mingle with a Puerto Rican woman or a black woman or a white woman or an Asian woman, whereas back in the days I couldn't look at a white woman; I couldn't look at an Asian woman . . . I had to stay within my race. Now it's all kind of people, you know what I'm saying? You got interracial couples doing what they do. You got men and women doing what they do; they approved gay marriage.

According to Ray, freedom in America means "no dictatorship, no particular, no communism you know . . . no particular . . . I mean you're free to vote, choose your friends, who you date, who you marry, and your food of course." This perspective, he told me, "stems from my upbringing . . . from my family and because they instilled those values in me, you know, according to, from the beginning of America, that was one of the basic rights that I tend to believe in." And Erica, a white woman, listed "the freedom to marry, you know, outside your race" as one of the first things that came to mind when thinking about America and the freedoms it guarantees.

To be sure, recognizing such freedoms did not necessarily mean personal approval of all practices. Some white interviewees objected to interracial marriage.[1] And Denzel—along with many others—did not support gay marriage. However, he and several others noted that one must distinguish between one's personal belief and the American social contract:

Two people have the right to do what they choose to; just because I don't like it don't mean it's right. Two people are grown, I'm not, I'm not their judge; I don't have to go deal with what they have to deal with on judgment day. That's, that's between them and God. Me, I know what I've got to do; God put man and woman here to be fruitful [and] multiply. He didn't put, he didn't make Adam and Steve; he made Adam and Eve.

Thus, as to what happens here, on this earth, America guarantees freedom, and this is of the utmost importance, "because," Ray continued, "you take a person's freedom away, what are you, what are you doing? You're caging them up like an animal. If I'm caged up like an animal, you're gonna treat me like I'm a, I'm a . . . to act like an . . . you see what I'm saying? If you don't cage me up, I'm free to roam around like I want, like a human being."

"Roam around like I want, like a human being": this was a phrase that made me pause and think. Without question, the people I met had a genuine, deep appreciation for human beings, of the physical ability to be wherever they want to be, whatever that might mean. In Linda's words, in the backyard of a Laundromat in Billings, "If we want to go out in the middle of nowhere and live like a hermit, we still have that choice." Sitting with us at the table, Roger, staring deep into the Montana horizon and listening to Linda speaking, concurred with a simple "yeah."

A final, prevalent explanation of the importance of moving about freely had do with hunting. "Is America better than most other countries?" I asked Jeff in Billings. "By far!" he replied. "Why do you say that?" He answered,

Because of the freedoms that you have here, to move around, to do what you wanna do, you know. I do a lot of hunting and fishing and hiking, so, you know . . . in a lot of places you can't do that . . . and the people here are generally pretty friendly and with all this stuff going around in the world today, we really don't have that except for 9/11, and ever since then it's been pretty calm.

I asked him how often he exercised those freedoms. "Well," he said, "I own my own boat . . . a little one; it's by the Snake River . . . so I do a lot of steelhead fishing every season. I mean three seasons every year, and then when I'm not fishing, you know, I camp." These were obviously things that one could do in other countries, I thought. I did not ask him about that but followed his statement with a second, standard question: Why did he say that he wanted to be a citizen of the United States and not any other country? "Too many people killing each other over there, blowing themselves up, you know."

In other countries, Jeff seemed to suggest, it is not easy to move around freely and hunt. A few months earlier, in Birmingham, Alex had described to me what freedom in America meant to him. What would happen if someone took that away from him? Hunting was again at the forefront of his thoughts: "I wont be able to, I won't be able to say what I want to say, I won't be able to do what I want to do, I won't be able to hunt, I won't be able to fish; if they took all my rights from me, then I'd be mad." He reiterated the importance of hunting in America when I asked him, moments later, whether his parents had raised him to be patriotic. He was indeed raised to be patriotic. What did that mean in practice? Hunting again appeared in the narrative:

Well, yeah, in ways like hunting and all, showing me I got the freedom to hunt and to fish and everything . . . stuff like that, more or less teaching me the right ways of life. Like, like saying, saying you can go shoot this deer, but don't go do it at nighttime, you know, or you'll get in trouble.

I would hear additional views of the relationship between physical freedom and patriotism. For several interviewees it in part had to do with the absence of downright widespread violence. Harley in Alabama for instance reasoned that the United States is the "home of the free! Home of the free!" because

the war ain't in on us; we ain't here fighting; we over there fighting. They don't come fighting us; we were there fighting them. See, we go to them; they don't . . . they gotta, they don't come to us; we meet them over there. That's the best part about it . . . Afghanistan, Iraq . . . now we gotta go fight ISIS before they come fight us. Yeah, I think we got a strong nation, and we the top of the line. And I think the United States is about the best place to be, the safest place to be. That's what I think . . . yeah and if they do come to us, then I might change my mind, I don't know. . . . Right, right now I'm saying, now it's about the best place for me to be, in my opinion.

Mental Freedom

Mental freedom is the second dimension of self-determination. It consists of the liberty to choose how we use our minds. Just as we should be able to roam freely with our bodies, to take them wherever we want to, to come and go, we should be able to take our minds wherever we wish. For the vast majority of the interviewees, such mental freedom is the essential and defining element of American society. Other countries do not owe their existence to it, nor do they honor it as much as the United States does. Of all the factors that explain the patriotism of the American poor, this was the most commonly and often most intensely affirmed.

Antonio in Birmingham captured remarkably well the essence of what I would hear throughout my travels: "It's good to be, to be able to use your own mind to think, make your own decisions without being forced to do something, you know. I think that gives us that right to have our own way of thinking that's, you know, not being in prison to me. In other countries I feel like they're in prison." Choice, then, is the critical element. "Free to make your own decisions . . . to think for yourself," said Nova, a Native American in Billings who works as a personal care assistant. Erica, the white Republican at a Birmingham's homeless shelter, emphasized the same ideas with slightly different words:

We have the option. We have the option to go to what church we choose; we have the option to pick our jobs; we have the option to choose our schools for our children; we have the option of where we can live. I think we have that in itself is so much more than a lot of countries have. . . . It's the heart of who we are, you know? Who we are. The freedom of being able to speak, the freedom of religion, the freedom to marry, you know, outside, your race, you know.

Choice is at the "heart of who we are." It was a remarkably concise statement, one that resonated powerfully considering the difficult circumstances Erica and many of the other interviewees were facing— homelessness, uncertainty about where they will find food next, and little to no income.

Choice is at the core of America because America recognizes it in its foundational documents. The readiness to see choice in the country's founding documents was especially prevalent in Montana. Most people there seemed keenly aware of the origins of the country and its promises. For Daniel, for instance, the principles the country was founded on were "freedom of speech, freedom of religion, you know, that's what they were being persecuted . . . and they were being taxed beyond belief by a king that was never involved in their life and didn't know anything about it."

References to the founding documents were frequent. Phil spoke at length about the Constitution and the Bill of Rights to explain why "freedom to me is choices, and America has one of the highest levels of choices." This was the thinking of Sean, too. I met him, along with his young daughter, in a Laundromat in Billings. A white man in his mid-forties, he was at the time employed by Target. Years ago he spent nine months as a soldier in the Middle East and was among those who invaded Iraq during the first Gulf War. He defined himself as very patriotic and had strong opinions about most topics we discussed. What did he fight for, in Iraq, I asked? What does America mean to him? His reply was representative of the views of many others. He was honored to be a US citizen "because of what the United States stands for. . . . Freedom, it stands for individual's rights that are guaranteed in our Constitution." When I asked him to elaborate on what he meant by freedom, he continued:

Freedom: being able to work where you choose to work, being able to become what you wanna become if you're willing to put in the work and the dedication and everything else you need to, to do it. Being able to say what you wanna say, being able to own a gun to protect yourself and your family. You know, basically we're the only country that has these rights guaranteed in our Constitution.

Fast Eagle similarly noted that "the Constitution, the freedoms that we have, very important, not only that, but, you know, being able to have choice. . . . I feel the way I feel, you know, 'cause some people don't have a choice. I'm thankful for that."

I would hear the same on the way back from Harlowton to Billings, when I drove past a very small village. One house caught my attention: quite run-down, it had a tall pole and a big American flag flying from it. I pulled over and eventually met Gil, a retired truck driver, and his wife, Becky. As we began talking, I asked them if they were patriotic and why they flew the flag in front of their home. Becky answered first by saying that her daughter's "ex-husband was in the military, in the army, and of course my dad, years ago, my dad was in WWII and he was a co-pilot and they flew from Seattle to the Aleutian Islands or Kodiak Island and delivered supplies all the time up there, and I'm very patriotic, I love my country, and that's why I fly the flag." Gil then said "the freedom." "Freedom to do what?" I asked. "Everything!" affirmed Gil. "Whatever we really want to do," added Becky. "Is there anything holding you back?" I inquired. "Nope!" said Becky. "Not us," interjected Gil with laughter. "I like the Constitution, the right to bear arms," he added. "You like that?" I asked. "Yes I do," Gil confirmed. Becky then revealed, with pleasure, that "in fact we both have a concealed" permit.

In the background or foreground of these reflections about the virtues of life in America were the limitations of other countries. By and large, there was a widespread conviction that many of the things one can do in the United States are not possible elsewhere. Perhaps it was a matter of degrees: fewer cultural, legal, or bureaucratic obstacles stand in the way—including, as I would hear in Montana especially, a less intrusive government (if not in practice, at least in theory). Or perhaps it was a question of formal guarantees in the founding documents. Or perhaps it had to do simply with basic safety. The interviewees did not elaborate extensively on this but certainly stated their views with little doubt in their minds.

Consider in this regard the words of Carlos, a young Hispanic in Billings, who proudly showed me his American eagle tattoo when I first approached him to see if he was patriotic. His love of country was a sign of his

respect for the freedom that we have here. A lot of people have taken that for granted and don't realize the freedom that we actually have that other countries don't have . . . oh, you know, freedom to have a job, you know, and make a pretty good living without the government, or someone stepping in, the freedom to get married on your own terms, the freedom to have kids on your own terms, the . . . the right and, you know . . . that goes with the honor, too. . . . You want to honor that, that aspect of what you have here.

Getting married, having kids, and having a job on "your own terms": one could argue that this sort of freedom is available in many other countries, too—especially democratic ones. But when pressed, it seemed that at least some of the interviewees believed American democracy to be a genuine exception in the world. Anne in Harlowton, for instance, when asked to explain why there is "not a doubt in my mind" that America is a better country than most other countries, explained that she had said that "because of the basis that America was built on. There . . . Israel is the only other real democracy on the map, in the world. And America. I don't think you can do better than that." Because she had excluded all of Europe, Canada, India, Latin America, parts of Africa, and other parts of the world from the realm of democracy, I felt inclined to ask Anne what political systems those other countries might have but realized I probably had the answer already when she followed her previous statement with, "I'm still, you know, I'm from the old school, and I don't think socialism works. Our way works." The view of America's exceptional protection of democratic principles was also shared, in a very matter-of-fact way, by Lynn, also in Montana, and again with a touch of libertarianism about recent government intrusions:

It's possible that I could have ended up anywhere in the world, wherever . . . you know, I could have been born anywhere in the world, and so many people are, so many people have no freedom at all, and some of it depends on whether you're a man or a woman, some of it depends on your race, some of it depends on your ethnicity, and I just think here, even though there are things that bother me here . . . we just have, we just have way more. Way more. I mean, I can go to church if I want to; I don't have to worry about somebody coming after me for that. I can, I mean, I can just . . . we can do most anything, I mean, obviously I've said I've seen them take away, make things more difficult in certain areas because of the whole safety issue, but when you look overall, I just . . . yeah, I got to go back to your question. I guess I can't think of any place else I'd rather live because . . . at this point in time I think we're still good, we're still good.

Back in Alabama, only one of the interviewees really brought up the country's founding documents and the limitations of other countries, and with that the historical context in which they were written and the importance of race, into the conversation. This was Eddie. His reflections on the matter are worth reporting here in some detail:

They're mostly embodied in the Bill of Rights and in our American Constitution. We have freedom of assembly, we have of speech, freedom of the press, and a lot of countries, these things do not exist. They just don't. And they keep a lot of countries, which we call quote unquote third world countries, they're run by dictatorships, military [mumbles]. When they have a cause or a need to suppress or repress or oppress the people for their own, surely own self-gotten gain, they are, they generally are repressed, the rights of the people. And this country resisted it, the king of England for those very reasons. Because he wanted to keep us as a colonized people they could oppress and rule, and fortunately we had some courageous men who dared stand up to the British Empire. And during the long history of this country, people of color have also weighed in and weighed in on these issues even though we didn't necessarily get them when we should have. Through our, our . . . continued pressure and social wrangling we now have close to what we would like in rights even though there's always work to be done. So this country was not built by one race of people alone; it started with a race, the white race who, who resisted the king of England on principle; there were men of Christian heritage who believed in liberty and freedom for mankind, which is embodied in the Constitution of the United States. We find these truths to be self-evident, that all men are created equal; and we are.

What specific types of mental freedoms did the interviewees have in mind? What seemed the most important? Some pointed to rather specific freedoms, such as spending one's "money like you want to. You don't have to give an account to anybody. . . . It's just various things that you can appreciate being a citizen of the United States," in Emily's words. In Harlowton, Jill talked about schooling: "This sounds kinda cliché in what we're talking about, but it's very free. I mean it really is. . . . We were one time a homeschooling family; I'm a huge advocate of the right to homeschool. And Montana is a very free state to do that in." For the most part, however, the key categories were broad and quite predictable.

One of the most frequently mentioned was freedom of religion. It was often the first on the list. Cole, the ex-convict in Billings, said, "I can't speak for nobody else, just for me; you know, I'm a Christian, so in America I'm not gonna get killed for being a Christian. . . . I have the right to, to . . . I have the right to worship who I want to worship." Emily, in Alabama, explained her love of America by singling it out "'cause it's the land of the free and free religion; . . . it's just a good country to be in. I mean, I've read up on different countries, and a lot of countries that I read up on, I been to, I can appreciate being American." The language would often be similar across all the respondents, but in some cases it proved more colorful than others. For Alex, for instance, America is held together by various freedoms, including that of religion:

A lot of religion . . . I mean . . . like the *Duck Dynasty*, you seen *Duck Dynasty*, haven't you? . . . They got mad because Phil prayed every night; after every show he would pray. I mean, that's his decision, not . . . that's his belief; don't knock his show because of that. That's stereotyping. That's it . . . let him be him.

Hubert noted that "you can worship anything you want here. [mumbles] Other countries . . . if you don't worship what they tell you to worship, they gonna kill you." Indeed, as Angie put it, the American guarantee of freedom of religion is so important to her "'cause I don't want to be forced in any religions; I don't want to be forced in anything. . . . I mean, as long as we're not going out doing crazy things."

A second major category concerned speech. For some, like Gabby, this actually included the ability not to speak if one so chooses: "You can choose not to if someone, if you ever go to court, you can choose to, it's the Fifth Amendment—I can't remember all the amendments; it's been too long. I think it's the Fifth; I think it's the Second. . . . I plead the Fifth basically. You can plead the Fifth, and you don't have to say anything." Phil seconded that thought with the comment that "the Bill or Rights also gives you the right not to do something." More often, though, it meant the ability to criticize the government without repercussions. As Cole put it, "I can say what I wanna say, you know. . . . We can have different views, different opinions, and this is . . . you know, we have that right whereas some countries you can't say nothing against the president or nothing against, you know." The freedom to criticize the government without reprisal was on Doug's mind, too:

Right of freedom of speech and to express yourself, freedom to talk against the government if you want to. . . . I mean, some other countries you cannot do that. You cannot do . . . you can't put down the leaders or contradict the leaders and all that. I mean . . . some countries you can't even take a camera; North Korea, that's a closed society. We are a more open society, and I mean, I mean . . . democracy is, our democracy is, is just about like the best in the world.

The Individual Above All

Underlying, often without explicit acknowledgment, both notions of physical and mental freedom was a deeper and more fundamental assumption: the paramount unit of human existence is the individual rather than any kind of collectivity, and America is the country, par excellence, that recognizes this fact. As Valerie put it, "Your individual is going to be your core, but you're going to build on that."

This insight translated into a set of closely related ideas. The first is that each person is unique. When I asked Shirley why freedom was so important to her, this was her reply:

For human expression . . . just for me to . . . be able to experience life in all its different shades. If we allow certain groups of people of certain ideas . . . to wipe out what we have as individuals. I mean, we, we weren't born a bunch of robots . . .'cause if we were meant to be all alike, we would all be alike, we would all look like each other, and we would all do the same things. That isn't how we are as humans.

The connection to America followed immediately:

The individual right for you to be able to experience life individually. And I believe that we'd fight to the death for that. . . . I think it's something that is . . . part of the air that when you get to America you might not . . . could have been . . . that part of you . . . a part of you lives or you imagine yourself . . . just what a dream, a fantasy, a thought . . . that you could come to America, and you could actually live that out. Whereas you might not actually be able to live that out somewhere else. Whatever it is.

The second idea was that any given person is equal, as a person, to anyone else. It followed that there are no fundamental differences between the least and most privileged members of society, something that Eddie was clearly pointing to when talking about racial equality, and a crucial idea that we discuss in more detail in the next chapter when examining how the interviewees reconciled their position with their patriotism. Perhaps Ray articulated this notion most clearly:

For me, yeah, it starts with the individual, naturally. And according to our Constitution, rules, and rights, you know . . . everybody is afforded that without question, and we supposed to be equal across the board as far as individuals, regardless of social status or whatever. I believe right that, that I can have a conversation not just with you; I could sit down, talk with the president of the United States or the queen of England on any given subject, you know. . . . I might not know the whole subject, but I can interject something in that subject 'cause they know stuff that I don't know, and I guarantee I know stuff that they don't know. We can always get individualized, but as a whole I can generalize with different individuals regardless of their social status, so I feel comfortable with that.

As it turns out, Ray's thought was not hypothetical: he recalled that when he was a young person in the military he shared a meal in Turkey with President Jimmy Carter:

And, yeah, we talked about numerous things, and, and he . . . I said, I said something like that's right, that's right, Mr. President, and he said, "You don't have to call me Mr. President; you can call me Jimmy." I said, "Thank you, Mr. President" [laughs]. Of course, nobody gonna call the president Jimmy! I thought it was funny.

The third idea was about authenticity: All people should be able to be true to themselves—to their uniqueness. Sidney cherished the "freedom of being yourself, freedom for not being condemned because of something that you choose to be or do." With that, of course, comes also responsibility. Here, too, America stands out. What did the flag represent to Kysha?

Awesome in that the red, white, and blue represent that we can be true, we can be true to ourselves. We can just explore. We can just be ourselves . . . right. And whatever challenge in life, you gotta overcome it. We're the country that give you a chance. If you don't make it, that's on you.

How, exactly, it came to be that human beings are endowed with these qualities was not something I inquired about. But a couple of people did give me some hints. God was certainly part of the story, as Sidney thought:

God gave us free will, and we should be able to do what we want to do; even if we choose to be gay, he don't make us serve him, so I don't see why certain countries you be killed because you want to serve him. . . . That's terrifying to think about . . . that's the best thing that we got—it's freedom. Because there's nothing like your freedom; it's like when your freedom gets took away, you feel encaged . . . like you in jail..

But there was also a sense that the individuality of each person is just a part of human nature. As Emma put it, it is "just part of being human to, to be able to think freely and to be an individual."

Love of Guns

Many of the people I met, especially in Montana, loved America *because* it guarantees the right to bear arms. And guns are necessary for freedom. Three narratives wove together guns, freedom, and America. First, America won its freedom from the British with guns. Guns were instrumental for the acquisition of freedom and thus represent freedom. Second, guns are a way of protecting one's freedom, and the freedom of loved ones, against evil people. Third, guns are essential for hunting, and hunting is an expression of freedom as well as independence. "[I] love guns," Daniel asserted in Billings; "they're the backbone of this country. That's the reason we have a country." With different words, Anne observed something similar in Harlowton: without guns "you're not your own self. You become a puppet, and I don't do puppets very well at all." She continued that you "gotta use your own thinker and decide for yourself what you can live with and what others can live with and what they can't." To my question of what "guns have to do with that," with being "your own thinker," she simply added, "Well, that's just part of the American way."

First, then, and in Montana in particular, several interviewees spoke of the connection between guns and the fighting spirit of the American revolutionaries. When I asked Becky outside her home in a small town between Billings and Harlowton how guns "go together with your love of country," she observed, "Well, that's, that's pretty much what our country was actually founded on. . . . The only way they could actually get freedom was to fight for what they believed in, and," she added with some rancor, "there are way too few people anymore that do that." The British tried to take away Americans' weapons, and freedom could be acquired only through the crafty manufacturing of guns and violent rebellion. As Sean, the white Iraq War veteran with his young daughter at the Laundromat in Billings, put it: "That's the whole reason the right to bear arms is in the Constitution, 'cause that's how Britain oppressed us, is we weren't you know . . . we had to, we had to make guns and own guns and everything else secretly so they didn't know we had them." So, freedom requires ownership of weapons, and this was the lesson that British oppression and the American Revolution should teach us, as Marshall reiterated in slightly different language:

I'm definitely for gun freedom. . . . Yes, even though, even though I'm not much for military action, I'm definitely for gun freedom. . . . Because you never know when you're gonna need to take military action. You might need it. There's a reason we were supposed to keep and bear arms. . . . Because when we, when we were oppressed by the British, one of the first things they did was they went and seized weapons, right?

Inherent in such thinking was the second, and most commonly mentioned, theme: personal protection as a fundamental right that, thankfully, America ensures. As Linda stated, "You know . . .'cause that, you know that's . . . I don't know, to me, part of being American is having the right to have guns if you want them . . . to protect yourself." Oppression can originate from any kind of source, not least the government. The essential point is that the power to defend oneself lies in the citizens, and nowhere else. Sean was clearest about this when explaining his opposition to gun control:

For the simple reason of that's the first step of oppression. Is a citizenship that isn't able to defend itself from its own government . . .'cause that's why, that's the whole reason we have in our Constitution the right to bear arms. It wasn't to hunt; it wasn't to . . . [it was] in case we were attacked so every, every citizen could be a soldier; it was so the citizens of a, of our country can defend themselves in the case the government tried to take over.

Since I could not imagine how armed citizens could resist the might of the American military, I asked Sean if his thinking was realistic. His answer revealed something important about the connection between arms and freedom and his pride in the country: the American military itself is a citizens' army whose loyalty is to the Constitution, not to the government. As Sean explained with pride,

The thing is, is . . . what people don't want to understand is we have a citizen military. We aren't made to serve. The people that are serving are volunteers; it's not like the government has the ability to, to go you do what we say or we're gonna kill your families. . . . And when you swear your oath in the military, you don't swear your oath to the government, you don't swear your oath to the president of the United States, you do not swear your oath to the Congress; you swear your oath to uphold the Constitution of the United States. And I'll guarantee you, yes, you're probably going to have some soldiers that follow the orders no matter what they're given to the letter, but you're gonna have a lot more soldiers who are gonna turn around and point a gun at that general's head when he says shoot that citizen. . . . And that is why I've not worried about us needing a bazooka or a tank or anything like that, because yeah, the FBI and the CIA have their toys, but when you have probably half the military of this country, you know, back its citizens, us having guns is gonna be enough.

The potential oppressor can be something other than the government. One person, Timmy in Billings, mentioned animals when camping in the wild: "I've carried a gun every time I've been to the mountains, I spend a lot of time in the mountains, I've never had to shoot a bear in self defense . . . but what happens that one time when, you know, I walk in between a mother bear and her cub without realizing it . . . you know, and it comes down to her or me?" But it was ill-intentioned people who were most typically seen as sources of trouble, and living in a country where guns are illegal will create, rather than solve, problems: "Who has an intent to harm you," Marshall reasoned, "they're also gonna have no problem with bypassing laws to go and get weaponry. They'll still be around."

Daniel had perhaps the most colorful explanation of how guns can help, thanks above all to the Second Amendment, which, on a libertarian note, he felt is under threat by the government:

I guarantee, your great-grandma jerks out a thirty-eight and shoots the hell out of somebody trying to rob her. It would break . . . somebody from messing with little grandmas anymore. You know you kill a few . . . [laughs] but no . . . there's not too many guns; there's too many people worrying about it, you know. And I can see why they're worrying about it 'cause they're trying to take over . . . the whole government is trying to take over to make us where they could control us, you know . . . so, since they can't take away the Second Amendment, the guns and everything like that, they've just decided to increase their felony charges, pretty much by their own laws; everybody gets a felony charge of some kind that takes away the guns [laughs].

His wife, Tanya, concurring, added a frightening personal anecdote: "I was somewhere two years ago, and a person came up behind me and hit me and slammed me to the ground. If I would have had a gun, I could have protected myself; I would have been allowed to carry a gun. . . . He broke my pelvis in three places. . . . I would have shot him if I had a gun."

Daniel had earlier expressed a belief in God and in the close connection between God and the country's origins. I was curious to know how he combined his devotion to God to his support of violence, even if for self defense. This led to a humorous, as well as revealing in its own right, exchange: "You're pro-gun, and you're pro-God. Don't those two things conflict each other? Shouldn't a pro-God person not be pro-gun?" "I don't know," he replied; "every angel I've ever heard of has got a flaming sword, so what's the damn difference? God never said you couldn't defend yourself; he said shouldn't commit murder." I responded, "He says you turn your cheek, doesn't he?" "Yes, he does," Daniel agreed, "but then you turn it. If they do it a second time, you shoot their ass!"

The images of encounters with violent people were often very vivid and raw. Cole, in Billings, offered another example:

Because I have, I have the freedom, I have the freedom, I have the right to bear arms to protect my property. Being from Texas, me personally, I believe in three things: I believe in God, guns, and the death penalty. If you come in my house, I don't care if you're male, female, white, black, Mexican, I'm gonna try to kill ya because you're, you're trying to harm my family. However, I think the biggest piece of, of trash is the people that, that bully people, that hurt people for no reason. I believe that if you take a life, you should be prepared to give your life because that person didn't get to choose whether he lived or died, but yet, you know, and, and I hate, I hate a thief, but I hate a liar even worse, and to me, you know, you are who you are, and if you say you're gonna do something, you do it, and that's what being American is all about.

He continued:

But I'm gonna turn this back around on you and whoever is transcribing this. . . . If you're asleep in your house, in your bed, with your wife that you just cherish, she is your best friend . . . gave you two or three or even one of the beautifulest kids you've ever seen . . . would you not want something to protect them? I mean, that's, that's kinda where it lays with me. I'm not gonna go attack nobody; I'm just not gonna let nobody attack me or my family.

I followed by asking whether "somehow you think that's an American freedom?" His reply was that "I, I really do, yeah." Timmy, standing next to him, then suggested that, in fact, "I think it should be a world-wide freedom."

Thus, America offers a possibility that other countries apparently do not. Jeff, at the Billings bus station, brought up England and the (now no longer true) fact that policemen would not carry guns:

Well, you know, even though everybody belongs here, there's people that don't wanna work, so they go out and steal, and you have the right to protect your property and your loved ones from evil people. And if people didn't have guns, right . . . just like England . . . people aren't allowed to have guns there . . . you know . . . and the cops don't even have guns . . . and I just thought that was weird, and look, look how the country is over there . . . people get blown up in Paris and wherever.

Jeff then compared it to Idaho, where "it's legal to carry a sidearm out on your" belt. I asked for more details:

Yeah, you just have to have a . . . concealed weapon card or a card that says you can carry that, you know . . . and you can go out to any store, any bar . . . but certain bars they'll make you take it off and put it behind the bar, you know, 'cause they don't want no incidents happening. And that's their right. . . . My neighbor, he wears his every day. . . . He was in the Marine Corps for twenty years.

I confessed to being a bit scared of the idea. Jeff tried to reassure me: "Oh you don't have to be scared; they ought to have permits, you know. You have to get a permit; you can't just do it."

With this idea of freedom and guns in mind, many interviewees felt that, if anything, more guns should be in Americans' hands. When I asked Emma, for instance, if she did not think that three hundred million in the country was not enough, she disagreed and then laughingly said, "I own probably twenty-five myself or something!" She then remembered with obvious pleasure that when she lived in Kennesaw, Georgia, "on their books it's a law that every home owner has to have a gun."

The third theme concerned hunting. We saw earlier that Alex in Alabama had effectively equated his understanding of freedom in America with hunting. But it was in Montana that people drew an almost survivalist narrative about hunting in America and thus also notions of tradition and family histories. Jill's description of the importance of hunting to her family offered perhaps the best example. After affirming that "I am pro-gun, yeah. My husband has a, a . . . he has a concealed weapons permit; we have guns in our home; we hunt," she proceeded to recall that

firearms have just been a part of our lives. My parents, my grandparents. You know . . . I, I couldn't tell you any generation in either side of my family or my in-laws that didn't hunt or provide dinner for their family. . . . Filling the freezer is a huge part of the year. So . . . that's a big part of that . . . yeah. And when you were talking about like the income . . . if it wasn't for hunting we would not have meat at all [in recent years]. And because we didn't have much money . . . but antelope or deer or elk in the freezer, you know . . . what are you gonna do? Buy chicken? Beef is unaffordable. And I'm the daughter of cattle ranchers. Like I, I, trust me . . . I know the beef industry, but if you're not in it, it is very . . . it can be unaffordable, and so that's probably an element of why back to your gun question, that kinda bring full circle of why I'm saying they are so important in our life. . . . Hunting is like a big family deal, like you have to understand that grandparents, aunts, and uncles, and you get together and, you know.

Hunting is part of the American way of life, and hunting requires guns.

Several others shared Jill's emphasis on the connection between guns, hunting, and survival. It was Daniel, however, who perhaps made the point most convincingly when he decided, at the end of our conversation, to head back into the house and return with a frozen, ten-inch salami made out of meat from an elk he had hunted months before. This is how they ate meat in his family, he said, handing the salami to me as a gift.

We Fought for This

A standard question in the interviews concerned the flag: What words or images come to mind when picturing a flag waving in the air? The question often evoked emotional responses and revealed something essential about the interviewees' love of their country. Most dealt with struggle. Blood was spilled for America's freedom. It was a fight, from the very beginning and ever since—through the Civil War, World War II, the civil rights movement, the Cold War, and now religious extremism. The patriotic pride of many of the people I met stemmed from the realization of what it has taken to obtain and defend that freedom.

A long history of struggle, then, mattered a great deal to many of the interviewees, even if the factual details were not always immediately clear. "We fought, our soldiers fought for that flag, our freedom and bloodshed; I mean that flag represents bloodshed for our freedom," Alex told me. "Whom did they fight?" I asked him. "Who did they fight? I don't know, like . . . it's been a while, like when they went to WWI and WWII, that was fighting for our freedom, to, to have our rights in the United States. That was trying to take over us, I guess; that's what I think I was getting out of it when I was in school and that we just had to fight for our freedom."

For Roger, in Billings, the first words that came to mind when visualizing the flag were "freedom" and then "wars": "Yeah, wars and the . . . Americans that gave their life up for their country. The American flag, I think what mostly stands for like the veterans, you know . . . they gave up their life for their country. Some come, come here and win a Purple Heart and all that, but they give up their life. I think of that when I look at the flag, you know?" The struggle for freedom, of course, began with the Revolutionary War, as Sean emphasized:

You know, the Revolutionary War and what we fought for to become a nation and, and, and why we wanted to get away from Britain because it, what you know . . . freedom of religion was one of it, but there was a lot more than that. You know it was . . . we were being oppressed. It was you're gonna live this way whether you like it or not and you're gonna give us all this money and everything else and deal with it. And we weren't even over in England.

The birth of the nation, then, was suffered. It came from struggle and required enormous sacrifice, as Doug described:

That sacrifice and the, the beginning of the nation, the beginning of the beginning. The very beginning of the nation, the Revolutionary War . . . when we was, we was building a nation and the conception of the flag within that fight. The sacrifice it took to . . . to gain independence. That maybe would come to mind when I, when I look at that flag.

That sacrifice would extend beyond the moment of the country's birth:

So, I mean, now, now when I said sacrifice, I was thinking about when I go back, I'm thinking about the generation who fought WWII, if that makes any sense to you. Sacrifice, those who had to go sacrifice and save the world from tyrants and, 'cause at that time it was a really turbulent time within world history and being an American and being, and, and America . . . and the part America played in that time of history to stop tyranny in the world.

The connection between national pride, freedom, and struggle became strongest in the case of the many interviewees who had family members who participated in the fight for liberty. Then, as Jill explained, it takes on an especially personal tone:

Well, my, my father-in-law was a WWII vet; he served in Europe. My grandfather served in WWII and Japan . . . and, you know, I come from cattle ranchers and horsemen and kind of elements of country, and I don't mean country with a capital "c," but country as in rural. Rural elements and I think that I, I want . . . we want our children to understand that this didn't come easy. You get to get up on Sunday morning and just decide there's seven churches, I think, here in town, go pick one . . . nobody cares. You wanna go, go be Catholic tomorrow, go do it. You wanna go to the venerated church the next Sunday, go do it, you know; nobody cares. And that didn't come without a cost, and I think also, I believe, you know, this is probably kinda capitalistic, but, you know, if you wanna go create a business and sell snow cones, go do it by all means. And that didn't come, you know, without some level of sacrifice, and, so it's really important to us that our kids walk in that and understand that.

Jill continued by underscoring again the premium she put on ensuring her children know the sacrifices their liberty took, eventually ending with an emotional, even if a non sequitur, description of her daughter being a rodeo queen one year, holding an American flag while the national anthem was playing:

Twenty-five to fifty years from now, and I wanna at least go to the grave knowing that we raised up a generation that remembers some of these elements in the event that they ever go away, and I think, I think those things are important. We have a son who just turned eighteen, and he joined the National Guard. He has one year of high school left, but the way he's doing it he will go to boot camp this summer, and then he will come back and finish his senior year of high school before going away for more training. And so I, I feel like maybe, you know, I feel like he, he's . . . probably walks in a lot of that patriotism too, you know; we have moments that I can't describe if you've never experienced them before like our, our daughter was a rodeo queen one year, and so there's this moment where she's carrying the flag in the rodeo arena and the national anthem is played and she's on her horse . . . you know that's . . . that's not something that, unless you've experienced.

In Alabama, Katie connected directly her love of country with the loss of a very close family member in 2005 who served in the military fighting in Iraq:

I, I care about the country. I mean, I've had a lot of my family members serve in the military, that served in Iraq and got killed. You know, fighting for our freedom and stuff. So yes, I believe in my freedom of speech, and I do believe in my freedom. And the people like, say, for instance, ISIS, you know, they're coming in here and destroying, and I'm glad that our country is standing for itself. . . . When I, like, picture the flag of the United States, you know, I know that I see a picture of my cousin [name] because I know that he served in the military and stuff and he got killed in Iraq for our freedom. . . . He was fighting for our freedom to be us and to be able to speak the words we want to speak and do the things that we need to do.

If family lives have been sacrificed for freedom in the Middle East in

the recent past, the same of course happened in Vietnam and previous wars. Angie, who spent a considerable amount of time defining her
love of country in terms of choices (which "are very important to me"),
thought, for instance, that her father had "fought" and died in Vietnam
"for our freedoms, to make sure we're not communists, we're not forced
into" something unwanted. She stated that American soldiers abroad
"keep us safe, protected"; the "flag," therefore, "represents our fallen
soldiers . . . because I know that whenever my dad died, that's what they
drape over your casket if you're a soldier."

Race, too, was seen as an important part of the unfolding of America's patriotic story. Eddie in particular elaborated specifically on this
when discussing the participation of Native American and black soldiers
in "every war" the country has fought, while ending with an interesting
reaffirmation of his hopes for continued racial progress in the country:

It may have been a handful, but American Indians have contributed something
to the country in their own fashion; and in every war that this country has
been involved in, black Americans have been involved in some way, so we,
we, supported the country with our blood and our young men and our labor,
and probably in the last sixty years I'd say it's when we kind of came of age as
a people; we broke down many barriers that had been erected. But all I believe
in, the spirit of American freedom and opportunity, we want it, freedom of
opportunity like any so-called American, and we want to treat it like other so-
called Americans.

Such images of blood and struggle deepened the respondents' love of
country. They made it easier to understand why Anne told me that "you
gotta know where you come from," so you appreciate how America's flag
has "earned the right to fly," that "it's a flag that needs to be respected."

These historical narratives were matched by a very strong conviction
that the struggle is far from over. The world is constantly threatening
freedom in the United States (and elsewhere). Courageous American
soldiers are putting their lives in danger every day in faraway places to
shield Americans from violent religious extremism, communism, and
other forms of oppression. Patriotism is a matter of honoring their service: it is almost a moral duty. Jeannie's thinking on the matter exempli-

fied this logic. What are the Americans fighting for, I asked her, in the Middle East? "Well, they're fighting for us, you know, and, and, and I mean it's either life or death down there. . . . They're protecting the flag, you know." I objected by saying, "But the Afghans are not here." She replied, "Well, I mean, I mean if they don't fight against them, then they're gonna come over and, you know." I was not sure what she thought would happen: "Take us, take our things?" "Yeah, yeah. Well, not just things, ourselves too." The American military preemptively goes into other countries, then, to avoid other people coming into the United States and depriving Americans of their way of life. This was a source of pride:

Yes, yes. I mean they don't, you know, it's hard to . . . let somebody go and not know if you're ever going to see them again or not, you know, but they're fighting for the country, and that's great, that's wonderful, that's, that's pride and respect, and, you know, it's . . . you got people, men and women fighting for the country, and that's great, you know.

The connection between the military, freedom, and pride would often emerge very early on in our conversations. Sidney, for instance, when asked "What does the US represent to you?," replied that "it is the war, how soldiers fight; I respect the soldiers, the veterans, and stuff for fighting for us, for the freedoms that we have." She then added, "I thank God for them wanting to put up their lives for someone like me." As to who might actually cause harm to Americans, Sidney reasoned that American soldiers abroad are "killing because they have to, to save the United States from being in, from, they saving us from the Russians." And Dennis answered, when asked why he was patriotic and why he liked the United States, "I mostly like them because of their strong military for protecting the country, you know, when they've been on top of stuff real quick, and that's the main reason I like them."

Such thinking had one important ramification: children should be taught, from a young age, to love their flag and country and to do so out of the realization of the effort it took to create all that is America, "so that our children understand," as Jill stated, "where they are and what they've been given." Nearly all the interviewees felt that the Pledge of Allegiance should still be recited in public schools. As Valerie, in Har-lowton, put it, in reciting the pledge, "the respect of the country, they learn to respect it. Respect the flag and the people. Because freedom isn't free. There's people out there that are defending our country, and they give their all, so . . . I think our kids should be well aware of that." Alex used very similar words: it will help children know "that they got the freedom that they got and what the, why we got that freedom, how we got that freedom."

With such knowledge, children will ideally develop the desire to take care of the country. As Alex stated, "Anything worth having don't come easy, and, and if you don't teach them to take care of their coun-try, well then they're gonna just tear it up, and, and the world's already messed up enough as it is." Indeed, pride in country is an important first step toward a righteous and productive life. "Yes," stated Sean,

I think we really do need to get back to teaching our young about taking pride in our country, taking pride in themselves, taking pride in accomplishments, you know, taking pride in, in working hard . . . because now we tell our kids it's okay just to show up. . . . Hey, you showed up, here's a medal . . . and I'm not saying we wanna tell our kids they're a loser, but I don't think telling every kid that you accomplished what you needed to by showing up is a good thing either.

In this regard, parents, too, have a responsibility to teach kids to honor their country and pledge their allegiance to it. "I bring these three words up with my kids all the time," stated Carlos: "loyalty, honor, respect. You should bring those three words and morals into every aspect you do in life. So if you're born in the United States of America, then you should be for America." This is how Angie described her educational efforts with her kids:

Because it's important to stand up for your country. My dad died fighting in the Vietnam War. He fought for our freedoms. . . . I do have a brother-in-law that's in Afghanistan right now, fighting for our country, so . . .'cause that's important to me to know the Pledge of Allegiance. Like I told you, I told my kids when they were babies. They knew it before they went to school. . . . They should know that. The same thing as me teaching them Bible verses; that's important to me.

It follows from this line of thinking that, if someone were to witness unpatriotic behavior on the part of children, such as failing to stand up for the national anthem, a reminder might very well be in order. This is at least what Chad, among several others, felt (although others thought that America even guarantees the freedom not to feel patriotic).[2] He recalled that at a recent music concert in town there was a kid who was not paying attention to the national anthem: "He just kinda goofed around, looking around, so I thumped him in the back of the ear and said, 'Hey, look . . . hey, look people have died for that flag, so . . . so show a little respect, you know? . . . People died for that flag; I mean people died for your freedom.'"

Confederate Glories, Montanan Libertarianism

While a good deal of the narratives about freedom and patriotism paralleled each other in Alabama and Montana, location mattered. In Alabama, several of the white interviewees gave considerable importance to the Confederate past. The logic, though not always transparent, was that the South fought for the very ideals on which the country was founded and that it was the North that, with its aggressive behavior, violated those ideals. Flying the Confederate flag along with the American flag therefore presents no conflict or contradiction, and love of country means also love of the South and what it stands for.

Freedom and the South go together in two different ways. First, since the early days of the republic, the South had a way of life based on rural values, including a life of hunting, agriculture, and family traditions—"all that country stuff that a country person would do," in the words of Alex. Freedom is an integral part of that, because the "country stuff" includes things that express and require freedom. They are somehow part and parcel of the same thing, as Alex stated when answering why he likes to wear a T-shirt with the Confederate flag on it. I asked him if that went against being American. He answered:

No, it's just a, it's just a heritage . . . Southern heritage . . . that's, that's what the heritage is; it's being country, doing and hunting and fishing. We got that freedom; we fought for that freedom to go out there and shoot a deer. I mean . . .

we got, got to obey by the laws, right . . . I understand. If nobody obeyed them laws, we ain't gonna have them deer to shoot and no fish to catch and nothing like that. That's why they got the laws, and I'm firmly for that, the laws, because we won't . . . oh, you can go shoot as many deer as you want out there; you can go out there and shoot all the deer you want, you know.

These were things he did as a kid, since he was seven or eight. As he rec-ollected those memories, he added, "Deer, hogs, we used to catch hogs all the time. . . . It was pretty fun; I liked it. But like we . . . we . . . if America wouldn't let us do that, then we'd be, it would be crazy."

I wanted to dig deeper into his thinking and asked whether, given what he said, a black person could wear a T-shirt with the Confederate flag. Consistent with his logic, he answered, "Yeah, and I know a lot of black people that do the same thing I do." They, too, live the Southern lifestyle. Concerning the possible contradictions between the American and Confederate flags, he saw none: "Yeah, I got, as a matter of fact, I got a shirt with an American flag and a rebel flag on it, and I had a bulldog in the middle of it." He then recalled an event he recently expe-rienced in Colorado, his home at the time of the interview:

And I wore it with my shirt one day, and oh . . . a black dude said, "Hey, homeboy!" . . . I turned around and looked at him, and he said, "That shirt you got on like . . . might get you called up;" I said, "What you talking about?" He said, "You might get shot for that." I said, "No I won't," and he said, "Yeah, you will, around here you will." I was like, what, that's crazy. I mean . . . it's just . . . looking at that thing, and it's racism . . . it ain't and that's the way I look at it.

Alex was not the only one to view the South, freedom, and American patriotism as intimately connected. Emma, too, shared that perspective. In her case, however, the key factor to grasp was that the North had sought to deprive the South of its ways, that it had attacked the South in an attempt to mold it to its liking—an action that was precisely the antithesis of freedom. She began by comparing patriotism in the South to that in Wisconsin, where she had lived years before:

Oh yeah, because, you know, in my family then men all served in the mili-tary, and patriotism is important in the South, it really is. I have lived in other places; I have lived in Wisconsin, and it is somewhat there, but we hold on to things more tightly in the South, even our Confederate flag, you know. . . . People don't understand that, but it's more about our heritage.

What was that heritage the South is holding on to? What did the Confederate flag represent? She felt that "a lot of people don't understand the meaning of it; they think it's racism, but it's not. It's just, you know, it's heritage and history and what, yeah . . . all my life, I've been taught to be patriotic and what it means to support America." She then offered an interpretation of the Civil War. For the South it was

to continue their way of life, to not be taken advantage of by the North, because my understanding, you know, was that it really wasn't that much about slavery; it was the North wanting the resources of the South. Because we had, you know, the great plantations; we had cotton, things that the North needed . . . and in the North they'll say, well, why do you, what do people in the South keep bringing that up? Well, because they attacked us . . . you know, we, you know . . . . we were attacked by them, that's why we bring it up.

The North, then, sought to take advantage of the South. The South simply wanted to continue living its life, one in accordance with genuine American principles. This was a second way in which freedom, the South, and patriotism are connected.

It followed that the American and Confederate flags "go together" and that there is no contradiction. Some people may not appreciate that, of course, but flying them together is absolutely acceptable. This is a point that Linda, in Montana but with Texas roots, also made: "Down in Texas we would be able to put out the American flag and also the Confederate flag at the same time. And a lot of people don't like the Confederate flag, but, you know, down there we have that choice." Besides, as Grace, the retired white cotton packer from Vernon, noted, "the Confederate flag ain't, is it not for the veterans?" If so, as she saw it, "they're trying to do away with the Confederate flag, and, and I just don't see that myself."

In Montana, antigovernment rhetoric infused a good amount of the patriotic narrative that I would hear (while, as we saw, in Alabama many interviewees actually expressed gratitude to the government for the aid it offers them, and made that part of their patriotic logic). In the minds of several interviewees, there exists a clear separation between the country and the federal government. What they love is the country—in particular its guarantees of freedom—and what they worry about is an overreaching federal government that is turning away from what the country was founded on. "The federal government is more and more and more involved in people's lives," Lynn felt, "and in all aspects of our lives and even just in what the states do." Sean put it in more ominous terms: "The way our government is heading, if things don't change, I think there's gonna be dramatic problems coming up very soon, because we are trying to steer away from our inalienable rights given to us by the Constitution, and our government is, is strongly trying to take those away from us." The overreach appears to have gotten worse in recent years. Why, for instance, did Carlos get such a prevalent American eagle tattoo on his leg?

The tattoo I got about six months ago. And I got it because I feel our country is in turmoil right at the moment, and I feel that us citizens need to step up and take back the country that, that the government has overrun. . . . I believe that the government has overrun the country; they, they're supposed to be working for the people, for us citizens of the United States of America, but they are not. They are working for themselves. . . . I believe it's up to us citizens and as people of the United States of America to step back up and try to help get this country back in order again.

The contrast between the country and the government was also very clear to Chad, who had just recently returned from an extensive deployment in Iraq. He expressed his readiness to go to war again, but with an important caveat: "I'll go to war; I'll go to war for the country. I will not go to war for this government. I, I . . . it's not Obama, don't get me wrong. It's the government's been messed up for a long time."[3]

Several areas of "intrusion" and "overreach" were listed. One was overregulation and abuse of regulatory power. Marshall, for instance, thought that if he were president, "I'd write an executive order canceling about ninety-five percent of the executive order power. . . . I believe those are overused. They've gotten to the point where they're infringing on freedom by trying to defend freedom. It defeats the purpose."

The language of "tak[ing] more control away from the government," as
Becky put it, would be repeated over and over. The solution for most
was to give people more freedom, or, at the least, "let the states control
more," as Gil reasoned: "It should be left up to the states. . . . That's
what it was actually designed for."

A second major area of concern had to with abusive security
practices—"they wanna know where everybody's at, at all times, and
how many people are in the United States. . . . I don't know, it just
didn't [used to] be like that," stated Autumn—and, with that, she noted
the current weakness of the American people in taking the country
back. Daniel thought that there is too much oversight, limiting one's
freedom to simply go about one's life:

Our personal . . . freedoms, our personal rights, they try to get . . . the government is trying to take care of everybody's business for them, and I don't, I don't
believe they should be involved in all they're involved in. . . . You go to get
pulled over for a traffic stop, and they're allowed to pull out a gun and shoot
you when you reach for your wallet. . . . You know, the government's got everyone scared that there's big terrorism scare, which is bullshit. . . . It's all just a
big mind thing trying to get control of the people, you know? We, we've always
been open to . . . you know . . . that's how Pearl Harbor happened. . . . We've
always been under the threat of that; it's 'cause we've had that country wide
open, we're free. They're taking that away slowly but surely.

When he continued by suggesting that the American people are "just
letting them take control," I asked him if he thought the government
had brainwashed the citizens of the country. His reply was, "I just think
they're weak ass damn people. Ain't nothing like they used to be." His
wife, Tanya, agreed, adding "pretty much!" Daniel then thought back to
the early days of the country:

They were strong people. You know, they were hardy that came over here in the
wilderness, scratched something up and then built something. But then again,
every time they got sick of it, they moved west. The worst thing to happen to
this country was the Pacific Ocean in my opinion, because they ran out of place
to go [laughs]. So now you turn around, and now you gotta deal with it, you
know.

The Americans who find all this objectionable, he continued, those with a sound understanding of the country's values, "the ones that do care get labeled as fanatics and homeland terrorists, and they usually lock their asses up."

The police were mentioned repeatedly as problematic. Darrius seemed particularly upset about this:

Phones, Internet, everything . . . heck yeah. Yeah . . . everyone can feel that kind of presence. Day to day, moving around, I mean, we're homeless and broke, so we don't really, we're not really in the limelight with anything; we keep to ourselves; we don't do drugs; we don't get in trouble, so . . . we just . . . we're very simple people, so we don't really feel that too much. . . . But the police and everything else in this country have gotten way more hard-core the last ten years. You've probably seen the news, like a lot more people have been getting killed by the police in this country lately, and that's because the culture that the police are being trained and raised in has totally militarized since the Gulf Wars. Totally militarized.

Darrius then offered a tangible example of what he meant:

Let me give you a really good example of this: on every police car back in the day, twenty to thirty years ago, it used to be written "to protect and serve." That's gone . . . a lot of police cars don't have that on their cars anymore. Why? I find that interesting, like little things like that have changed. A lot of people don't notice, but things have definitely changed in this country.

Others complained about unnecessary checks, shootings—"it's been a lot of death here by cops' hands in the last five years. The number is extreme, even in Laurel [Montana] there's been two in Laurel in the last four years. And it's just ridiculous," Autumn stated. It was, however, Kevin who, perhaps, put it most succinctly, even if a bit vulgarly: "If they cast their eye on you, for lack of a better word . . . forgive me for sounding impolite, but you're fucked."

There were several other areas of libertarian patriotic concern. Having to pay for health insurance felt like a major breach of the American promise of freedom for Sidney. A bloated welfare state that supports lazy people was another. The freedom of parents to discipline their kids with spanking—without it being called child abuse ("you could spank your kids . . . but now they are watching every little move you make," complained Sidney; "you discipline your kids . . . DCS or Child Protective Services, boom, right there!" complained Oscar)—was mentioned by at least six interviewees in Montana. Finally, of concern to some, were taxes—both the amounts levied and the way it which the money was spent. Jill felt, for instance, that "the government is a machine out of control. A machine that was created out of necessity; you have to have some sort of order to the chaos, but I think it's gotten out of control. . . . Taxes are creeping up!" Her distrust was shared by Cole, who certainly had no taxable income at the moment but felt resentment about the "the misuse of management of my funds."

The feeling in Montana was quite clear. Deep, genuine patriotism has to do with a love of freedom, and the government intrusion into that freedom should be noticed and resisted.

CHAPTER 7

RECONCILING POVERTY AND PATRIOTISM

We began with a puzzle. America's least well-off are very patriotic. Although they receive less help from their country and face dimmer prospects of upward mobility, they are more patriotic than the poor in other advanced countries. Even though they hurt, in many instances their patriotism exceeds that of wealthier Americans. Why do poor Americans love their country so much?

The focus of my conversations with the sixty-three interviewees in Alabama and Montana was to discover the nature of that love. I asked directly about their appreciation of the country. The previous three chapters reported on their views. Toward the end of nearly all the conversations, however, I also had the opportunity to investigate matters from a different, and potentially more sensitive, angle: Did the interviewees not think that there was a contradiction between their patriotism and the struggles that they have experienced living in America? Why did their personal situation not negatively affect their views of their country? I was aware that what seemed like a puzzle to me might not have seemed like one for them. I treaded carefully and, as with the other parts of the interviews, sought to listen to, to grasp, what people were saying.

The responses proved multifaceted and fascinating. Either they made the question of the respondents' poverty *irrelevant* for their love of country, or they pointed to enough *hope* for the future to make the current situation seem temporary and therefore acceptable. The interviewees talked about the fairness of outcomes in life, their sense that new opportunities were about to come along (especially if one was walking with God), a conviction that everyone is worth the same regardless of wealth, and, finally, the admission that the United States is really the only country they know. Taken together, these answers helped complete the picture of the depth and coherence of the patriotism of America's poor. One's precarious circumstances are no grounds for doubting the greatness of the country, or, as Will in Birmingham put it, "You be loyal to your country because you have a great love for it, I mean, even though you're not living at that standard, middle class or higher class."

To Each His Own

Virtually all of the people I met took ownership of the trajectories of their lives. This was consistent with well-known survey data showing that most Americans believe that one's fate is the result of one's own choices and not external circumstances, such as family upbringing, one's neighborhood, luck, or even God, and with a deeply rooted and old-standing belief in American society about the importance of personal responsibility.[1] Such thinking meant that the interviewees simply did not attribute their current economic challenges to the government or the country more generally. While many certainly stated that there is excessive poverty in the country and the government could do more for its people, this did not translate into viewing their problems as anything more than the result of their own choices and actions. They could therefore be poor *and* patriotic.

If everyone can make it in America, failure to make it is a person's fault. Consider in this regard Cole's assessment, in the streets of Billings, of his own situation:

The biggest part about being homeless is, is not letting yourself go down because if you appear to be homeless, people are gonna treat you like you're homeless because they're always willing to throw a label on ya and they're willing to judge ya even though they sit up and say, oh no, I hope you're safe, and they're in their nice warm bed and you're sleeping in the park. . . . However, it is not their fault that I made the choices, I made the decisions. Every day I have a choice; I have a decision I can do right or wrong, and when you do wrong, you have to pay the piper. I've dug a hole, I'm homeless, I'm a convicted felon; I'm, I'm fighting drug addiction, alcoholism; however, I am almost three years sober, and, and I love my sobriety.

Failure, Kysha said in Birmingham, "it's on you . . . it's on you . . . you got a chance like anyone else." Those who fail do so because they "get discouraged like I did. Perfect example is my portrait and my artwork. . . . Everybody got a chance. Some people don't wanna do right. You gotta realize that. You're mixing dinner with the sweets."

The history of segregation and slavery in the South came into the picture for some. But for most, there has been enough progress that its legacy should no longer be considered a justification for failure. I asked Harley, a black man in the South, whether those who fail in America should "be resentful toward the country." His reply was that "it's their fault, it's their fault." He continued:

Gotta be bad choices. They didn't get denied, so gotta be bad choices. I would say back in the sixties or something like they, they got denied. I resent the country for that, you know. Because the president didn't have to let that happen, what happened in the South, you know. He could've stopped that a long time ago . . . but right now, I wouldn't say that right now. I still say it's a good place; I love it. I'd suit up right now [for the military].

So, for Doug, another black man in the South, "if you fail like I failed, it's my own fault. I failed, more than one time." Indeed, Fast Eagle in Montana, too, despite all the injustices Native Americans to this day have experienced, shared this view:

I believe that a lot of people have the same . . . we may not come from the same backgrounds [but] . . . we all go to school, we all, you know . . . we're all given the same opportunities to be able to do that, you know. So some people come from hard backgrounds and are very, they succeed in life . . . you know, and the choices that they make go to that, so some people come from very fortunate backgrounds growing up as kids, and they make bad decisions and end up in a different position, so to me it's about the choices that you make.

Rainbow, also a Native American in Montana, felt exactly the same way: "No, I think that everybody is responsible for their own, for their own."

There can obviously be little conflict between one's situation and love of country if the responsibility for that situation rests on the individual's, not the country's, shoulders. Eager to probe into this logical connection, I asked directly, when the situation made it appropriate, whether there was a contradiction in what I had been hearing from respondents regarding their situations and then their patriotism. The answers were consistent, as with Sam, at Birmingham's bus station. "Right," he said, "no contradiction there. It makes sense." Shouldn't they be more upset with their country, I inquired? "No," he replied, "they can do more for themselves; they could do more for themselves, you know?" Or, as Alex put it in the same station a bit more crudely, "Get up and get your ass up and go get a job and man up and go get . . . get right you know. That's your fault, not the government's fault . . . and don't blame it on the president; that's your fault you ain't got money. Everywhere is hiring every day. Anybody can get a job anywhere." He added these reflections on his own life: "I've been in pain, and I've been, been down in the dumps, you know . . . but it's my fault 'cause I chose that life. The government didn't choose it for me; the government didn't say, hey, look you're gonna be on dope for this many years and you're gonna, you ain't gonna have nothing." Consistent with this viewpoint, not one of the interviewees seemed to question how rich people acquired their wealth. While certainly some expressed concern with the number of Americans who live in poverty, there was accordingly no resentment toward the country, the government, or the system. Yes, while many thought, like Cole, that "low-income or middle America built America," there was also a sense that top earners simply deserve their income. Why? Because they have earned it.

Valerie's thoughts in Harlowton offered an example: "Those people with the money have earned it. So what do we want them to do, just give it away? And there are a lot of those people with money that are giving it away." An element of choice is again at play, as Jeff, sitting in Billings's bus station, explained: "People make their own life, and they make their own money the way that they wanna make it and however much they wanna make it." As he went on, Donald Trump came to mind:

And, you know, by going to school, by going to college, by going to training, you know . . . to become something. . . . You do what you want, like what you feel you can wanna live on. You know, like Donald Trump, self-made mil-lionaire, billionaire . . . built Trump castle and Trump . . . whatever . . . casinos and, you know, builds up his empire on real estate, and he did that with hardly anything.

Choice was also on Timmy's mind, as we discussed matters in front of his dry house in Billings:

People can choose what, what income level they're in. . . . If you're in a lower income level, you can go to school or change jobs to change your income level. You know, and I mean, also at the same time higher-income people can make dumb choices and lose all their money, so . . . I think it is all up to the person's choice on how they decide to live their life and what level they want to be at. Some people are content living homeless on the street and don't want to do anything else.

Thus, rich people choose to succeed and are willing to work hard for it. "They did it themselves," stated Paula. "It's something they learned. And they got wealthy. They went to work and did it."

With that said, some of the interviewees could certainly see that ad-verse circumstances can prove difficult to overcome. At the same time, they also insisted that a path to success is always available, as Jeff did:

'Cause, you know, they're . . . they don't seem to get it in their head that they can do something else that's better, you know, than . . . and they, they grow up like that 'cause their mom and dad's like that, you know. And their mom and dad split up, and they're just living with their mom. . . . Dad goes to prison for however long and goes back and forth . . . and that, that's what that kid grows up to learn. . . . But then there's some that fight their way out of that, you know, and become professional football players or basketball players or go to college and become somebody. I mean . . . nobody is, is really stuck in one place if they don't wanna be. Choices.

There is always, in other words, a way out. Emily, for instance, explained to me that, "while some people don't understand" the importance of showing up on time and ready to work, throughout her life she always made a point of being timely and prepared. Indeed, our interview at the Birmingham Public Library was such an example: "Just like you told me, you said be here at three o'clock. I was here; I think I was here before three o'clock. I mean, I'm just like a timely person; I mean, I didn't know what all the interview was on or about, but when I read this and the lady told me, said, "Yeah, Miss, look over this" . . . I called the number and I was here on time. I mean, anything you wanna do, you just got to get up and do it." Indeed, for Paula, a middle-aged white woman in Birmingham who described herself as a Democrat, even growing up in abusive families is surmountable. As she put it, "I know there's rehab to get well."

Such an interpretation of wealth (and wealth differences) could obviously not lend itself to a criticism of the country. If, as Katie told me, the first thought that comes to mind when seeing a fifty thousand–dollar car drive by her is that, "Yep, they earned it," people obviously get what they deserve. If not even luck seems a factor ("Don't you think some people are luckier than others?" I asked Katie and Hubert; "No" and "nope" were their answers), then there is little one can attribute to external causes. Failure and success result only from a person's choices. And freedom to choose is precisely what makes America so special.

Preparing for Better Things

"Americans," Erica thought, "are much more optimistic than Europeans; they're much more positive than them. There is a sort of hopefulness, yeah." I encountered such optimism repeatedly in Alabama and Montana. In most instances, the interviewees had suffered from poverty and difficulties for years and decades. Yet many seemed hopeful about the future. Several were in fact planning for a turnaround while describing their situation as a transitory problem. Some felt strongly that God played an important role in their lives and stressed their eagerness to lead a more righteous and productive life. The promises of a better tomorrow helped diminish the weight of today's problems. Patriotism under such circumstances may not be all that surprising. Resentment toward one's country seems less likely when optimism offers prospects of brighter days ahead.

Several interviewees described their plans or hope for a turnaround. I met Fiona in the Harlowton library, where she went to apply for public assistance. Divorced, having lost her job, and having made very little money all her life, she had no source of income. Previous jobs paid little: "Pretty much my entire life I've been living right below or just a hair above poverty level according to US standards." She was taking care of a foster child, which made things all the more difficult. This is how she made sense of her situation at the time of the interview:

Unfortunately, I'm unemployed at this point, but this you know . . . it's a temporary thing for me, and I know that . . . I myself being unemployed right now, I spoke with [the town librarian] about this for the first time in my life. I'm fifty-one years old; I have applied for public assistance because I have a child to take care of. I'll get another job; it's just going to take me . . . to make sure he's taken care of.

Things, in other words, were not permanent, and a job, for sure, will materialize down the road, although patience is of course in order. Fiona spoke with pride of her upbringing and her parents teaching her and her siblings independence and pride: "My parents raised us, like I said, we're all of us kids were independent; we took care of ourselves; we still do. I . . . we're proud." She spoke as well of her dislike for those who depend on "government handouts. . . . It just seems like too many people are wanting it done for them, instead of doing it for themselves."

Fiona seemed confident that something good would come along soon: she seemed to count on it. Given her past record of employment, her hopes may have been realistic, though even with a job she probably would not leave poverty far behind her. Many others shared that positive and hopeful spirit. Alicia, in Birmingham, for instance, reflected on lifelong struggles and her determination that she will find her way out one day, precisely in response to my questions about the strength of her patriotism. "Do you ever doubt," I inquired, "your love of the States? In other words, do you ever sit down and say, 'Do I really know why I love the States'? Has that thought ever occurred to you?" Her reply was revealing:

No, because I've been going through some things as a child, you know, growing up in a rough neighborhood. Now I'm in a shelter at thirty, I'm on SSI [Supplemental Security Income]; that's something that I don't want to continue to be on all my life. I don't want to limit myself to just that amount of money. I've really . . . I've had time to think about all that . . . been thinking about how can I get myself out of this situation and get myself a better life.

If Alicia's plans sounded vague at the moment, others were far more specific. Marshall, who had described his homelessness in Montana as a "sabbatical" from things that gave him a great amount of freedom, said that "right now I'm working on developing a mobile video game for kinda smart phones, tablets . . . that kind of thing. I'm actually developing it on my smart phone, so I carry it with me and work on it when I want." Kysha held on to her hope that her artwork would one day attract attention, despite some real setbacks:

But as you can see, I wait 'till I get this age to start writing poetry and drawing. I haven't been drawing about a month, but I was told that when I sent a picture in, I have no talent, so that discouraged me. Other . . . other than that, I . . . I feel greatly about all. . . . I already know a lot of people want me to succeed; they want me to; they want me to be . . . they want me to publish my things and do right. . . . I'm not even worried right now 'cause I'm single; I recorded a Christmas CD last year. . . . I got a lot going for me. God blesses all of us with talent.

In some cases, the "next thing" was actually just about to start—a concrete reason indeed for optimism, especially if "destiny" or "fate" was responsible for the turnaround. Will, for instance, told me how he was able to secure the landscaping job he would be starting the next day. "So," he told me, "I've been using the temporary [job placement service], which is not really a consistent job, but it's something, and, so that's, today actually I walked out from one of these shelters here. I was stopping by to grab something to eat and walked right into a job." "Oh, wow, how so?" I asked. He replied:

Well, a guy was standing right around the corner, happened to be a veteran, and he has a landscaping . . . so I'm going to start that in the morning . . . just happened. . . . Well, I had called him, but I couldn't find out what the guy . . . I was looking and he was looking for me, so we kinda walked into each other. Well, fate.

Benevolent fate smiled on Will, but the optimism was perhaps the strongest among the interviewees who saw God working in their lives. Then they also spoke of difficulties, of course, but also of a sense of purpose, of a healthier and more rewarding life—all perspectives that would make a negative patriotic narrative all the more unlikely. Denzel's account of his relationship with God offered a telling example. Before his encounter with God, five years ago, he did "everything. Drinking, clubbing, staying out a lot of the night, not wanting to go to work." Then he had a motorcycle accident and broke his ankle. At that moment, his life took on a new direction, and with time (God's time, not Denzel's) things got better:

And I couldn't walk for a year and a half, so, during that year-and-a-half process, God said, "I'm going to sit you down so that you gonna learn to listen to what I tell you." And I went from there. So I picked up the Bible, started reading the Bible, started walking with God, praying about certain things that get better in my life . . . it has. I mean I see it, but it has, it's gotten better. It's getting better now, but it's getting better in his time, not my time.

Difficulties mix with hope, and struggles are met with faith in God's work. A tough life thus becomes more tolerable, especially since God continues to give signs of support and care, as Will's words suggested:

I believe there's a God, yeah, I do. He blesses me, despite that I'm down. I'm blessed. I still get, I, when I had nothing, no work 'cause I got laid off, I got blessed with a car, you know. I was walking down, and my lady friend was coming from this local park over here, and I was walking past this church, and something decide—I guess my spirit—and said "look!" I saw this pastor putting hinges on the door, and I was, like, asked a gentleman about a car, but I was walking on the sidewalk, and as I was walking, the building is out of sight now. . . . I told her, "Stop, stop, something tell me to go talk to that guy about a car," and I walked over there, and he said, "No, we actually don't do cars here," he said, "but I tell you what, I'm gonna give you a number and you call this number." And I did, and they sent my application the next day and said, "Yeah, we have a car ministry," and three months later I got a Mustang.

It was a remarkable story. "And it was given to you?" I asked. "It was given to me," he replied. Will could see God's help in the interview itself, in fact:

Something inside of me that guided me that way, just like it guided me to you. It did. I wasn't, I was gonna go in another direction, and I actually had, needed twenty dollars for . . . I had, I needed some gas, and I was gonna go. I wasn't gonna come this way, but I said I'm gonna go by this part, and something made me come to the library, and then I go there and pick up a DVD for the month of December and usually I just walk off, but there was this paper, and I couldn't see anything. I didn't have my glasses, so I'm squinting, and it say—I put my glasses on—and it say twenty-five dollars; he got me, this is what I need. You know man . . . that's how it happened, same thing with the car. Same way with the [landscaping] job today 'cause I was inside, and the guy said, "Where are you coming from?" and I was walking right in, and I was starting and then walked around the corner and walked dead into the guy. So, yeah, I'm a religious man, and I can go on and on about different things like that. I mean, I have a book of [mumbles] about how that came about. Yes, I believe in it.

So, in times of trouble, God comes to the rescue. Indeed, as Kysha put it, God will give you double for your trouble: "I got the worse hand though," Kysha reflected, "but don't bother me 'cause I know God got something good for me. . . . He someone give you double for your trouble. And I believe that . . .'cause I know I'm a good person."

Similar stories of having fallen and getting a lifeline from God would be repeated everywhere I went. My conversation with Cole, in Billings, on this point combined in a particularly rich way the narratives of God, hope, and love of country:

I'm forty-four years old, and I work fast food at KFC, and I quit Denny's washing dishes and because I know, like Timmy says, it's not forever. However, there is no job I am too good for and in, so when you're . . . you get the mind frame of you're too good for something, that's what's gonna come back and bite you in the butt because how bad do you want this. . . . I was sleeping outside covered in snow; the next day I got some dry clothes, I prayed—me personally—I prayed to God. I said either give me the power to just sit here and take whatever life has to offer or give me the strength to get up and do something about it. Soon after, I'm . . . I'm getting enrolled in my GED. I'm back . . . I get into college, and I got about a fourth-grade education, and I go from simple arithmetic to college algebra in one year. . . . However, I wasn't working; school is the only thing that I did, and I did literally study seven, eight, ten, twelve hours a day, and I made that my job, but he [Timmy] is absolutely one hundred percent, right and that's what makes this country so great. Anybody can do anything.

Life remains difficult of course. He now sleeps "on the floor of a church that, that I'm grateful enough to, to . . . he lets me sleep there, but it's no picnic. It is no easy walk in the park." But he has God to hold on to:

Without God, what would you have? I wouldn't have nothing, you know. God is my one and only, my higher power who I choose to call God because in order for me to get my life on track and get my life right, I had to get right with God first and foremost. Only thing I can do is make errors, make mistakes, stumble and fall, but with God I can stand up and walk. . . . I can do anything.

God saved Sidney, too, the thirty-two-year-old white woman who spent three years in Arizona in prison for drug offenses (and who began smoking marijuana at the age of nine):

'Cause God changed my life . . . for the better. Because I was one of those angry, hateful people that were doing the wrong thing, and now I just try to, try to always live today to be better than yesterday and to help whoever I can in any way, just by saying a nice word or being . . . open a door for somebody, or give somebody a smile. . . . I read it [the Bible] every day; it roughly takes twenty minutes. I do that first thing in the morning when I wake up, start my day out kinda changing my thinking if I try to go south, try to get bitter or angry or anything. So . . . I do that, and I still have a lot of work, a lot to work on.

I sensed on several occasions that God functioned as the lifeline for some of the people I met, as with Eddie:

I try to carry myself in a humble way in the world because God has looked out for me through a lot of stuff. I'm fifty-six years old. I could not make it on my own all this time, and that's me. . . . I've had my discouraging times, and when I get like that, I try to dig inside and find my God connection and, and tap that spirit in me that says, get up, Eddie, you know, don't give up and let's try again.

In fact, for some, even the troubles themselves are a way for God to show people their way. Denzel reasoned as much:

No, not always, but it comes a time in everybody's life when God has to knock you down to a point where he says, "I'm going to put you in a position where you have to lean on me, where you'll trust me," and when it came to that point in my life, God knocked me down, and I said, "God, I can't take no more; I can lean only on your understanding so I can trust you." And from that point on I had to change my life. Stop doing what I wanted to and start doing what he wanted. Read the Bible; it's not about me every day; it's about what I can do for everybody else every day.

Did some doubt God? Alex admitted to but also learning not to do it again:

I've . . . I've doubted it, I've doubted it before, and I shouldn't have 'cause I've been proven wrong too many times. Like, when I fell off that scaffold, they told me I'd never walk again, and I'm walking. . . . When I was in Colorado, I wasn't cussing, but I . . . I was running out of gas and everything and was going down the road, and something told me to pull in at the gas station. This was when I was about to run out of gas, and I had two kids and my old lady, and I told them guys, "If you're real . . . prove me right now, and I swear to God make me a believer right now; I said for real make me a believer. I will . . . I'll know pulling in a gas station." And a man handed her all the money, handed me money. . . . That was . . . that was like . . . blowing my mind.

These were powerful statements of hope and determination. Many of the respondents had not given up at all. They were working, or trying to work, at improving their lot. They were poor but still hopeful. And this combination of factors surely helped them not doubt the worthiness or greatness of their country.

We Are All Worth the Same

Psychologists and sociologists have argued since the 1960s that a feeling of relative deprivation—the sense that others are doing much better than oneself—can lead to deep disgruntlement toward the status quo in society and fuel a desire to revolt.[2] We have already seen that inequality in America did not seem to bother most, if not all, of the respondents: by and large, they believed that people get what they deserve and that anyone can make it in America. If poverty is a choice, the system should not be blamed. But another, and related, logic was also commonly shared among many of the people I met.

This logic reached back to the core belief that each person on this earth has the right to live and be. The idea was that, regardless of wealth, education, looks, or any other metric of success, we are all *worth* the same. No individual counts more than another. What this means, exactly, needs analyzing, of course. Yet it is easy to see how it might mitigate any negative feeling one might have toward one's country because of personal economic hardships. Those hardships become less relevant in one's calculation of love of country if in fact they do not constitute the whole picture of one's sense of self. If the poorest Americans—or, indeed, if the poorest person on earth—are worth the same as the president of the United States, then why should their economic circumstances affect how they see their country? Moreover, if the American social contract, at its heart, is founded on this very recognition of the worthiness of every life, one's love of America is quite easy to understand. Becky articulated this most clearly in just a few words: "I think everybody is equal on their own space, and . . . nobody's life is worth anymore than anyone else's. And that's part of what our country is based on, I think, too."

Discussions around worth came up in all the interviews when I explored notions of whether an American life is worth more than the life of a person from, say, Somalia or Iraq—countries where the United States has conducted killings with drones. It was then that the logic of equal worthiness of all human beings was articulated consistently by many of the interviewees. I would extend my question to Americans, and whether all Americans are worth the same. The answer was almost always yes.[3] That logic had a couple of key components.

The first is that we are all living beings: a life is a life, so each person counts as one. As Valerie put it, "Every life is worth the same. Black, white, yellow." Race does not matter, and the same is true for one's occupation, as Cole noted without losing the chance to express his dislike of the police: "A life's a life. . . . There's good and bad in every race . . . every profession, there's good cops, there's bad cops, we hate the police, but what would this world be without them?" Indeed, the worth of a life cannot be measured, as Chad observed: A "life is a life. I don't care who you are, you know. . . . You can't put a number or a worth value or whatever." Thus, as Paula answered when I asked whether anyone's life is worth as much "as the life of, say, President Obama," "Yeah, we are people. We're people! I don't care if you're the president or somebody poor down here. . . . We're all people." It follows, as Jeff stated, "I think everybody's life is important." Indeed, to consider one person's life as more important than another is deeply wrong, as Shirley noted: "No, no. No no. Because to do that is to devalue human life, period. All life matters. Every bit of it because if you . . . . we don't, we don't understand all the time how fragile the fabric of life is, and, and at times we, we've gotten away from valuing the life itself." A deep appreciation for life seemed to be key, as did the belief that the material or other differences we often think so important are actually in the end irrelevant, because, as Carlos noted, we are ultimately all looking to do the same thing:

Because we're all human beings. We're all made of the same flesh. We're all made of the same blood and bones, organs. . . . We're all humans, you know; we're all trying to live on this earth the best that we can and without dying or starvation or, you know, poverty. We're all trying to make a living in this country or this, this world, so, no, I think every human life is valuable.

The second component involved God. We are all worth the same because we are all equal before God—something that, according to some, the Constitution itself recognizes. Sean reasoned, for instance,

In God's eyes, yes, nobody's life is worth more than another person's life. I mean, I, it's . . . now, if that person's trying to kill me or is trying to steal from me or trying to take my rights or, or is coming in here and living off of me, is their life worth less? No . . . but if somebody's trying to kill me, am I not gonna kill them back? Yes. If somebody's trying to steal from me and they're non-American and they're here illegally, yes, I'm gonna say he needs to be deported. But is his life worth less? No . . .'cause what I said; nobody's life is worth any more than anybody else's. It's just like, you know, it's . . . sorry but . . . Barack Obama's life is not worth any less than the homeless veteran sleeping on the streets . . . [and this is based] on God, 'cause honestly, the Constitution to a part is based . . . on the Ten Commandments, to an extent. I mean, I wouldn't say it's verbatim, but it is, it's . . . it's that all men are created equal in the, in, in . . . inalienably . . . everybody is the same. Nobody is better than anybody else.

Grace similarly felt that "no, I don't think we [Americans] are worth more, and, ask God, we're all one." Daniel echoed this when stating that a "human life is a human life. God don't know what country you live in."

Yet I felt the power of such thinking especially when it came from Ryan, a forty-year-old white man who had just been released from prison in Birmingham. I spoke to him at the bus station, as he was moving on to his life as a free man: "All life should be treated equally. . . . No man's life is better than my life." "Why?" I asked. "Because we was made by the same man. . . . Jesus Christ . . . created us all." Indeed, as Kysha put it, differences in worth cannot exist for a Christian, "not from the Christian aspect, no, 'cause we're all the same in God's sight. We're all the same. All human beings are valuable. Even animals . . . I don't mistreat my animals."

Such strong beliefs in equality at almost existential or spiritual levels, matched by the recognition that America happens to be the country to be founded on the premise of such equality ("I think everybody's equal, you know; it's just . . . in their own country they don't have as much freedom as we do. And that's 'cause of the government," in Linda's words), likely dampens the implications of income or other inequalities for one's love of country. It reduces the significance of material or other circumstances when it comes to patriotic considerations. Put differently, given that so many of the poor Americans I met believed themselves fundamentally equal to the wealthiest or otherwise better-off Americans, it should not be too surprising that they saw little tension between their conditions and their patriotism. On the contrary, given the country's own commitment to that fundamental equality, they had every reason to feel committed to, and supportive of, their nation.

This Is All I Know

Lesser philosophical considerations also offer clues into why America's poor have no doubts about their patriotism while they suffer economic hardships and receive relatively few benefits from their government when compared to the poor in other advanced countries. When asked about other countries and what they may offer, the most common response was an acknowledgment of limited comparative information quickly followed by a reassertion of one's love of the United States: yes, it may be the case that elsewhere is better, but America is all one knows, and America remains a great country anyway—with the proof sometimes being that one has never really felt the need to leave.

Marshall captured exactly this line of reasoning when stating, "I don't know any different, personal . . . firsthand experiences of anything better, 'cause I haven't been out of the country because I haven't had any reason to leave . . . and that's, that's something that speaks for itself right there!" The words of Jeannie, in Vernon, showed the vacillation between recognizing one's limited knowledge and reasserting nonetheless love of country:

Yes, like I said, I mean, I wouldn't know; I don't know nothing about the other countries. Would I want to explore, well sure, you know. And just see how different the government or the, you know, people are down there. You . . . I really just, I shouldn't have said that maybe because I don't know, but I think the United States, like I said, I don't know nothing about it, but I love America.

Carlos, in Billings, followed exactly the same pattern, in this case when responding to my suggestion that much of what he said about his love of the United States, and especially the freedoms it guarantees, can also be found in neighboring Canada:

I don't really know, honestly, to tell you the truth. You know . . . I haven't read a whole lot of studies on Canada. . . . I believe that they are, just from what I've heard . . . I know a lot of people say that they're going to move to Canada if Trump gets elected [laughs], but I don't know. . . . I believe that, you know, Canada is an open country too, so . . . but like I said, I haven't done much of that . . . and I'll be honest with you, I don't know about all the freedoms in all the other countries . . . but I was born and raised here, and I know, I know the freedom that this country was built on, so that's one of the things that I do love about it.

Yet not all the interviewees were so comfortable with their limited experiences and knowledge. Some clearly wished for more exposure. Alicia, for instance, reasoned that she is patriotic

because I guess it's the only place that I know. I grew up in the projects; my mom was a single parent, and I have never been anywhere but here. I never had a chance to experience anything else but this; it's sorta that, all I know . . . I don't know nothing else; it's all that I know. And I always dreamed as a little girl that I wanted to grow up, become a nurse or a traveling nurse, so I can go see other parts of the world because I know this is not all it could be. But I haven't been able to do that because my mom was a poor mom. She had four children. Her husband left her when I was one; she struggled; now I'm struggling, which is sad. This is all I know. But my heart desires to know more.

Others, perhaps less directly than Alicia, also indicated a slight discomfort with their limited experiences by saying that they could not possibly feel otherwise given their personal histories and lives. Doug, for instance, stated,

I mean, I mean, that's all I know. If you . . . if that's all you know, you don't know nothing . . . anything else. All I know is to be . . . is US citizen. I never been, I never had dual citizenship. . . . I've never traveled extensively. I have read things about other countries, but I've never got up and try to understand. . . . I don't know anything; I don't know anything else but to be an American.

Deep roots in one place, and what those mean for one's desire to see something else, were also mentioned. Denzel reflected on this very point:

I have more roots here than anywhere else. Now it would be different if I was an army brat, where my parents used to travel from state, from country to country to country. . . . I wouldn't know what to find, but by me being raised in America, being born in America, coming up in American ways, yeah, I have roots and I have ties here. If I was born in Asia or somewhere, I'd have roots and ties there. . . . Americans they like pork, ham, sausage, bacon . . . whatever, pork chops. . . . You can't go get, I'm not saying you can't go get it in China or somewhere, but it's not the same. It's not cooked the way, the way you know, the way you cook it here. It's not cooked over there that way. So . . . you got roots; you got cultures that you have to go by, follow certain guidelines.

More knowledge would be welcome, then, but one is unfortunately limited by the circumstances. As Valerie put it, "It's the only country I know. It's the best I know," and, as Shirley admitted, "America is all of that that I've experienced. Even though I've been to different cities and different states, that's really all that I've experienced. Now had I been, had I been well traveled, then I probably could give you a different understanding from that. But I have never been outside of America. So this is all that I know."

The inevitability of one's patriotism was felt perhaps even more strongly by those with personal and family histories in the military. One cannot feel too distant from the United States when generations of relatives have sacrificed their time and sometimes lives for the country. Sean, for example, had this realization:

> It was one of those things. . . . My father was in the military, my grandfather was in the military, my uncle was in the military, you know, so it's one of those things it does; it does run in my family. I'm the only one that's never went in the army, but it is definitely something that's in my family, and, yeah, we, we, we do hold, we do have, hold a special esteem for our country. . . . We want to serve it.

Similarly, Rainbow, when talking about the reasons for her patriotism, pointed out that "both my stepdad and dad served in the military. I have a few other relatives that have served in the military, so that's very near and dear to me."

In any case, it should be noted, even with no international experience, the news from other countries confirms one's attachment to the United States. What about European countries? As Lynn told me, "The ones you hear about the most are the ones where the huge, the huge issues are." Concerning Asia and Oceania, Charlotte said, "Well, I, I can't say for sure about New Zealand or Japan, 'cause I haven't lived there, but you take Communist China and places like that, and, and I definitely know that what they do is monitored . . . so, you know, and there might be a better place." Things are even clearer regarding the Middle East and countries like Pakistan. Did Roger really have no reason to expect more from his country? Did he not feel a need to reconcile his low-income status with his love of country? The answer was negative: "It's 'cause I don't have to; I don't have to worry about walking out, walking out of my door and a . . . worrying about a bomb dropping on me. . . . Yeah, you know, and Saudi Arabia . . . not Saudi Arabia, but Iran, Iraq, all that. I don't have to worry about whether or not I'll make it across the street without getting shot . . . not like ISIS going on and all that, you know . . . being worried to walk one block to visit your uncle or something. You might not make it."

And while the news from abroad is bad, in America one is taught to believe from a young age, "since grade school," in the words of Jill, "to believe." Given all this, it makes perfect sense that poor Americans should love their country. There is, in fact, no real tension between their financial or economic conditions and their ardent patriotism. Their belief in the greatness of America, their love of country, is rooted in part at least in a singular understanding—learned at a very young age and seldom challenged by exposure to something different—of their nation and its virtues.

CHAPTER 8

AN UNSHAKABLE BOND

The sight of run-down towns and neighborhoods in America is unfortunately a common one. Anyone traveling by road in any part of the country in little time will encounter visible signs of decline: dilapidated homes, streets full of potholes, semiabandoned parks, old cars, and predatory loan businesses.[1] The most powerful country on earth, with soldiers in more than one hundred countries and vast amounts of wealth, has large segments of the population struggling to make ends meet and ensure a better future for their children. Their country helps them but does so in more limited form than what happens in other advanced nations. At the same time, in the same towns and neighborhoods, expressions of patriotism often abound. There seems to be little doubt in their residents' minds that America is a great country, deserving of loyalty and admiration. There is a sense that people feel blessed, even lucky, to be citizens of the United States. As we have seen, statistical data confirm this impression: 80%–90% of America's poor are very patriotic. The figure exceeds that for the poor in other advanced countries. It is also in many instances higher than the already high figures for working-, middle-, and upper-class Americans.

Why such patriotism? What is its nature? What do struggling Americans love about their country? We know quite a lot about American patriotism in general, but very little attention has been paid to the country's least well-off. We should know more about their beliefs and mind-sets: much, as we have seen, depends on their patriotism—from the social cohesion of the country to its sense of self and identity in the world. The sixty-three conversations I held in urban and rural Alabama and Montana offered illuminating, powerful, and sometimes very moving insights. We can reflect here on the key results.

Patriotic Narratives

The patriotism of America's poor has deep, strong roots. The personal economic and financial situations of the people I met seemed to have no negative import for their love of country: they were not an issue. The opposite actually appeared to be the case: precisely because they were struggling, many found solace and reassurance in being American. Explanations of their love of country came easily, with enthusiasm, conviction, and no hesitation. In most cases, I seemed to be inquiring about something essential and taken for granted: being American was an integral and important part of one's identity. Many were keenly aware of the country's history. While America has surely struggled along the way—with racial issues and class inequality, for instance—it has been from its very start an extraordinary country. Indeed, it has promised its citizens something unique and special. Because of this promise, the country is securely lodged in people's consciousness and hearts. My conversations in Alabama and Montana revealed a good deal about what that promise entails.

Three narratives emerged. First, the United States offers hope to each and every American; in fact, it offers hope to every human being on earth. The country represents a deliberate effort to unshackle each individual's existence from the repressive forces that have hurt peoples throughout history. It entails therefore a special sort of social contract, one that sets it apart from every other country or previous society. It also manifests itself into an active and practical role of the United States on the world stage as a generous and honorable nation ready to do the right thing. Considerable misunderstandings and beliefs about the flaws of other countries certainly abounded, and factual inaccuracies about the United States were often mentioned. But many of the people I met also had a legitimate understanding of history—in Montana, for instance, many spoke accurately about the American Revolution, while in Alabama important facts about the civil rights movement were often brought up.

Such hope mattered a great deal to the interviewees: it spoke to them directly. When much in life is otherwise challenging, belonging to the country that is the world's shining city on a hill acquires powerful appeal. It can also be a source of dignity. The fact that the interviewees saw God playing a role in the country's birth and evolution added further intensity to this narrative: America—with its special qualities—is God's country. The United States is special because God has made it so. Its people, in turn, worship God. The interviewees—especially the older ones—placed a premium on such closeness to God: being on God's side offers reassurance, a sense of protection, and even optimism. Again, the thinking was not always lucid. Some of the interviewees struggled to explain why, if God loves every human being the same, there should be differences between Americans and everyone else. But these were considerations raised by my own asking: they did not, on their own, trouble anyone in any real sense. For many, the United States, with its divine destiny, simply offers an almost transcendental sort of hope for its citizens, because of its ideals but also its generosity and commitment to humanity—all things of great value for those struggling to go through their day fed, clothed, and sheltered.

This first narrative was accompanied by an equally powerful, second one: Despite the interviewees' own travails, America remains the land of milk and honey. To many of them, for obvious reasons, this felt reassuring. There is tremendous wealth in the country—more so than anywhere else. There is also a good deal of support available. The country offers all kinds of help, and public goods—such as free Internet access at libraries and paved roads—abound. Sure, some other countries in the world are wealthy, but none matches America's riches. I was reminded of this especially in Alabama. All one has to do is take advantage of this. Everything is within reach. Inequality—something with significant destabilizing potential—was of little concern.[2] Anyone can make it, for the opportunities are there, and responsibility ultimately lies within each of us. The fact that people from all over the world seek to come to

America is proof of the opportunities it offers. Many of the interviewees expressed a sense of contentment. There is something awesome about America, even in terms of its natural beauty and resources, and daily experiences of access to its wealth—through charity, public services, and other means—make living, or surviving, in the country both possible and a privilege. Indeed, living in America is one of the luckiest things that can happen to a poor person.

The third narrative was the most frequently mentioned. This is the land of individual freedom: the country of physical and mental self-determination. Nothing is dearer than freedom, for life and being a human being require it. America guarantees it. In so doing, America protects the most precious thing anyone can have. The interviewees were keenly aware of their rights, and it seemed that their freedom acquired even more importance because they lacked most other resources. In Montana, such discussions of freedom took on a libertarian tone; in Alabama, black interviewees often recalled the overcoming of slavery and segregation. Here the interviewees saw themselves again reflected in the American social contract: they saw in it an essential part of themselves and as something that they are ready to protect fiercely. Deprived of much else, the interviewees placed enormous importance on being free.

When discussing freedom, many—especially in Montana—placed a special value on their ability to own guns. There was a clear logic to this: with guns, one can protect oneself and one's family from intrusion and oppression and also survive by hunting and feeding oneself. Guns represent freedom, and freedom represents the human spirit. America's guarantee of gun ownership amounts to a protection of one of the most fundamental aspects of being human. Once again, America stands out from other countries in the protection of what is the most dear to human beings: the interviewees saw themselves in this guarantee and believed that guns could not be owned elsewhere in the world. The fact, moreover, that some had served in the military, and that many belonged to families with a history of service, added further intensity to these feelings. I was reminded often that the country began with a violent revolution, spurred by English monarchical oppression and its confiscation of firearms. Freedom was something that was dearly fought for, with many Americans sacrificing their lives for it along the way. Importantly, this line of thinking at times mixed with more local narratives—of Confederate glories in Alabama and of rugged individualism in Montana.

If there was ever any doubt in my mind that people's economic difficulties could undermine Americans' faith in, and love of, their country, my direct questions about this erased any such doubt. People get what they deserve, I was repeatedly told. The future is looking bright anyway. And, perhaps most crucially, we are indeed all worth the same: A life is a life, and one's economic conditions, or race for that matter, do not define one's value. There is no difference between a homeless person and the president. America is the one country to recognize this essential fact. Other countries perhaps might, too, to some extent, but it is difficult to discern if one has never visited them.[3]

Thus, these patriotic narratives, when taken together, point to a fundamental aspect of the patriotism of America's poor. As much as the interviewees belong to America, it became clear to me that America also belongs to them. The Americans I met found themselves reflected in their country's founding documents and symbols. America is about its people—it is their creation; it is something set up by the people to safeguard and celebrate each person's life. A commitment to America is therefore a commitment to oneself and to everyone else in the compact: all stand equal before the country, and the country stands equal before every American. Difficult personal circumstances cannot easily shake such a sense of mutual belonging between people and country. On the contrary, tough times can further intensify one's identification with America.

Such a perspective is quite consistent with the historical development of the country, as historians and sociologists have written: America has belonged, from its very inception, to the people. It is a populist, pragmatic sort of project.[4] It was so from its very beginnings: rather than an accomplishment of the elites, as was the case for England, France, and Russia,[5] America's sense of nation and the potential for an unprecedented sort of society was perhaps the only thing that the new-comers shared with one another as they set out to create a new social experiment. "The seed population, so to speak," writes Greenfeld, "to begin with consisted of citizens of a nation who brought the conviction of their nationality with them to a new continent"; those citizens "reconfirmed the commitment of the new society to the original principles derived from the old one [England], and determined that it would henceforth develop toward ever closer alignment with them." Hence, it quickly became the case that "liberty and equality, for Americans, became self-evident."[6] This was clear from the very early days of the country. The words of a young Samuel Dickinson, one of many representatives of the new nation,[7] uttered during a July 4 oration in 1797 in Massachusetts, offer one of many examples: "I need not spend any time to prove the equality of men, or the inalienable rights of humanity. . . . You my countrymen know the reality. They are a sacred deposit in the bosom of every American."[8] All Americans, clearly, belonged to the experiment. This very idea would be repeated throughout the history of the country—from the Civil War and the words of Abraham Lincoln at Gettysburg to the wars of the twentieth century, the civil rights movement, and the country's reaction to the terrorist attacks of 9/11.[9]

In sum, the bond between the interviewees and America seemed utterly strong, personal, and multifaceted. Some of what we learned resonates with many of the insights put forth in existing research on American patriotism and on group cohesion discussed in Chapter 3. This suggests that there are connections between that research and the views of poor Americans. The interviewees spoke about the dignity and rights that America's founding documents give to each individual (insight 1), the American Dream (2), self-determination (3), and the bond between God and the country (4). They also spoke about the inherent inclusiveness of America's social contract (5) and showed a fairly calculative appreciation of the benefits of being an American (9). They exhibited as well a fair amount of misconceptions about other countries, what they have to offer, and some of the limitations of the United States itself (8). Only two of the insights—having the feeling that one

contributed to the building of the country (6) and a desire to rationalize one's unfortunate circumstances by loving the country (7)—did not
seem relevant: little that was said offered evidence in the direction of
either point.

Yet, even for all the relevant evidence, little in the existing research
could have predicted the specific articulations and expressions that the
interviewees would share with me in our conversations. When, for instance, freedom in America is equated with one's ability to sleep undis-
turbed in open fields in Montana or hunt for survival, when one feels
that America respects individual rights because of lenient prison sen-
tences and the second chances it offers to recovering addicts, or when
the benefits of living in America are calculated by taking into consideration the availability of water in public libraries, the terms "freedom,"
"rights," and "benefits" acquire very particular meanings. The same can
be said about terms such as "inclusiveness," the "American Dream," and
"divine." The interviewees wove these and other conceptual threads together in unique, unexpected, and often moving fashion. They provided
very particular content, as it were, to those broader ideas.

There was also much that went beyond the insights of existing research. There was little that could have prepared me, for instance, for
the hope that believing in America gives to its poorest members, for the
admission that, when all else is a struggle, belonging to what is understood to be the greatest country on earth gives one an enormous psychological lift.[10] Even if we turn to the most recent best sellers exploring
the mind-sets of economically marginalized Americans, such as J. D.
Vance's *Hillbilly Elegy* or Nancy Isenberg's *White Trash*, the dominant
feeling described is one of gloom and lost hope.[11] The same can be said
of the many mentions of the country's physical beauty, the depth of the
interviewees' knowledge about its history and evolution, the remarkable
but often unfounded optimism that things are just about to get better,
or the feeling that one has an obligation to love the country because
of the personal sacrifice of generations of Americans, many of whom
are relatives or ancestors. Those were aspects of patriotism that only in-
depth conversations could reveal. And only those conversations could

shed light on the fact that, ultimately, in the minds of many there is no tension between their difficult personal situations and their deep love of country—that, in fact, quite the opposite could be the case, and being poor might even intensify one's appreciation for the country. Thus, traveling and talking with sixty-three exceptional and insightful Americans afforded me a truly revealing window onto something that no consultation of any existing research could ever have done.

Broader Considerations

We conclude by thinking about the broader implications of the findings in this book. Three overarching observations are in order.

The first concerns inequality and politics in America. Numerous observers and scholars have wondered why America's underclass has tolerated the large and growing gap between the rich and the poor, the displacement of wealth it entails, and the related reduction of employment opportunities. Why is it, some have asked, that America's poor do not revolt? What keeps them in place, still willing to participate in American society? This is a good question to pose. One common explanation points to "false class consciousness"—a duping of the poor into a state of complacency and ignorance. The argument, discussed in Chapter 3,[12] sees the poor as passively accepting what the elite tell them. Incapable of assessing their objective conditions, they embrace without too much thinking the idea that everything is okay. Inequality, they are told, for instance, is not excessive, and the American Dream is still very much alive. Patriotism might in this way be part of the story; as a way to pacify their spirits, poor Americans are simply made to believe in the greatness of their country.

My encounters and conversations, however, indicated something quite different. There was certainly, in the minds of the people I met, an acceptance of the social order, and many were holding on to sometimes rather inaccurate views of other countries and the United States. But this did not mean that their love of country lacked genuine and deliberate foundations. I met reflective, intelligent, and wide-reaching minds who were aware of their situations and deeply felt a true sense of appreciation for the United States. They separated their personal situations—which the majority of respondents viewed as the result of their own choices and not larger forces—from their understanding of the American social contract, which by and large they described with accurate historical knowledge and thoughtfulness. One might criticize them for their steadfast commitment to the country despite what they are experiencing, but these were deeply held views that many interviewees were able to explicate and discuss at length.

As I assumed from the very start of the project, then, there would be much to learn from my conversations. I felt humbled, moved, and impressed by the people I met. My takeaway was that America's poor—at least many of the patriotic ones—do not revolt because, in part, they remain deliberately attached to their country and because the ideals of America are the people's ideals. We should allow for the possibility that America's poor truly identify with their nation—indeed, this serves as a key element of their sense of worth and dignity. For the moment, these seem like unshakable foundations. There remains a genuine, bottom-up attachment to the country—something of fundamental importance if one wishes to understand the strong glue that keeps America together.

The second point has to do with the possible evolution and uses of the patriotism of America's poor. What seems utterly unshakable today may, in fact, be challenged one day, alter in content, or be leveraged in novel ways that affect its tone and character. Change can happen. The situation of the least well-off has been worsening over the last decades. Governmental policies have hurt those with limited financial means. Inequality in the country is very high. The recovery from the Great Recession has done little to help the poorest citizens. People are strained and struggling. Three of the interviewees I selected, by design, were not patriotic: for the record, I report in the Appendix their thinking and feelings, along with the reservations some of the other interviewees occasionally expressed during our conversations.

These dissonant voices offer insights into possible things to come. Could prolonged challenges and growing inequality change, one day, either the intensity or nature of the devotion to their country of those at the bottom of the economic hierarchy? Could they make it much more difficult for poor Americans to separate, as the interviewees did, one's circumstances or the country's government from the country itself—and thus no longer benefit from the valuable psychological lift that being American offers? A concurrent sense that the standing of the United States on the world stage is diminishing may make such a shift in thinking more possible.[13] It is not easy to imagine what the impact of such disillusionment might exactly be. But it will probably be significant. The more idealized America is, the bigger its potential to disappoint. With everything else in life proving so difficult, a turn away from America could prove greatly disruptive at the individual and collective levels.

A different sort of change is also a possibility. A steadfast commitment to America on the part of the worst-off always has the potential to be appropriated by populist political leaders eager to advance a different vision of the country. Such politicization could have real and large-scale consequences. What would that mean for the poor themselves—their sense of satisfaction in life, hopes, and aspirations—and the country—its stability, identity, and even place in the world? Could that appropriation or politicization, in turn, also alter the very nature of that patriotism?

One need only think of Donald Trump's successful 2016 presidential campaign, with its "Make America Great Again" slogan. It strategically leveraged the patriotism of poor (and not poor) Americans with considerable success by speaking to some of its strands while capitalizing on the significant amount of popular discontent with the political establishment and the country's economic conditions.[14] In so doing, it amplified, altered, and reworked those strands to diagnose problems, advocate for certain policies, and make certain claims about other countries. Something similar can be said of Bernie Sanders's campaign, though of course there were major substantive differences between the two camps. It is not too difficult to see, then, how the patriotism of America's poor could take on different forms and how this could have major implications that would reverberate well beyond any one section of American society. This is certainly something quite pressing that deserves further reflection.

The final point concerns differences in patriotism among the poor and across economic classes in the United States. The interviewees, though selected purposely from particular locations in Alabama and Montana, numbered sixty-three. This is a good number for studies of this kind, but it seems appropriate to wonder what additional narratives might emerge from extending the interviews to other sites in the country. Any one location has its own history, economy, political climate, traditions, ethnic and racial makeups, and other distinctive characteristics. What would those narratives add to the picture presented in this book?

While, in turn, it seems reasonable to expect middle- and upper-class Americans to subscribe to some of the narratives we heard in this book—such as those around freedom or guns—the specific articulations of those narratives are very likely to vary. Being free, for a wealthy American, probably carries very different connotations than for a homeless person wondering where the next meal will come from. Owning a gun may be valued across the economic spectrum because, among other things, of its indispensability for hunting. But hunting itself may be more recreational and not be so closely associated with survival for wealthier Americans. In addition, some of the narratives we encountered may simply not be shared by many of those who enjoy more financial resources. For instance, the feeling that one has nothing left to lose and that being American offers one's remaining hope and sense of dignity is probably absent among those who have more money.

How patriotic narratives across economic classes in America may overlap, parallel, contrast, or even complement each other remains an open and very important question. Understanding these dynamics would offer additional, and very useful, insights into what we may call the architecture or physiognomy of American patriotism. It would highlight the multifaceted nature of patriotism, and national identity more broadly, in America and, possibly, more generally. It would show how similar ideals are adapted and integrated into specific class milieus. In sum, research on this aspect of patriotism is obviously, still, very limited. Much work clearly lies ahead.

Appendix

The Appendix is divided into three sections. In the first, I examine the views of three interviewees who felt ambivalent toward or simply opposed the idea of being patriotic. In the second, I specify in detail the methodology used for conducting and examining the content of the interviews. The third section lists all the interviewees (by pseudonyms) and their basic demographic data and location.

Dissonant Voices

As we learned in Chapter 2, depending on how we measure it, 80% to 90% of poor Americans are patriotic: they believe in the greatness and often superiority of the United States. This book's objective was to discover the nature of that patriotism. But, by design, not everyone I met was resolutely supportive of the United States. Most were for sure, but I selected two interviewees in Alabama (Jake and Michelle) and one in Montana (Kevin) specifically because they expressed ambivalence toward, or outright rejection of, patriotic ideals. As Shirley herself noted, "Not everybody is on board with 'I love America.'" I wanted to hear what clearly nonpatriotic Americans had to say. In addition, several of the other interviewees at times qualified their love of country—by noting, for instance, cracks in the cultural and political foundations of the country. While it would be impossible to observe patterns or identify general narratives from their statements, it seems worth discussing their primary points of objection.

The statements included here add valuable counterpoints to the positive picture that emerged from the interviews throughout the chapters.

Depending on one's perspective, these counterpoints could be described in a variety of ways, from cynical and disillusioned to sober and realistic, resentful, pessimistic, resigned, or smart. If the glass seemed full or half full to nearly all the interviewees in this book, to a few it felt half empty or outright empty. Such thinking aligned more directly with what we learned about the poor and the challenges they face in America.

First, there was some cynicism about the very idea that America is a great country. Jake, a young white male recently released from prison in Alabama for possession of Xanax, simply scorned the idea of patriotic love:

I just don't like the connotation of saying like, you know, we're the greatest country on earth, like, once again that, that makes me think about preppy guys at school that play football and shit, you know? Greatest country on earth; these guys suck . . . this country is second place; this country is third place.

There is something too top down and authoritative about the flag and love of country: "It just seems more like, like overall more like a dictatorship type thing." He continued:

Most of the influence I've gotten over the years has either been, well, I rejected influence from my family, and I, I mean from music that I listen to, and I'm not saying that I'm totally ignorant other than what I've heard in, like, rock songs or anything, but sorry, I . . . I just, I just . . . everything about politics makes me sick, just the way that, that I mean I understand lying. I understand doing stuff for social points and, and all that, but I just I don't like it. Yeah, and I mean the way that I see it, my vote doesn't really make a shit for, you know, as far as what's going on anyway. I know they say every vote counts or whatever, but I don't give a shit.

He talked about "apathy," and the fact that he played "music, that's all I really" do. On that note, he thought very little of the national anthem: "It's just annoying, 'cause it's an annoying song." Asked if he cared for the American flag, his reply was that he did not:

The flag, no, in fact I'm, I was in a band in Florida that was called Downer Syndrome. It was like a Nirvana cover band/punk original band, and we would, you know, put up flags and everyone would sign 'em, and that's not, I didn't think that was like a, I say we would put up flags, someone would put up flags, and we signed it one day, and everybody thought that was really fucked up, and, I was like, we're just signing our names on it. I mean, we'd write things, like, I wrote "Jake does drugs" . . . stuff like that.

Would he ever fight for America? His answer was no: "I, I just would not give up, put up my life for, I mean, I value my life much more than the idea of, of, you know, utopia America, whatever you wanna call it. . . . Kinda like the *Desperate Housewives* picture of living. . . . I don't know it's, it's kinda disgusting to me." In fact, when he thought of the flag, the image that came to mind was one of "bullies . . . yeah, yeah. And the way we are about wars and fuck with us and you'll find out what happens."

Consistent with this critical outlook, Jake also asserted that he would not teach his daughter to be patriotic. It is important "not to just accept what's presented to you at face value 'cause that's not always what you get." Authority should be questioned so that "you actually know what's going on and make your decisions based on what you know and not just what you've been fed."

The cynicism extended to the poor Americans themselves who are patriotic. They are deluded and romantic, who cling to unrealistic images of the United States. Kevin, the part-time construction worker in Billings, offered observations on this point:

They're buying into what America used to be . . . because upward mobility used to be huge, huge in America. . . . I would say that Americans probably buy into that 1950s idyllic . . . idyllic suburbia white picket fence, all of that . . . and you gotta look at what the world was like in the 1950s. America was the sole, was the sole country that emerged from the Second World War as being on top. Russia, devastated. Germany, devastated because they fought Russia, which the Americans probably don't ever probably get to fully . . . appreciate is just how many bodies were thrown at each other on the Eastern Front. Western Front was a side show. . . . To get back to that, though, the United States was on . . . we were reaching our peak in the 1950s.

Concerning their interpretation of their own undesirable situation, "unfortunately the poor only blame themselves," while also hanging on to "warped" ideas of America, such as the notion that "it was founded by Christians." "I mean," Kevin continued, "Thomas Paine wasn't a Christian. . . . Jefferson has gone on record several times, you know, extolling the virtues of having a separate church and state." The foundational assumptions of America's greatness and its roots are thus inaccurate and questionable.

Second, this overarching skepticism gave way to a list of specific ailments that are crippling America. Many of the interviewees saw problems. Darrius, along with several others, especially in Montana, felt that, because of 9/11, "which changed everything in this country, America has fallen from its grace." It is far from being the land of freedom it once was. We encountered some of this thinking when exploring the libertarian rhetoric in Montana. A good many more felt that the country lacks a certain moral rectitude. Americans, for instance, seem to no longer care for each other, as Chris, the retired truck driver in Birmingham, noted:

People, back in the day, we helped each other, you know. We helped each other. You know, person didn't have no food, you give them food. They haven't anywhere to sleep, you give them somewhere to sleep. You know, people don't do that now. . . . You know, we just so angry. . . . . We just don't . . . we don't, we don't help each other.

Instead of supporting each other, Americans are now hurting one another. "Living in America," explained Darrius, "is like living in a . . . how can I put this . . . like, it's like a dog eat dog, a dog eat dog world kinda thing. Like eat or be eaten like . . . nowadays in America it's very primal."

Everyday violence and crime are undermining basic social solidarity. Entire neighborhoods are unlivable. Cole recalled being in Dallas: "I promise you, every night. Every night in my house it was . . . boom, boom, boom, boom, boom. Well, I lived across from some, some low-income housing, and, and there's nothing but drugs and gangs and drive-by shootings and police killings." The situation in Birmingham was apparently not much different. "Black on black, white on white," Paula lamented. "You know, then they kill each other. . . . They kill the opposite. That's not, that's not a good time around here." But the problem is across the nation—something that led Chris to leave his truck-driving job he had for many years:

Because it's dangerous . . . more dangerous now than when I first started [driving]. You didn't know anything about people breaking in your truck . . . but now, you know . . . he might take your life about something you can't do nothing about. So, you know, I just . . . I just . . . it was time for me to get off the road.

The inflow of illegal immigrants does not help either, according to Katie and a few others. Schools, for instance, need metal detectors because of people coming "from Mexico; they come from anywhere . . . they come from everywhere."

The decline in moral rectitude is reflected as well in a generalized laziness, a willingness to accept free "handouts" from the government—something that goes directly against the basic grain of the country's founding values and something that people in Montana especially brought up. The laziness is widespread, including among the young, as Carlos, who was facing the loss of his bank job in the coming months, lamented:

I think that, today's, especially today's youth, I would say probably a generation ago up until now gonna be going further, they have lost all aspects of what America means, you know? They think that everything should be given to them. You know, and they think that everything needs to be, to be handed to them without them having to do any hard work at all for it, and if they don't, they throw big fits and all of a sudden now we've got all these people that are, that are hurt . . . mostly hurt because they're being told no to.

The result is that America's citizens have lost a certain "something" that once defined them. Again, the interviewees in Montana were especially likely to mention this. As Carlos continued,

It's like, you know, my dad raised me with a switch, with a belt, and brought me up on the morals of always treat the elderly correctly, always treat women correctly, and always treat your parents correctly. And that was instilled in me since the day I was born, and that's how I am today, too, you know. I don't abuse women, I don't abuse the elderly, and I'm raising my two kids on my own . . . and so in today's day and age you don't see a whole lot of kids that are willing to do that, you know . . . because the parents just don't want to take that step up. They want everything to be handed to them. Like I said, the citizens of the United States have lost something, we've lost something; I don't know exactly what it is, but we've lost it.

Jill, in the real estate office in Harlowton, had similar concerns and some ideas about what might bring that "something" back to America:

The solution is to, I think, come back to a . . . a different level of moral consciousness. You know, I think part of . . . I'll give you a very good example, talking to young people in high school, the idea of having a job . . . I, I can't believe how many high school kids in our little class school here don't work in the summer. You've gotta be kidding me; why would you not require your child to produce something, even a few hours a week? What are they doing with that time? Well, they're either doing two things: nothing, slugging through the summer, or they're doing these intensive nothing sports, sports, sports and how many of . . . what do you think the percentage out of that school, you know, of fifty kids that pro athletes are gonna burst out of that. . . . I think that's really reflective of America in general. Like, get up and produce something wonderful today, and I think that's the moral conscience I'm talking about.

The laziness, and with it a lack of appreciation for the country and the hard work it is built on, extends to adults, too, only to connect again to the younger generations. Chad's thoughts on the matter offer a good example:

It's getting, I think it's getting worse . . . like I said earlier, we allow people to sit around on welfare all day long, you know, and some people do, do drugs on welfare, and I think we should have a piss test for it. . . . I don't think welfare should be constant, you know; it should be like here's five years, and by that time you should be off; if not . . . you gotta figure out something else in your life. Right now we don't have any . . . it doesn't feel like patriotism is a real big thing. You know, kids step on the flag, that kinda thing, like someone fought for your freedom, just so you could do that. I understand it's not a crime or anything like that, but I mean . . . seriously somebody died so you could do what you're doing today. And that's just . . . like you never know . . . like maybe their cousin, maybe their grandfather was a veteran . . . pretty much you're, pretty much you're stepping on them.

More hard work, then, and less largesse from the government, are in order: "I tell ya, I, I think we got a great country," stated Anne, the former director of Harlowton's Senior Citizen Center, "and we need to get back on the right track . . .'cause all this socialism talking now. . . . I ain't, never was, in love with Hitler and his methods or any of them. Look at those countries, good Lord." So, for many, the way to get the country back on the right track is to recognize, as Fiona said, that "there's too many people out there that play the poor-me game," too afraid to be "prideful." Americans, "one hundred years ago, they were hardier," and a return to that is what is needed.

The lack of moral rectitude was seen in another respect: a country deep in debt. If the United States, asked Ryan in Birmingham, "was so, so great, why are we in so much debt to China? You know what I mean?" Sean, the Gulf War veteran in Billings, worried that "we're spending . . . we're already spending money we don't have. We're borrowing more money from China. . . . I mean China owns us at this point." A corrupt government is part of the problem, according to Fiona: we are "probably paying our politicians" too much. "A lot of them," Grace, the retired cotton packer in Vernon thought, are "just dishonest. . . . Well, Obama sure hasn't done anything for us. He's spent all the money going on trips; he's got the United States in bad debt. I think that some of it was ruined before he went in office." Corruption, of course, is a sign of deeper ethical problems. It involves an unhealthy attachment to money, which the country as a whole suffers from, as Ryan noted: "There's a lot of love of money . . . I mean that's a, you know, a sin, a sin in the Bible. Money is . . . the love of money is root of all evil. And it is, you know that as much as I do."[1]

Something else seemed to undermine faith in America's greatness: a sense that, while there is considerable suffering in the country, resources and attention are instead going to people in other parts of the world. There is a feeling that, as Alicia stated, things seem to be "falling apart." As Fiona stressed, "We have starving children right here in America that need to be taken care of." Oscar, too, noted that "we've got kids over here that are starving to death, ain't got no family, ain't got no money and are starving in the United States." Homelessness is pervasive. The "situation of veterans," Logan told me, "it's terrible." The list went on.

Despite such problems, there was a sense that the government and

American society in general are not living up to their obligations toward their people. As Fiona stated, "There's too many illegals coming that are taking away benefits from our own people that need it. . . . We tend to take care of other people instead of taking care of our own . . . and I don't see our government doing a whole lot about that. But they'll be the first to go wherever, you know." There is almost a moral failure to act. The country seems to care more about the needy in other countries than the ones here. Gabby's words were representative in this regard:

I want to say the way the country, the way America is going right now is very disappointing to me. I would think, I mean, we're trying to help other countries when we're suffering. So how about we focus on making, how about we focus on trying to help ourselves before we're giving all this money to France, Paris? Everybody else that needs money . . . they should spend less time trying to help other countries and just try to, try to get, try to fix America first, before trying to fix everybody else's problems. . . . There are homeless people that are starving, and we're too busy helping people in Africa that are starving. . . . I'm sorry, I mean, they're their own country; they, they need to take care of their own. America is not Africa, America is not Afghanistan, America is not China; it is America.

Not surprisingly, the president, too, was called into question. Anne stated, for example, that "we don't elect a president in this country to fuss about global problems; we elect him for America. For our people, for our way of life and our government. But that's not how they do things anymore."

All this suggests that doubts about America certainly exist. For most of the interviewees, these were primarily side considerations— something that the country should address, especially if it is to remain the greatest nation on earth. For the strongest dissenting voices, however, it meant a rather different attitude toward the country and its greatness. As Michelle, the former McDonald's manager who recently resigned from her job because of unlivable wages, put it, "Okay, I love . . . don't get me wrong, I love the United States, but if it was up to me, personally, I would go to another country." Such a sentiment is certainly worthy of note.

Research Methods

Chapter 3 spelled out the logic used for selecting interview sites in Alabama and Montana and for finding and selecting interviewees at each site. Here I offer more information on the interview process, questionnaire, and methodology for coding the transcriptions of those interviews.

Interview Process and Questionnaire

The interview process involved sixty-three persons. The interviews typically lasted thirty to forty minutes. I held forty-one one-on-one interviews and eleven interviews with couples (generally because I approached them as couples and began my conversation with them together). The couples were sometimes friends, sometimes partners. Thirty-one interviewees were in Alabama, and thirty-two in Montana. The majority were in urban settings, but some (six in Alabama and six in Montana) in rural ones (specific ZCTAs and locations are identified in Chapter 3). The interviews were digitally recorded (audio only) on a computer and smart phone and then uploaded and transcribed. The names of all interviewees were recorded but changed in this book to ensure anonymity. All interviewees signed a form acknowledging that their statements might appear in this book. I asked some interviewees if they would be willing to have their pictures taken and possibly included in this book. Those who agreed signed a form where this was specifically stated. The interviews were approved by the Behavioural Research Ethics Board of the University of British Columbia and the Internal Review Board of Bates College (where I have affiliations and the sources of funding for the interviews) to ensure compliance with ethical standards. All interviewees were provided with a consent form (approved by the University of British Columbia) for them to keep, where the nature and purpose of this study were spelled out, along with the institutional contact information.

The interviews were open-ended and semistructured. They took place in a variety of locations (public libraries, bus stations, Laundromats, etc.). The questions were organized into four sections. Those in the first section related to basic demographic data (name, gender, age, racial background), work experience, family situation, and political orientation. They also included questions about income (to ensure that respondents were indeed below the poverty line as defined by the US Census Bureau) and patriotism (using primarily the GSS questions we considered in Chapter 2 on whether a person would rather be a citizen of the United States than of any other country and whether the United States is better than most other countries on earth). I selected two respondents in Alabama and one in Montana who were nonetheless not patriotic, because I was interested in catching at least a glimpse of alternative narratives.

The second section probed deeply into the nature of the respondent's patriotism. Included were open-ended questions about the images and associations that came to mind when thinking about the American flag, the qualities and traits of the United States as a country, the worthiness of American lives, the values we should teach our children, the patriotism of family members, scenarios where American citizens show little interest in patriotism, and other related topics. The discussions often evolved into deeper explorations of one's upbringing, volunteering and military service, religion, American history and traditions, what American soldiers fight for and protect Americans from, the benefits of living in the United States, and numerous other issues.

The third section included comparative questions and was designed to invite respondents to explain how they viewed the United States relative to other advanced and developing countries in the world and whether many of the positive qualities they attributed to the United States could also be attributed to other countries. Here, I also shared basic comparative data about other OECD countries with more generous welfare policies, clear commitments to freedom, lower crime rates, and other appealing characteristics to test further the respondents' logic.

In the fourth section, I posed to the respondents questions concerning the struggles and challenges they face and their devotion to the United States. The objective was to see how they reconciled, if they did, their dire circumstances with their resolute appreciation of their country. I closed by asking how America could be improved, to learn more about their knowledge of their country and their perspectives of how its shortcomings could be addressed.

I strove to have the interviews be as relaxed, informative, and open-ended as possible, with me occasionally sharing personal information to make the interviews more conversational and fluid—in line with existing academic recommendations for successful in-depth interviewing.[2] My expressed intent was to *learn* what the interviewees thought and felt, to probe into their thinking, and to arrive at a solid understanding of their mind-sets. I reassured the respondents that there were no right or wrong answers and that I was interested in them and their thoughts. Perhaps as a result, many of the interviewees seemed at ease sharing personal feelings and anecdotes, and several of the interviews took on an unexpected emotional quality. Most, if not all, of the respondents appeared to enjoy the experience, with some stating that the questions made them reflect about their own beliefs, upbringing, and perspectives on the world.

Any interviewing process is subject to limitations and potential biases. One potential problem was that the recruitment fliers posted prior to my arrival at different public locations (schools, community centers, etc.) mentioned twenty-five dollars as compensation for the time given. Obviously, this very likely tempted some not very patriotic people to volunteer anyway for the interview. As it turned out, the fliers proved effective in Alabama only: in Montana, no person called me ahead of time to schedule an interview. I dealt with the incentive problem in Alabama by screening potential interviewees over the phone prior to my arrival there with questions about their patriotism. Overall, only around a quarter of the sixty-three interviews were scheduled ahead of time. The vast majority, therefore, were set up on-site and only after an initial, informal screening on my part.

A second potential problem is that it is quite possible that some respondents gave answers that they felt seemed desirable, given the nature of the project, rather than accurate descriptions of their mind-sets and thoughts. This is a known problem in this type of study and can be addressed by presenting the interviewees with follow-up questions about the same topics, to test repeatedly for consistency over a particular theme.[3] Reaching "saturation" in the sorts of answers I heard early in my investigation (i.e., after five to ten interviews in each state, I repeatedly encountered the same themes, feelings, and ideas) indicated to me as well that the respondents were genuinely forthcoming and transparent.

A related challenge was that, because of my nonnative accent, respondents might have felt a need to somehow speak more positively about their country than might have otherwise been the case: One likes to impress foreigners, and criticizing one's country might be easier when speaking with compatriots. In actuality, many of the respondents seemed genuinely passionate about the United States and emphatic in their appreciation of their country. The extended nature of the interviews, coupled with the fact that I have lived in the United States for more than thirty years and know the culture of the country, also allowed me to delve deeply into the respondents' answers and the logic behind their statements. The conversations often took on a personal, relaxed, and intimate quality; there was accordingly little to suggest that the interviewees were somehow stating things that they did not truly feel. Moreover, virtually all respondents had something negative to say about the United States as well and quite often qualified their positive statements with important caveats. I am therefore very confident in the authenticity of what the interviewees shared with me.

Coding Methodology

The interviews were transcribed (a total of 894 single-spaced pages) by a research assistant and then uploaded and coded using a qualitative data analysis program called NVivo. I developed an initial coding scheme using thematic categories that I expected (based on the insights developed from existing research in Chapter 3 and in light of the first twenty or so interviews) would help identify relevant passages around the nature of the respondents' patriotism and the logic behind that patriotism. After reviewing all the transcripts and applying the original coding scheme to selected transcripts, I revised that scheme multiple times to make it as precise, unambiguous, and revealing as possible. The research assistant was trained to execute the coding. Following some of the most recent methodological guidelines for such an analysis, I coded in parallel selected transcripts separately to ensure consistency and precision.[4] As the assistant then proceeded to code, I examined all transcripts on my own and manually coded each one. The result was two full, and separate, codings of all the transcripts. With those in hand, I felt confident that no relevant statement from any of the interviewees was overlooked or misunderstood.

The coding scheme utilized twenty-eight major categories—that is, sets of keywords or concepts—and twenty-four subcategories (more specific renditions of those keywords and concepts). One of these subcategories broke down into further and more refined categories. The major categories clustered around four broad themes, which eventually informed the titles and content of Chapters 4, 5, 6, and 7 of this book: (1) the United States represents the last and best hope for humanity (and for the respondents themselves); (2) the United States is still the land of great riches and wealth; (3) the United States is, by design and because of its foundational social contract, the land of freedom; and (4) how the respondents reconciled, if they in fact did, their poverty and dire circumstances with their love of country.

The Interviewees

Tables 3 and 4 list the interviewees, alphabetically, in Alabama and Montana, respectively. All names are pseudonyms, but the basic demographic and location information is accurate.

Name*	Gender	Race/Ethnicity	Political Orientation	Veteran	Age	Employment Status	Location
Alex	Male	White	Republican	No	27	Injured during brick laying	Birmingham, Greyhound bus station
Alicia	Female	Black	Democrat	No	30	Trying to get GED	Birmingham, homeless shelter
Angie	Female	White	Republican	No	36	On disability (brain tumor)	Birmingham, Greyhound bus station
Antonio	Male	Black	N/A†	No	53	Unemployed (odd jobs, putting up tents for events)	Birmingham Public Library
Charlotte	Female	White	Republican	No	60	Runs a barbecue cafe	Vernon barbecue café
Chris	Male	Black	N/A	Yes	60	Trying to get disability; previously a truck driver	Birmingham Public Library
Dennis	Male	White	Conservative	No	69	Cast-iron-pipe worker	Birmingham, homeless shelter
Denzel	Male	Black	N/A	Yes	54	Seasonal jobs; puts up tents	Birmingham Public Library
Doug	Male	Black	Democrat	Yes	59	Temporary work for the VA	Birmingham Public Library
Eddie	Male	Black	Liberal	Yes	50s–60s	Off-the-book odd jobs	Birmingham Public Library
Emma	Female	White	Republican	No	49	Helps with town newspaper	Vernon Public Library

Table 3. Interviewees in Alabama, December 2015.

* All names are pseudonyms; † Not asked; ‡ Not patriotic.

Name*	Gender	Race/ Ethnicity	Political Orientation	Veteran	Age	Employment Status	Location
Emily	Female	Black	Democrat	No	72	Used to work for printing company	Birmingham, homeless shelter
Erica	Female	White	Republican	No	57	Unemployed; worked as a caregiver	Birmingham, homeless shelter
Gabby	Female	White	Independent	No	27	Unemployed; previously in fast food	Birmingham, Greyhound bus station
Grace	Female	White	Republican	No	72	Retired; former cotton packer	Vernon Public Library
Harley	Male	Black	Independent	Yes	60	On food stamps; served in the army	Birmingham Public Library
Hubert	Male	Black	Doesn't know	No	63	Retired; former construction worker	Birmingham Public Library
Jake‡	Male	White	N/A	No	24	Out of jail (heading to court)	Birmingham Greyhound bus station
Jeannie	Female	White	Democrat	No	30s–40s	N/A	Vernon, clothing store
Katie	Female	White	Democrat	No	35	Trying to get disability; former prostitute, worked in fast food	Birmingham Public Library

Table 3 (continued). Interviewees in Alabama, December 2015.

* All names are pseudonyms; † Not asked; ‡ Not patriotic.

Name*	Gender	Race/Ethnicity	Political Orientation	Veteran	Age	Employment Status	Location
Kayla	Female	Black	N/A	No	82	Retired; former bus driver	Vernon Public Library
Kysha	Female	Black	Independent	No	62	Retired; previously in nursing and former security guard	Birmingham, homeless shelter
Logan	Male	White	Democrat	No	41	Laid off (worked in industrial air-conditioning installation)	Birmingham Public Library
Michelle‡	Female	Black	N/A	No	50	Quit working at McDonald's after 21 years; fighting for a raise	Birmingham, homeless shelter
Paula	Female	White	Democrat	No	53	On disability	Birmingham Public Library
Ray	Male	Black	Democrat	Yes	56	Partial retirement after 18 years in US Army	Birmingham Public Library
Ryan	Male	White	Left leaning	No	40	Just got out of jail	Birmingham Greyhound bus station
Sam	Male	Black	Democrat	Yes	60	On Social Security and military benefits	Birmingham Greyhound bus station

Table 3 (continued). Interviewees in Alabama, December 2015.

* All names are pseudonyms; † Not asked; ‡ Not patriotic.

Name*	Gender	Race/ Ethnicity	Political Orientation	Veteran	Age	Employment Status	Location
Shirley	Female	Black	Independent	No	46	Unemployed; previously worked in restaurants and in retail	Birmingham Public Library
Tom	Male	Black	Democrat	No	76	Retired; former truck driver	Vernon Public Library
Will	Male	Black	Democrat	Yes	56	Laid off but starting new job; served 6 years in US Marines	Birmingham Public Library

Table 3 (continued). Interviewees in Alabama, December 2015.

* All names are pseudonyms; † Not asked; ‡ Not patriotic.

Name*	Gender	Race/ Ethnicity	Political Orientation	Veteran	Age	Employment Status	Location
Anne	Female	White	Mostly Republican	No	74	Retired; former director of Senior Citizen Center	Harlowton Senior Citizen Center
Autumn	Female	White	N/A†	No	20s	Banquet server	Billings, Laundromat
Becky	Female	White	N/A	No	60s	N/A	Small town between Harlowton and Billings
Carlos	Male	Hispanic	Democrat, but lately Republican	No	20s or early 30s	Regional financial manager; going to lose job soon	Billings, Laundromat
Chad	Male	White	Republican	Yes	26	Farm inspector	Billings, Laundromat
Cole	Male	White	Republican	No	30s	Works at KFC	Billings, street
Daniel	Male	White	Varies	Yes	50s	Floor installer; was in US Army 11 years	Billings, Laundromat
Darrius	Male	White	Varies	No		Cook	Billings, Laundromat
Fast Eagle	Female	Native American	N/A	No	30s	Works at front desks at hotel	Billings, Laundromat
Fiona	Female	White	Varies	No	51	Just lost her job	Harlowton Public Library

Table 4. Interviewees in Montana, April 2016.

* All names are pseudonyms; † Not asked; ‡ Not patriotic.

Name*	Gender	Race/ Ethnicity	Political Orientation	Veteran	Age	Employment Status	Location
Gil	Male	White	N/A	Yes	60s	Used to be a truck driver	Small town between Harlowton and Billings
Janice	Female	White	Varies	Yes	22	Was in US Army, now a care professional at a retirement home	Billings, Laundromat
Javier	Male	Hispanic	N/A	No	26	Works in roofing	Billings, Laundromat
Jeff	Male	White/ Native American	Democrat	Yes	59	Truck driver; in US Marine Corps 5 years	Billings, bus station
Jill	Female	White	Independent/ Conservative	No	40s	Real estate agent	Harlowton, real estate office
Kevin‡	Male	White	Independent/ Libertarian	No	20s	Works in construction	Billings, Laundromat
Lanai	Female	Asian	Republican	Yes	20s	Housekeeper at VA	Billings, Laundromat
Linda	Female	White	Varies	No	50s	Laundromat owner	Billings, Laundromat
Lynn	Female	White	Independent	No	65+	Retired farmer	Billings Public Library

Table 4 (continued). Interviewees in Montana, April 2016.

* All names are pseudonyms; † Not asked; ‡ Not patriotic.

Name*	Gender	Race/ Ethnicity	Political Orientation	Veteran	Age	Employment Status	Location
Marion	Female	Native American/ Irish	Independent	No	38	On Social Security	Billings Public Library
Marshall	Male	White	N/A	No	32	Unemployed; works on a new smart phone application	Billings Public Library
Nova	Female	Native American	Democrat	No	33	Personal care assistant	Billings, Laundromat
Oscar	Male	Hispanic	N/A	No	56	Concrete finisher	Billings, Laundromat
Phil	Male	White	Varies	No	60	Retired cartographic technician for US government	Billings Public Library
Rainbow	Female	Native American	Democrat	No	42	Unemployed	Billings, Laundromat
Roger	Male	White/ Native American	Republican in the past	No	70s	Retired	Billings, Laundromat

Table 4 (continued). Interviewees in Montana, April 2016.
* All names are pseudonyms; † Not asked; ‡ Not patriotic.

Name*	Gender	Race/ Ethnicity	Political Orientation	Veteran	Age	Employment Status	Location
Sean	Male	White	Independent	Yes	45	Works at Target; 9 months deployed and invaded Iraq during first Gulf War	Billings, Laundromat
Sidney	Female	White	N/A	No	32	Stay-at-home mom	Billings, Laundromat
Tanya	Female	White	Democrat	No	50s	Secretary	Billings, Laundromat
Timmy	Male	White	Varies	No	44	Owns construction company, but on probation and without work	Billings, street
Todd	Male	White	N/A	No	20s	Banquet server	Billings, Laundromat
Valerie	Female	White	Independent	Yes	74	Retired; served in US Navy 2.5 years	Harlowton Public Library

Table 4 (continued). Interviewees in Montana, April 2016.

* All names are pseudonyms; † Not asked; ‡ Not patriotic.

Acknowledgments

My thanks go, above all, to the sixty-three interviewees in Alabama and Montana who were willing to share their insights, thoughtfulness, life stories, and love of country. I learned from them and was humbled by the depth, genuineness, and optimism of their feelings toward the United States and life more generally. The interviews took place in public or open spaces such as Laundromats, bus stations, libraries, a senior community center, a homeless shelter, a used-clothing store, fast-food restaurants, and the front yards of homes. Most were not scheduled ahead of time. Approached unexpectedly by me as they were going about their daily lives, the interviewees proved incredibly kind and generous. Their ideas, thoughts, and sentiments are at the heart of this book.

On many occasions, I had to request permission to spend time and conduct interviews on certain premises. Ahead of my travels, I contacted staff at numerous venues to see if they could post interviewee recruitment fliers in visible places and outlets. My requests were met with kindness and a willingness to help. I am grateful for their support.

I conceived of this project while at the University of British Columbia in Vancouver, Canada. Its Department of Sociology was my academic home from 2013 to 2015. Numerous faculty members there provided me with priceless insights and suggestions, including Catherine Corrigall-Brown, Amin Ghaziani, Neil Guppy, Wendy Roth, and Rima Wilkes. Two remarkable doctoral students, Kamila Kolpashnikova and Andrew Patterson, offered feedback as well as research support. I am grateful to all of them for their help. Some of the funding for this project came from the Faculty of Arts at the University of British Columbia. This book could not have been written without that support.

At Bates College, where I returned in 2015, colleagues in the Department of Sociology—Emily Kane, Michael Rocque, and Heidi Taylor—and numerous undergraduate students helped me hone the project. Special thanks go to Leah Humes for her invaluable research assistance—transcription of all sixty-three interviews and coding of the resulting transcripts. Her tasks took months and hundreds of hours, and Leah delivered flawlessly even as she worked on her own undergraduate degree and thesis. Excellent ideas came as well from the Causal Inference Seminar Series group at Bates, to whom I presented the work in March 2016. Bates helped substantially with funds to cover the costs of the project: without those funds, this project could not have been completed. Impeccable administrative support came from Denise Begin.

One of the perks of being an academic is to have access to a network of people with brilliant minds who are happy to comment on, and provide ideas about, one's work. I benefited immensely from the feedback of Andrew Blom, John Campbell, Lisa Ceglia, Emil Dabora, Jonathan Eastwood, John K. Glenn, Liah Greenfeld, John Hall, Kevin Kraft, Patrick Lohier, Todd Pietruszka, and David Schab at various stages of this project.

The most an author can ask for is to have a committed, insightful, and even-handed editor. At Stanford University Press, Jenny Erin Gavacs matched precisely the ideal of a great editor. I am thankful to her for her guidance and recommendations in the early phases of this project: she encouraged, challenged, and aided me in innumerable ways. Kate Wahl, editor in chief at the press, shared, in the later writing stages, ideas and wisdom that only a seasoned editor with a commanding view of the publishing industry can offer. I am grateful to her for her input and support.

As part of the editorial process, the manuscript was shared with anonymous referees at the proposal and written stages. All provided me with very useful advice and suggestions. I took those to heart and hope to have incorporated them successfully. I thank them for their time and ideas.

Writing a book for me is akin to entering a long tunnel: while I am in there, my mind and energies are invariably devoted to reaching the end. While this helps to propel me forward, it does mean that often I am not as present with my family as I would like to be. This time around, my children, Sofia and Luca, were old enough to understand the nature of the work and offer their own valuable reflections and suggestions. Angela, my wife, who is accustomed to my distractions, not only generously endured them but offered countless suggestions, insights, and ideas from the earliest to the final stages of this project. And my mother-in-law, Nettie Jean, helped a great deal by covering for me at home while I was traveling to conduct the research for this book. The project unquestionably took its toll, and I am very grateful to my family for being so helpful and patient.

Notes

CHAPTER 1

1. The names of all interviewees have been disguised. See the Appendix for a list of the interviewees (by pseudonyms) and their basic demographic background.

2. See Yahoo! News, 2015.

3. Putnam, 1993; Misztal, 1996; Durkheim, 2014; Simmel, 1950.

4. Delhey and Newton, 2005, 323–324.

5. Della Fave, 1980.

6. *Economist,* 2014.

7. Edsall, 2015.

8. Reich, 2014.

9. *Economist,* 2016a.

10. Teachout, 2009, 177.

11. Defense Manpower Data Center, 2011.

12. *Economist,* 2015.

13. Watkins and Sherk, 2008.

14. See National Priorities Project, 2011. The military does not provide data on recruits' household incomes, so analyses of recruitment patterns rely on other data that the military offers (such as the zip codes of recruits).

15. White, 2008; Jordan, 2014.

16. Consider that in 2015 the basic pay in the army for a new recruit was $18,378, far below the US federal guideline minimum of $24,250 for a family of four if they are to live above the poverty line. See US Army, 2015. For older data, see Schmitt, 1994.

17. See, for instance, the 2015 Pew Research Center survey on America's global image, showing that a median of 69% of respondents across the world hold a favorable opinion of the United States, with a median 63% believing that the country respects the individual liberties of its citizens. See Wike, Stokes, and Poushter, 2015. A 2013 Pew Research Center survey also found that "respecting individual liberty remains the strong suit of America's image."

See Pew Research Center, 2013. And a 2001 poll indicated appreciation of America as the land of opportunity. See Pew Research Center, 2001.

18. Keller, 2015; Pew Research Center, 2011.

19. US Census Bureau, 2014a.

20. Abramsky, 2013, 10.

21. See US Census Bureau, 2014b.

22. *Economist*, 2010; Bloome, 2015.

23. Pew Research Center, 2015; see also NPR News, 2015.

24. Tirado, 2014; Abramsky, 2013.

25. Anderson, 1983; Gellner, 1983; Greenfeld, 1992; Malesevic and Hall, 2005.

26. Greenfeld and Eastwood, 2005.

27. Walt, 2011.

CHAPTER 2

1. US Department of Health and Human Services, 2015.

2. See, for example, Prasad, 2012; and Steensland, 2007.

3. Esping-Andersen, 1990; DiPrete, 2002.

4. Kenworthy, 2014.

5. Hill, 2013; Brin, 2012.

6. Woosley, 2008.

7. *Economist*, 2012; McCall, 2013, 221.

8. Kraus and Tan, 2015.

9. OECD, 2013a.

10. Causa, Dantan, and Johansson, 2009; *Economist*, 2012.

11. Jäntti et al., 2006.

12. Corak, 2006; *Economist*, 2012.

13. Grawe, 2004. A study published in 2014 in the prestigious *American Economic Review* found that intergenerational mobility is particularly low in especially deprived areas of the country: those experiencing high residential segregation, high inequality, worse public schools, less social capital, and lower family stability. Poor Americans who do experience mobility seem to come, therefore, from places that are, to begin with, better off in broader terms. If correct, the study helps us appreciate the especially difficult situation experienced by poor Americans who are stuck in their ranks. See Chetty et al., 2014.

14. Waldron et al., 2004; Gershuny and Fisher, 2014.

15. Estimates calculated using data from OECD, 2015a.

16. Gershuny and Fisher, 2014.

17. For the latest OECD data, see OECD, 2016.

18. OECD, 2013b.

19. In fact, the bottom fifth of households in terms of income have seen

their income almost stagnate between 1979 and 2007 (with an overall income growth of only 16%; the figures for the middle fifth, highest fifth, and top 1% were 25%, 95%, and 281%, respectively). See Ungar, 2013.

20. Ishio, 2010.

21. See Koch, 1996, 21; and Meier-Pesti and Kirchler 2003, 686.

22. To be sure, some scholars have used "nationalism" and "patriotism" in exactly the opposite way, with the former referring to a sense of superiority and dominance over other nations and the latter signifying a people's identification and love of country. See, for instance, Feshbach, 1994; and Peña and Sidanius, 2002. It is ultimately a question of terms and labels, and what is simply needed in any given study is definitional clarity upfront.

23. This was a drop from the 100% of the earlier wave but remains very high. A similar drop can be observed in Germany and other countries, most likely due to the financial crisis of 2008–2009.

24. Question V211: "How proud are you of your nationality?" and Question V238: "People sometimes describe themselves as belonging to the working class, the middle class, or the upper or lower class. Would you describe yourself as belonging to the:"

25. The June 2–7, 2015, Gallup Poll found that a remarkable 54% of Americans are "extremely proud" to be American, and another 27% are "very proud." With another 14% reporting that they are "moderately proud," the poll results paint a very patriotic picture of the American people—and one that is very similar to pre- 9/11 levels. See Swift, 2015.

26. Computed from the General Social Survey for the years 1996 and 2004. Variables: *Subjective Class Identification* and *Agree America Is a Better Country*. If we consider those "agreeing" and "strongly agreeing," the total for lower-class Americans was 80%; for the working class, 79%; for the middle class, 80%; and upper class, 83%. Those in the lower class thus stand out, in relative terms, for "strongly agreeing."

27. Variables: *Subjective Class Identification, Race of Respondent, Political Party Affiliation, Gender of 1st Person, Expanded NORC Size Code (rural includes towns between 2,500 and 9,999 people, smaller areas, and open country; urban includes cities of 50,000–250,000 and greater than 250,000 people), Respondent's Religious Preference, Age of Respondent,* and *Agree I Would Rather Be a Citizen of America.*

28. See Ishio, 2010. However, this line of research does not focus on poverty as such. Moreover, the definition of "patriotism" in those studies is more akin to that used in this book for nationalism: a sense of identification with a country rather than a belief in its superiority.

29. See Swift, 2015.

30. General Social Survey, Variable *Respondent's Religious Preference.*

CHAPTER 3

1. See, for instance, the twenty-three-nation study conducted by the National Opinion Research Center at the University of Chicago in 1995 (see University of Chicago News Office, 1998; and Smith and Jarkko, 1998), and its final wave in 2003 (Pardys, 2008), both of which found Americans to be the most patriotic citizens in the sample. See, as well, the World Values Survey, 2010–2014 (Wave 6), in which Americans were among the most likely to express pride in their country (Variable 211), with 87% reporting to be either "very proud" or "quite proud" of their nationality. This exceeded the percentages in countries such as Germany, Japan, the Netherlands, China, and Brazil.

2. Hall and Lindholm, 1999, 92; Kohn, 2005, 291; Wilsey, 2015.

3. Baldwin, 2009.

4. Hall and Lindholm, 1999, 92. See also Lieven, 2012.

5. Bodnar, 1992, 16.

6. Teachout, 2009, 5.

7. Ibid., 6.

8. Greenfeld, 1992, 31.

9. Kohn, 2005, 291.

10. Kraus and Tan, 2015, 110.

11. Hall and Lindholm, 1999, 18.

12. Hauhart, 2015, 65. Some researchers question whether the belief in the American Dream is still as widespread, after the Great Recession, as it has been for much of the country's history.

13. Greenfeld, 1992.

14. Hall and Lindholm, 1999, 91.

15. Pew Research Center, 2011.

16. Wald and Calhoun-Brown, 2014; Wilsey, 2015

17. Bellah, 1967.

18. Gaddie and Goidel, 2015.

19. O'Leary, 1999.

20. Teachout, 2009.

21. Wilkins, 2002; Teachout, 2009.

22. Bodnar, 1996a.

23. For claims by women, see Morgan, 2005; for claims by Native Americans, see Rosier, 2012; for claims by the Kentucky State Militia, see Gallaher, 2003.

24. Rosier, 2012, 10–11.

25. Ibid., 1.

26. Robbins, 2013, 1.

27. Ibid., 9.

28. Ishio, 2010, 70.

29. Jensen, 2008.

30. Jensen, 1996, 139.

31. Jensen, 2008, xi.

32. Duryea, 2013, 150.

33. Ibid., 138.

34. Ibid., 154.

35. Ishio, 2010.

36. Bageant, 2007, 6.

37. Peña and Sidanius, 2002, 783; see also Sidanius and Pratto, 1999.

38. Sidanius et al., 1997, 106.

39. For an overview of the theory and its evolution over time, see Van der Toorn and Jost, 2014.

40. Jost et al., 2003, 13.

41. Ibid.

42. Van der Toorn and Jost, 2014, 416. This research comes at times with caveats. Newman, Johnston, and Lowe (2015), for instance, have recently argued that, in the presence of extreme inequality in their local environments, poor Americans do tend to become disillusioned with the existing order of things. Theories of false consciousness no longer holds in those cases.

43. Marx, 1972; Marcuse, 1964; and Mannheim, 1985.

44. Chomsky, 1999, 2011.

45. See, for instance, Frank, 2004.

46. Meier-Pesti and Kirchler, 2003, 688.

47. Computed from data from the General Social Survey for the years 1996, 2004, and 2014. Variables: *Subjective Class Identification, Agree I Would Rather Be a Citizen of America,* and *Region of Interview.*

48. See, for instance, Davidson, 1996, 9; Gallaher, 2003, esp. chap. 4; and Kimmel and Ferber, 2000.

49. ZCTAs often overlap with the ZIP codes used by the US Postal Service but were developed by the US Census Bureau for statistical data collection rather than efficient mail delivery.

50. US Department of Health and Human Services, 2015.

51. US Census Bureau, 2017.

52. For practical purposes of reaching in a reasonable time those rural areas from my selected cities (Birmingham and Billings), I limited my choice to rural areas between seventy and two hundred miles outside those cities.

53. See Kane, 2012, 219.

54. See US Department of Health and Human Services, 2015.

55. Campbell et al., 2013, 350.

Chapter 6

1. Grace, for example, said, "No, I don't think blacks should marry whites.

I think that the good Lord would have made us all the same color if he meant that. . . . The Bible's strictly against it. And I am too." Why, I asked, was this the case when the Bible says that in God's eyes we are all the same? "It just looks to me like they're downgrading themselves," Grace said. This applied to both white and black people.

Of course, this sort of sentiment was more widely shared among white respondents in Alabama. Charlotte in Vernon, for instance, said, "I think white need to stay with the white and black need to stay with the black. That's the way, that's the way I was raised." I then asked, "What happens if they intermingle?" "Well," she answered, "that's . . . [laughs] that goes in their book, and they have to answer for it. I put it that way. I don't . . . it's like, this is my book, and I have to answer for what's in it, you know, I can't answer for nobody else. But to me, I wouldn't." Or consider the words of Alicia in Birmingham: "God say that he don't agree with it; he's destroyed the city of Sodom and Gomorrah for it, and I don't see why the government so wanted such high standards and have authority to legalize something that God say he don't agree with. I don't understand it so, no, I don't think they should have legalized it; I think that was wrong. I do."

2. Autumn, for instance, valued a child's choice over mandating recitation of the Pledge of Allegiance: "I don't want my daughter to believe in anything that she doesn't want to believe in. She knows . . . the only thing that I push upon my daughter and I don't even push it is let . . . I just let her see by what my actions are, and that's up, getting up and hitting my knees every morning and praying, and she'll pray with me sometimes, and whether she does that or not . . . but I want her to know that I have a God that I believe in. That's the only thing that I care about. . . . As far as something that she should believe in the United States . . . that's not a for sure thing. It might fail her at one point in time, and I'm not gonna force her to believe in something like that."

In regard to children, there was for the most part a consensus that they should be taught patriotism. But the interviewees felt more ambivalent about adults and the possibility of unpatriotic behavior. While not approving of it, many felt that being free in America includes not having to demonstrate love for the country. As Harley put it, "To each his own. You can't make somebody like something if they don't wanna like it. So, fine with me."

3. A few people in Alabama also expressed concerns about the government and its betrayal of the country and its core values. Emma, for instance, stated, "I, I think that we've gotten away from the ideals that the country was first founded, and I, I don't think we've got the same quality of leadership that we had."

CHAPTER 7

1. See, for instance, Brewer and Stonecash, 2015.

2. Walker and Smith, 2002; Dudley and Miller, 1998.

3. Ray was one of the few who felt differently when contemplating a scenario of a drone attack and whether he would prefer the loss of life to be local or that of an American citizen. As he put it, "A life is a life . . . but, a drone attack and someone dies in the Middle East . . . [laughs] of course I'm partial to Americans. . . . I, being an ex-military, I still got military in my blood . . . and ninety-nine point nine percent of Americans are actually good Americans, you know?"

CHAPTER 8

1. The BBC's Michael Goldfarb (2016) recently wrote a powerful piece on the plight of American towns.

2. Tocqueville, in his classis *Democracy in America*, put forth the idea—today known as the "Tocqueville effect"—that great levels of inequality makes inequality itself more accepted, while in those places where equality is great even small levels of inequality are seen as an injustice (1840, 272). The logic might apply here.

3. The notion that limited options in life can promote contentment with one's lot, while more choices, which typically come with wealth, generate anxiety, might be relevant here. Social theorists from Durkheim (1979) to Greenfeld (2013) have proposed as much.

4. Hall and Lindholm, 1999, 91; Bodnar, 1996b.

5. Greenfeld, 1992, 277.

6. Ibid., 403, 409.

7. See also Slauter, 2011, 88–89.

8. As quoted in Greenfeld, 1992, 409.

9. Bodnar, 1996b, 3.

10. In a new book, Greenfeld stresses that awareness of being a part of a nation, in any country, gives citizens a sense of dignity—something that most human beings did not have prior to the rise of modern nation-states. She then states that "dignity is addictive" and that in "modern society people will never agree to be deprived of their dignity, which they acquired with national consciousness" (2016, 14). In societies where the idea of equality is most entrenched in principle (as in the United States), this sense of dignity is especially pronounced. This is certainly consistent with what we heard in the interviews.

11. Vance, 2016; Isenberg, 2016. See also Hochschild, 2016.

12. See Chomsky, 1999, 2011.

13. Considerable data on education, income, health, and other areas point to a country in decline. See, for instance, Coplan, 2015. Many Americans seem

to be noticing: see, for instance, Tyson, 2014, and survey data pointing to a drop of 10 percentage points (for the period 2011–2014) in the share of Americans who think that their country stands above all others in the world.

14. See, for instance, *Economist,* 2016b.

APPENDIX

1. At a more personal level, more for pragmatic than moral reasons, some of the interviewees worried as well about personal debt, especially as it concerns students. Kevin noted that "there's a lot of low income and a lot of people in huge amounts of debt, especially people that are graduating right now." Indeed, Darrius observed, "That's a big, that's a big problem. It's a huge problem in this country. Every college student gets out of college with a debt that's impossible to pay in a short period of time . . . and so every one of them has that problem."

2. See Kane, 2012, 226; for an extended discussion on the topic, see Rubin and Rubin, 2012.

3. See Campbell and Pedersen, 2014, 351, for suggestions on how to probe further into any given statement during interviews.

4. Campbell et al., 2013.

References

Abramsky, Sasha. 2013. *The American Way of Poverty: How the Other Half Still Lives.* New York: Nation Books.

Anderson, Benedict. 1983. *Imagined Communities.* New York: Verso.

Bageant, Joe. 2007. *Deer Hunting with Jesus: Dispatches from America's Class War.* New York: Crown Publishing Group.

Baldwin, Peter. 2009. *The Narcissism of Minor Differences: How America and Europe Are Alike.* New York: Oxford University Press.

Bellah, Robert N. 1967. "Civil Religion in America." *Daedalus* 96 (1): 1–21.

Bloome, Deirdre. 2015. "Income Inequality and Intergenerational Income Mobility in the United States." *Social Forces* 93 (3): 1047–1080.

Bodnar, John E. 1992. *Remaking America: Public Memory, Commemoration, and Patriotism in the Twentieth Century.* Princeton, NJ: Princeton University Press.

———, ed. 1996a. "The Attractions of Patriotism." In *Bonds of Affection: Americans Define Their Patriotism,* edited by John Bodnar, 3–18. Princeton, NJ: Princeton University Press.

———. 1996b. *Bonds of Affection: Americans Define Their Patriotism.* Princeton, NJ: Princeton University Press.

Brewer, Mark D., and Jeffrey M. Stonecash. 2015. *Polarization and the Politics of Personal Responsibility.* New York: Oxford University Press.

Brin, Dina Wisenberg. 2012. "Among Rich Nations, U.S. Retirement System Needs Work." CNBC, April 16. http://www.cnbc.com/id/46795823.

Campbell, John L., and Ove K. Pedersen. 2014. *The National Origins of Policy Ideas: Knowledge Regimes in the United States, France, Germany, and Denmark.* Princeton, NJ: Princeton University Press.

Campbell, John L., Charles Quincy, Jordan Osserman, and Ove K. Pedersen. 2013. "Coding In-Depth Semi-Structured Interviews: Problems of Unitization and Inter-coder Reliability and Agreement." *Sociological Methods and Research* 42 (3): 294–320.

Causa, Orsetta, Sophie Dantan, and Åsa Johansson. 2009. "Intergenerational

Social Mobility in European OECD Countries." *OECD Economics Department Working Papers* 709:1–44.

Chetty, Raj, Nathaniel Hendren, Patrick Kline, and Emmanuel Saez. 2014. "Where Is the Land of Opportunity? The Geography of Intergenerational Mobility in the United States." *Quarterly Journal of Economics* 129 (4): 1553–1623.

Chomsky, Noam. 1999. *Profit over People: Neoliberalism and Global Order.* New York: Seven Stories Press.

———. 2011. *How the World Works.* Berkeley, CA: Soft Skull Press.

Collins, Jane, and Victoria Mayer. 2010. *Both Hands Tied: Welfare Reform and the Race to the Bottom in the Low-Wage Labor Market.* Chicago: University of Chicago Press.

Coplan, Jill Hamburg. 2015. "12 Signs America Is on the Decline." *Fortune,* July 20. http://fortune.com/2015/07/20/united-states-decline-statistics-economic/.

Corak, Miles. 2006. "Do Poor Children Become Poor Adults? Lessons from a Cross-country Comparison of Generational Earnings Mobility." *Research on Economic Inequality* 13:143–188.

Davidson, Osha Gray. 1996. *Broken Heartland: The Rise of America's Rural Ghetto.* Iowa City: University of Iowa Press.

Defense Manpower Data Center. 2011. *Appendix B: Active Component Enlisted Accessions, Enlisted Force, Officer Accessions, and Officer Corps Tables.* http://prhome.defense.gov/portals/52/Documents/POPREP/poprep2011/appendixb/appendixb.pdf.

Delhey, Jan, and Kenneth Newton. 2005. "Predicting Cross-national Levels of Social Trust: Global Pattern or Nordic Exceptionalism?" *European Sociological Review* 21 (4): 331–327.

Della Fave, L. Richard. 1980. "The Meek Shall Not Inherit the Earth: Self-Evaluation and the Legitimacy of Stratification." *American Sociological Review* 45 (6): 955–971.

DiPrete, Thomas A. 2002. "Life Course Risks, Mobility Regimes, and Mobility Consequences: A Comparison of Sweden, Germany, and the United States." *American Journal of Sociology* 108 (2): 267–309.

Dudley, Ryan, and Ross A. Miller. 1998. "Group Rebellion in the 1980s." *Journal of Conflict Resolution* 42 (1): 77–96.

Durkheim, Émile. 1979. *Suicide: A Study in Sociology.* New York: Free Press.

———. 2014. *The Division of Labor in Society.* New York: Free Press.

Duryea, Scott N. 2013. "Genuinely American: Croatian-American Race, Manhood, and Nationalism in Postwar Pittsburgh." *Studies in Ethnicity and Nationalism* 13 (2): 138–157.

Economist. 2010. "Upper Bound," April 15. http://www.economist.com/node/15908469.

———. 2012. "Like Father, Not like Son." October 13. http://www.economist.com/node/21564417/print.

———. 2014. "Why Aren't the Poor Storming the Barricades?" June 21. http://www.economist.com/blogs/democracyinamerica/2014/01/inequality-0.

———. 2015. "Who Will Fight the Next War?" October 24. http://www.economist.com/news/united-states/21676778-failures-iraq-and-afghanistan-have-widened-gulf-between-most-americans-and-armed.

———. 2016a. "The Rise of the Far Right in Europe." May 24. http://www.economist.com/blogs/graphicdetail/2016/05/daily-chart-18.

———. 2016b. "Both Economic Hardship and Racial Divisions Fuel Support for Donald Trump." October 22. http://www.economist.com/news/finance-and-economics/21709018-both-economic-hardship-and-racial-divisions-fuel-support-donald-trump-subtract.

Edin, Kathryn J. 2015. *$2.00 a Day: Living on Almost Nothing in America*. New York: Houghton Mifflin Harcourt.

Edsall, Thomas B. 2015. "Why Don't the Poor Rise Up?" *New York Times*, June 24. http://www.nytimes.com/2015/06/24/opinion/why-dont-the-poor-rise-up.html?_r=0.

Esping-Andersen, Gosta. 199. *The Three Worlds of Welfare Capitalism*. Princeton, NJ: Princeton University Press.

Feshbach, Seymour. 1994. "Nationalism, Patriotism, and Aggression: A Clarification of Functional Differences." In *Aggressive Behavior: Current Perspectives*, edited by Rowell L. Huesmann, 275–291. New York: Plenum Press.

Frank, Thomas. 2004. *What's the Matter with Kansas? How Conservatives Won the Heart of America*. New York: Henry Holt.

Gaddie, Keith, and Kirby Goidel. 2015. "The American Nationalism Problem." *Huffington Post*, December 6. http://www.huffingtonpost.com/keith-gaddie/the-american-nation-probl_b_8733102.html.

Gallaher, Carolyn. 2003. *On the Fault Line: Race, Class, and the American Patriot Movement*. Lanham, MD: Rowman and Littlefield.

Gellner, Ernest. 1983. *Nations and Nationalism*. Malden, MA: Blackwell.

Gershuny, Jonathan, and Kimberly Fisher. 2014. *Post-industrious Society: Why Work Time Will Not Disappear for Our Grandchildren*. Working Paper No. 2014-03. Oxford: Centre for Time Use Research, Department of Sociology, Oxford University.

Goldfarb, Michael. 2016. "Returning to an Ohio Town on the Decline." BBC News, July 1. http://www.bbc.com/news/election-us-2016-35653619.

Grawe, Nathan D. 2004. "Intergenerational Mobility for Whom? The Experience of High- and Low-Earning Sons in International Perspective." In *Generational Income Mobility in North America and Europe*, edited by Miles Corak, 58–89. Cambridge: Cambridge University Press.

Greenfeld, Liah. 1992. *Nationalism: Five Roads to Modernity*. Cambridge, MA: Harvard University Press.

———. 2013. *Mind, Modernity, Madness: The Impact of Culture on Human Experience*. Cambridge, MA: Harvard University Press.

———. 2016. *Advanced Introduction to Nationalism*. Northampton, MA: Edward Elgar.

Greenfeld, Liah, and Jonathan R. Eastwood. 2005. "Nationalism in Comparative Perspective." In *The Handbook of Political Sociology*, edited by Thomas Janoski, Alexander M. Hicks, and Mildred A. Schwartz, 247–265. New York: Cambridge University Press.

Hall, John A., and Charles Lindholm. 1999. *Is America Breaking Apart?* Princeton, NJ: Princeton University Press.

Hauhart, Robert C. 2015. "American Sociology's Investigations of the American Dream: Retrospect and Prospect." *American Sociologist* 46 (1): 65–98.

Hays, Sharon. 2003. *Flat Broke with Children: Women in the Age of Welfare Reform*. New York: Oxford University Press.

Hill, Steven. 2013. "The Myth of Low-Tax America: Why Americans Aren't Getting Their Money's Worth." *The Atlantic*, April 15. http://www.theatlantic.com/business/archive/2013/04/the-myth-of-low-tax-america-why-americans-arent-getting-their-moneys-worth/274945/.

Hochschild, Arlie Russell. 2016. *Strangers in Their Own Land: Anger and Mourning on the American Right*. New York: New Press.

Isenberg. Nancy. 2016. *White Trash: The 400-Year Untold History of Class in America*. New York: Viking.

Ishio, Yoshito. 2010. "Social Bases of American Patiotism: Examing Effects of Dominant Social Social Statuses and Socialization." *Current Sociology* 58 (1): 67–93.

Jäntti, Markus, Knut Roed, Robin Naylor, Anders Bjorklund, Bernt Bratsberg, Oddbjorn Raaum, Eva Osterbacka, and Tor Eriksson. 2006. *American Exceptionalism in a New Light: A Comparison of Intergenerational Earnings Mobility in the Nordic Countries, the United Kingdom and the United States*. IZA Discussion Paper Series (1938), 1–40. http://ftp.iza.org/dp1938.pdf.

Jensen, Kimberly. 1996. "Women, Citizenship, and Civic Sacrifice: Engendering Patriotism in the First World War." In *Bonds of Affection: Americans Define Their Patriotism*, edited by John Bodnar, 139–159. Princeton, NJ: Princeton University Press.

———. 2008. *Mobilizing Minerva: American Women in the First World War*. Urbana: University of Illinois Press.

Jordan, Miriam. 2014. "Recruits' Ineligibility Tests the Military." *Wall Street Journal*, June 27. http://www.wsj.com/articles/recruits-ineligibility-tests-the-military-1403909945.

Jost, John T., Brett W. Pelham, Oliver Sheldon, and Bilian Ni Sulliva. 2003.

"Social Inequality and the Reduction of Ideological Dissonance on Behalf of the System: Evidence of Enhanced System Justification among the Disadvantaged." *European Journal of Social Psychology* 33 (1): 13–36.

Kane, Emily. 2012. *The Gender Trap: Parents and the Pitfalls of Raising Boys and Girls.* New York: New York University Press.

Keller, Jared. 2015. "What Makes Americans So Optimistic? Why the US Tends to Look on the Bright Side." *The Atlantic,* March 25. http://www.theatlantic.com/politics/archive/2015/03/the-american-ethic-and-the-spirit-of-optimism/388538/.

Kenworthy, Lane. 2014. *Social Democratic America.* Oxford: Oxford University Press.

Kimmel, Michael, and Abby L. Ferber. 2000. "'White Men Are This Nation': Right-Wing Militias and the Restoration of Rural American Masculinity." *Rural Sociology* 65:582–604.

Koch, Cynthia M. 1996. "Teaching Patriotism: Private Virtue for the Public Good in the Early Republic." In *Bonds of Affection: Americans Define Their Patriotism,* edited by John Bodnar, 19–52. Princeton, NJ: Princeton University Press.

Kohn, Hans. 2005. *The Idea of Nationalism: A Study in Its Origins and Background.* New Brunswick, NJ: Transaction.

Kraus, Michael W., and Jacinth J. X. Tan. 2015. "Americans Overestimate Social Class Mobility." *Journal of Experimental Social Psychology* 58:101–111.

Lieven, Anatol. 2012. *America Right or Wrong: An Anatomy of American Nationalism.* Oxford: Oxford University Press.

Malesevic, Sinisa, and John A. Hall. 2005. "Citizenship, Ethnicity and Nation-States." In *The Handbook of Sociology,* edited by Craig Calhoun, Chris Rojek, and Bryan Turner, 561–578. London: Sage.

Mannheim, Karl. 1985. *Ideology and Utopia: An Introduction to the Sociology of Knowledge.* San Diego: Harcourt Brace Jovanovich.

Marcuse, Herbert. 1964. *One-Dimensional Man.* Boston: Beacon Press.

Marx, Karl. 1972. *The Marx-Engels Reader.* Edited by Robert C. Tucker. New York: Norton.

McCall, Leslie. 2013. *The Undeserving Rich: American Beliefs about Inequality, Opportunity and Redistribution.* Cambridge: Cambridge University Press.

Meier-Pesti, Katja, and Erich Kirchler. 2003. "Nationalism and Patriotism as Determinants of European Identity and Attitudes towards the Euro." *Journal of Socio-Economics* 32:685–700.

Misztal, Barbara. 1996. *Trust in Modern Societies: The Search for the Bases of Social Order.* Cambridge: Polity Press.

Morgan, Francesca. 2005. *Women and Patriotism in Jim Crow America.* Chapel Hill: University of North Carolina Press.

National Priorities Project. 2011. "Military Recruitment 2010." June 30. https://www.nationalpriorities.org/analysis/2011/military-recruitment-2010/.

Newman, Benjamin, Christopher Johnston, and Patrick Lowe. 2015. "False Consciousness or Class Awareness? Local Income Inequality, Personal Economic Position, Belief in American Meritocracy." *American Journal of Political Science* 59 (2): 1–15.

NPR News. 2015. "Pew Research Report Finds Most Americans Are No Longer Middle Class." *All Things Considered*, December 10. http://www.npr.org/2015/12/10/459250001/pew-research-report-finds-most-americans-are-no-longer-middle-class.

OECD (Organisation for Economic Co-operation and Development). 2013a. *Economic Policy Reforms 2013*. Paris: OECD.

———. 2013b. *How's Life? 2013: Measuring Well-Being*. Paris: OECD.

———. 2015a. "Average Annual Hours Actually Worked per Worker." Accessed December 30. https://stats.oecd.org/Index.aspx?DataSetCode=ANHRS.

———. 2015b. *In It Together: Why Less Inequality Benefits All*. Paris: OECD.

———. 2016. "OECD Income Distribution Database (IDD): Gini, Poverty, Income, Methods and Concepts." November 24. http://www.oecd.org/social/income-distribution-database.htm.

O'Leary, Cecilia Elizabeth. 1999. *To Die For: The Paradox of American Patriotism*. Princeton, NJ: Princeton University Press.

Pardys, Sara. 2008. "World's Most and Least Patriotic Countries." *Forbes*, July 2. http://www.forbes.com/2008/07/02/world-national-pride-oped-cx_sp_0701patriot.html.

Peña, Yesilernis, and Jim Sidanius. 2002. "US Patriotism and Ideologies of Group Dominance: A Tale of Asymmetry." *Journal of Social Psychology* 142 (6): 782–790.

Pew Research Center. 2011. *Angry Silents, Disengaged Millennials: The Generation Gap and the 2012 Election*. November 3. http://www.people-press.org/files/legacy-pdf/11-3-11%20Generations%20Release.pdf.

———. 2013. "America's Global Image Remains More Positive Than China's." July 18. http://www.pewglobal.org/2013/07/18/americas-global-image-remains-more-positive-than-chinas/.

———. 2015. *The American Middle Class Is Losing Ground: No Longer the Majority and Falling Behind*. December 9. http://www.pewsocialtrends.org/files/2015/12/2015-12-09_middle-class_FINAL-report.pdf.

Prasad, Monica. 2012. *The Land of Too Much: American Abundance and the Paradox of Poverty*. Cambridge, MA: Harvard University Press.

Putnam, Robert. 1993. *Making Democracy Work: Civic Traditions in Modern Italy*. Princeton, NJ: Princeton University Press.

Reich, Robert. 2014. "Why Aren't We Having a Middle Class Revolt?" Alternet, January 27. http://www.alternet.org/news-amp-politics/why-arent-we-having-middle-class-revolt.

Robbins, James S. 2013. *Native Americans: Patriotism, Exceptionalism, and the New American Identity.* New York: Encounter Books.

Rosier, Paul C. 2012. *Serving Their Country: American Indian Politics and Patriotism in the Twentieth Century.* Cambridge, MA: Harvard University Press.

Rubin, Herbert J., and Irene S. Rubin. 2012. *Qualitative Interviewing: The Art of Hearing Data.* Thousand Oaks, CA: Sage.

Schmitt, Eric. 1994. "As Military Pay Slips Behind, Poverty Invades the Ranks." *New York Times,* June 12. http://www.nytimes.com/1994/06/12/us/as-military-pay-slips-behind-poverty-invades-the-ranks.html.

Sidanius, Jim, Seymour Feshbach, Shana Levin, and Felicia Pratto. 1997. "The Interface between Ethnic and National Attachment: Ethnic Pluralism or Ethnic Dominance?" *Public Opinion Quarterly* 61 (1): 102–133.

Sidanius, Jim, and Felicia Pratto. 1999. *Social Dominance: An Intergroup Theory of Social Hierarchy and Oppression.* Cambridge: Cambridge University Press.

Simmel, Georg. 1950. *The Sociology of Georg Simmel.* Edited and translated by Kurt Wolff. Glencoe, IL: Free Press.

Slauter, Eric Thomas. 2011. *The State as a Work of Art: The Cultural Origins of the Constitution.* Chicago: University of Chicago Press.

Smith, Tom W., and Lars Jarkko. 1998. "National Pride: A Cross-analysis Survey." National Opinion Research Center, University of Chicago, May. http://gss.norc.org/Documents/reports/cross-national-reports/CNR19%20National%20Pride%20-%20A%20cross-national%20analysis.pdf.

Steensland, Brian. 2007. *The Failed Welfare Revolution: America's Struggle over Guaranteed Income Policy.* Princeton, NJ: Princeton University Press.

Swift, Art. 2015. "Smaller Majority 'Extremely Proud' to Be an American." Gallup, July 2. http://www.gallup.com/poll/183911/smaller-majority-extremely-proud-american.aspx.

Teachout, Woden. 2009. *Capture the Flag: A Political History of American Patriotism.* New York: Basic Books.

Tirado, Linda. 2014. *Hand to Mouth: Living in Bootstrap America.* New York : G. P. Putnam's Sons.

Tocqueville, Alexis de. 1840. *Democracy in America.* London: Saunders and Otley.

Tyson, Alec. 2014. "Most Americans Think the U.S. Is Great, but Fewer Say It's the Greatest." Pew Research Center, July 2. http://www.pewresearch.org/fact-tank/2014/07/02/most-americans-think-the-u-s-is-great-but-fewer-say-its-the-greatest/.

Ungar, Rich. 2013. "The Crisis Is Here for Millions—Income Inequality Now Set to Wreak Its Ugly Revenge." *Forbes,* March 19. http://www.forbes.com/

sites/rickungar/2013/03/19/the-retirement-crisis-is-here-for-millions-income-inequality-now-set-to-wreak-its-ugly-revenge/.

University of Chicago News Office. 1998. "Americans Are World's Most Patriotic People, National Research Center at the University Chicago Finds." National Opinion Research Center, University of Chicago, June 30. http://www-news.uchicago.edu/releases/98/980630.patriotism.shtml.

US Army. 2015. "Benefits." Accessed December 30. http://www.goarmy.com/benefits/money/basic-pay-active-duty-soldiers.html.

US Census Bureau. 2014a. "Welcome to QuickFacts." Accessed December 30, 2015. https://www.census.gov/quickfacts/.

———. 2014b. "Table H-3: Mean Household Income Received by Each Fifth and Top 5 Percent." Accessed December 30, 2015. https://www.census.gov/data/tables/time-series/demo/income-poverty/historical-income-households.html.

———. 2017. "Community Facts." American FactFinder. Accessed March 13. http://factfinder.census.gov/faces/nav/jsf/pages/index.xhtml.

US Department of Health and Human Services. 2015. "2015 Poverty Guidelines." September 30. http://aspe.hhs.gov/2015-poverty-guidelines.

Van der Toorn, Jojanneke, and John T. Jost. 2014. "Twenty Years of System Justification Theory: Introduction to the Special Issue on 'Ideology and System Justification Processes.'" *Group Processes & Intergroup Relations* 17 (4): 413–419.

Vance, J. D. 2016. *Hillbilly Elegy: A Memoir of a Family and Culture in Crisis.* New York: HarperCollins.

Wald, Kenneth D., and Allison Calhoun-Brown. 2014. *Religion and Politics in the United States.* Lanham, MD: Rowman and Littlefield.

Waldron, Tom, Brandon Roberts, Andrew Reamer, Sara Rab, and Steve Ressler. 2004. *Working Hard, Falling Short: America's Working Families and the Pursuit of Economic Security.* The Working Poor Families Project, October. http://www.workingpoorfamilies.org/pdfs/Working_Hard.pdf.

Walker, Iain, and Heather J. Smith. 2002. "Fifty Years of Relative Deprivation Research." In *Relative Deprivation: Specification, Development and Integration,* edited by Iain Walker and Heather J. Smith, 1–9. Cambridge: Cambridge University Press.

Walt, Stephen M. 2011. "The Myth of American Exceptionalism." *Foreign Policy,* October 11. http://foreignpolicy.com/2011/10/11/the-myth-of-american-exceptionalism/.

Watkins, Shanea, and James Sherk. 2008. "Who Serves in the U.S. Military: Demographic Characteristics of Enlisted Troops and Officers." Heritage Foundation, August 21. http://www.heritage.org/defense/report/who-serves-the-us-military-the-demographics-enlisted-troops-and-officers.

White, Josh. 2008. "Army off Target on Recruits." *Washington Post,* January

23. http://www.washingtonpost.com/wp-dyn/content/article/2008/01/22/AR2008012203326.html.

Wike, Richard, Bruce Stokes, and Jacob Poushter. 2015. "America's Global Image." Pew Research Center, June 23. http://www.pewglobal.org/2015/06/23/1-americas-global-image/.

Wilkins, Roger W. 2002. *Jefferson's Pillow: The Founding Fathers and the Dilemma of Black Patriotism.* Boston: Beacon Press.

Wilsey, John D. 2015. *American Exceptionalism and Civil Religion: Reassessing the History of an Idea.* Downers Grove, IL: InterVarsity Press.

Woosley, Matt. 2008. "World's Best Places for Unemployment Pay." *Forbes,* June 27. http://www.forbes.com/2008/06/27/unemployment-benefits-world-forbeslife-cx_mw_0627worldunemployment.html.

World Values Survey. 2010–2014. "WVS Wave 6." http://www.worldvalues-survey.org/WVSDocumentationWV6.jsp.

Yahoo! News. 2015. "Most Dangerous Cities in America." November 10. http://news.yahoo.com/most-dangerous-cities-in-america-1297176524619830.html.

Index

Class and Power in the New Deal: Corporate Moderates, Southern Democrats, and the Liberal-Labor Coalition
G. William Domhoff and Michael J. Webber
2011

Social Class and Changing Families in an Unequal America
Edited by Marcia J. Carlson and Paula England
2011

Dividing the Domestic: Men, Women, and Household Work in Cross-National Perspective
Edited by Judith Treas and Sonja Drobnič
2010

Gendered Trajectories: Women, Work, and Social Change in Japan and Taiwan
By Wei-hsin Yu
2009

Creating Wealth and Poverty in Postsocialist China
Edited by Deborah S. Davis and Wang Feng
2008

Shifting Ethnic Boundaries and Inequality in Israel: Or, How the Polish Peddler Became a German Intellectual
By Aziza Khazzoom
2008

Boundaries and Categories: Rising Inequality in Post-Socialist Urban China
By Wang Feng
2008

Stratification in Higher Education: A Comparative Study
Edited by Yossi Shavit, Richard Arum, and Adam Gamoran
2007

The Political Sociology of the Welfare State: Institutions, Social Cleavages, and Orientations
Edited by Stefan Svallfors
2007

On Sociology, Second Edition
Volume One: Critique and Program
Volume Two: Illustration and Retrospect
By John H. Goldthorpe
2007